In
GOD'S
EYES

In God's Eyes

Learning to See Yourself as God Sees You

Chevis Brooks

Author Academy elite

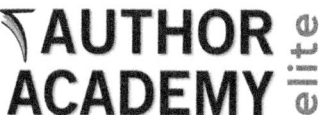

Printed in the United States of America 2017 First Edition

Subject Index:
Brooks, Chevis
Titile: In God's Eyes: Learning to See Yourself as God Sees You
Christian 2. Inspirational 3. Personal Growth

Paperback ISBN: 978-1-64085-129-0
Hardback ISBN: 978-1-64085-133-7
LCCN: 2017914587

Author Academy Elite, Powell, OH

ENDORSEMENTS

"In God's Eyes," my good friend Chevis Brooks details how God Himself views us as His Children. In a time full of *trials*, this book will assist the reader in being *triumphant*. We all need a self confidence boost occasionally and understanding that God sees each of us through the perfect "filter" giving us the courage to "GO." Grab a highlighter and notepad and dig in to this incredible teaching.

Richie Hughes
Author: Start Here, Go Anywhere
Richiehughes.org

Chevis is one of the most strong-willed people I have ever met and had the privilege of coaching. Over the years, I've been fortunate enough to have a "front row seat" to his life and have watched him literally let God "take the wheel". He went from struggling at a young age for acceptance and searching for validation through man to finding his one true validation: God. His subtitle, "Learning to See Yourself as

God Sees You", is a perfect description and testament to the path I've watched him walk out. His contagious passion and persistence to give others what he has been given is inspiring and truly heart-warming. I'm certain you will be blessed by his life and words just as I have.

Clint Spencer
Head Strength and Conditioning Coach
CFL (Canadian Football League)
Saskatchewan Roughriders

Enlightening, inspiring, thought provoking, and profoundly important. . . . *In God's Eyes* provides a blueprint for seeing yourself as God sees you! This is such a timely book in so many ways for Christians today. If you read this book with an open mind and a willing spirit Chevis' words will equip you with the tools to take your relationship with God and others to a deeper and more meaningful level. God has gifted Chevis with a prophetic voice to speak truth in order to equip people to live out their lives with Godly purpose and fulfillment. He writes with a level of transparency and raw honesty that anyone can relate to and his life stories, advice, and illustrations hit home in meaningful ways. *In God's Eyes* truly delivers godly wisdom and fresh insight to scripture. It›s a must read and then a must read again!

John Paul Burdashaw
Executive Pastor
Crosspointe Church

Jesus tells us that the greatest commandment is to love the Lord your God with all your heart, and with all your soul, and with all your mind, and the second is, love your neighbor as yourself. Everything starts with love and specifically with the love of God. If we are called to love our neighbor as we love ourselves then it is imperative we allow ourselves to love ourselves. Having known Chevis over the past fifteen years,

I've personally watched him transform from lost to found, from a life full of uncertainty to a life full of clarity, and from not knowing love at all to knowing the love that created all. In these pages, Chevis Brooks takes on three of most difficult questions for any of us to answer, but also three of the most important questions individuals will ever ask themselves. So, whether you're a business person, a mature Christian, or even an unbeliever, you will be encouraged and inspired to come to know the love of God fully, which leads to the love of self and in turn leads to the love of others.

Mario Hood
Next Generations Pastor
Church On The Living Edge

Chevis Brooks asks some challenging questions but helps answer them with vulnerability and transparency from his own life experiences. I'm confident this book will help the reader discover the extreme importance of seeing oneself from God's perspective! Read it and learn how to begin your journey with God toward contentment and productivity.

Jimmy Harper
Campus Pastor
Lee University

Chevis Brooks has overcome adversity in so many ways. I've seen it firsthand. Now he's giving the blueprint to how he has found his identity not in the things of this world, but in the very One who created him.

CJ Blount
Associate Worship Pastor
Church of the Highlands

To my daughter, Avery (aka: A-Bear):
I look at you and I see God's "Masterpiece".
My prayer is that you will learn to see the same.
I love you.

CONTENTS

NOTE TO THE READER

As you dive into this book, you'll soon notice a somewhat unpredictable "pattern" of reading and experience, meaning, some chapters you'll be able to ingest casually and digest easily while other chapters will be much more challenging. This was all done by intentional design as I wanted the "flow" of the book to be in sync with the "flow" of my life and, what I believe, is the "flow" of life at large. While we (myself along with the proofreaders and editors) did our best to make it grammatically perfect, I made the decision to keep the overall tone imperfect in hopes that my life could be one you could relate to and, in turn, open your heart to because my desire is to make a difference in the world. And, I realize such a pursuit begins with making a difference in *your* world — the world of the individual — first. As one of my hero's often says, "Transformed people transform cities" (Bill Johnson, Pastor of Bethel Church in Redding, California). My hope is that the lessons within the book will bring some type of transformational value to you just as they have to me. Thanks so much for being willing to open your mind and heart to the contents in the following pages and for allowing me to be the real *me: inconsistent, passionate, and vulnerable.* Beloved,

I do not cease giving thanks for you, while making mention of you in my prayers; that the God of our Lord Jesus Christ, the Father of glory, may give to you a spirit of wisdom and of revelation in the knowledge of Him. *I pray that* the eyes of your heart may be enlightened, so that you will know w*hat is the hope of His calling, what are the riches of His glorious inheritance in the saints, and what is the surpassing greatness of His power toward us who believe. (Ephesians 1:16-19).*

INTRODUCTION

You. This was the answer I gave to a good friend (who is also a believer) as an introduction to what this book would be about when it was still in its infancy stage (as an idea).

"You need be careful!" he said. "That sounds like some personal development one-liner from one of those motivational gurus".

To which I responded, "It is. His name is Jesus".

Looking at me like I had three-heads, I felt the need to explain.

"What are the two greatest commandments?" I asked him.

He thought for a second and said, "The first is 'Love the Lord your God with all your heart, mind, soul, and strength and the second is 'Love your neighbor as yourself'".

"That's exactly right" I replied and proceeded by asking him, "Can you tell me the last two words of everything you just said"?

He thought about it for a moment and said, "**AS YOURSELF**".

I smiled, offered no response, and patiently waited on his next objection (I knew there would be one because old thinking, like old habits, die hard). He argued, "No. It all starts with loving God first".

I kept smiling and asked, "You think so?" To which he responded with a passionate, "YES!"

I said, "You're the reason I'm writing the book".

Slightly offended, he retorted, "What are you talking about"?

(Laughing) I told him, "I agree that it all starts with God, however, I disagree that it all starts with us loving Him first".

I could see a shift in his thinking beginning to occur as I continued, "Actually, it is the exact opposite: **It all starts with God loving us first**".

Despite the confused countenance on his face, he was intrigued enough to ask, "Can you explain?"

As a response, I began putting "pen to paper" and the explanation became the book that you are now holding in your hands (and that he is holding in his).

1

THE FORGOTTEN
COMMANDMENT

"Learning to love yourself, it is the greatest love of all."

—MICHAEL MASSER

If I asked you to name all of the things you love, how long would it take you to name yourself? Or, would you name yourself at all? If you're anything like I used to be, or like the vast majority of humanity still is, you most likely wouldn't make it onto your own list. And, the reasons you wouldn't are as plentiful as the day is long — your father walked out on you, your mother gave you up for adoption, your spouse cheated on you, a family member sexually abused you, the congregation you served faithfully for decades *voted* you out, your friend betrayed you, your mentor told you it's wrong, your religion taught you that in order to truly love God then you have to hate or despise yourself. These are all convincing excuses, but none were convincing enough for God to remove you from His list, which means you must re-think who and/or what you've allowed to determine yours and, as an obedient response, re-write it so that it begins to look more like His.

WHY

Within the last couple of years, I've experienced an emerging desire, or dare I say, an emerging calling to give people permission to love themselves. As uncomfortable, contrary, and risky as it feels to promote such an agenda, I feel it's quickly becoming a must — something I can't deny doing — because I know from first-hand experience what it's like to not love yourself. You see, I've been abandoned by my own father, rejected and kicked out of churches, disappointed by coaches and mentors, cheated on by girlfriends, lied to, stolen from, slandered, and betrayed by close friends, and fired by employers. I know the deep pain of standing in the rain to wait on a father who promised he's coming this time only to be left waiting . . . again. I know what it's like to seek counseling from a pastor for your struggles only to be told you're "full of the devil" and "if you don't turn it around God is going to take everything from you". I know the confusion of coming home to a box at your front door packed full of your belongings, left there by a "spiritual mother and father" who promised to always be there for you. I know the disappointment of starting a business with your best friend, opening a bank account with both of your names on it, funding the account for start-up capital, only to realize two months later that more than half was taken (aka: stolen) with no explanation. Trust me, I know all-too-well the brutal realities of people and their actions that all scream, "You're not lovable". Don't get me wrong, I've not always been the victim. I also know what it's like to be the one that abandons, rejects, disappoints, cheats, lies, steals, betrays, and fires. Once again, a list of actions that leave you saying and believing, "you don't deserve to be loved"– that leave you asking *why*.

This was the cycle of my life (even after I became a Christian) for many, many years until I came across what I've come to call "The Forgotten Commandment", found in what we have commonly referred to as *The Greatest Commandments*, which says,

> *"Love the Lord Your God with all of your heart, mind, soul, and strength. And, love your neighbor as yourself (Luke 10:27)".*

There it was hidden in plain sight: the answer to *why*. *Why* all those people hurt me and *why* I would hurt others. The answer to *why* anybody does anything to anybody. It all comes back to a love for oneself.

I DON'T LIKE LOVE

Before I go any further, I have a confession that I need to make. Anyone close to me will tell you that my passion is not as much about love as it is about what love leads to. Ashamedly, I have to admit that love messages are among my least favorite to hear or study. Bored, uninterested, and nauseous are a few of the adjectives that I've used in the past to describe my feelings concerning this particular topic. Perhaps, a little too loudly, as some 'brothers and sisters in the faith' have offered their unsolicited advice as reasons for my extreme lack of interest ranging from some buried hurt in my past that I've not been willing to confront, to being prideful, to simply being a male. Not sure I agree with any of it, although, I did spend a considerable amount of time trying to rid myself of every conceivable past pain I could think of in an effort to make myself *like* love. Heck, I even made up some hurts along the way just in case I missed any. After many wasted attempts, I've come to the conclusion that my indifference has nothing to do with my past, or my pride, or my gender. It's just who I am and that's ok. Why? I've learned to love who I am. Not someone else's version of who they think I should be, but I've come to a place of really loving me. I love that I'm not interested in "love" as a message, I love that I'm no longer moved by those who tell me something is wrong with me because of it, and I love that I don't *like* love. I like to love but I don't *like* "love" as a discussion.

Love is a word that we, in the American culture, use as a blanket of sorts to cover anything and everything that captures our attention or peaks our interests. For example, we say, "I love my wife" and "I love pizza". While it's understood that we mean something different depending on where our love is directed, the true essence of its impact is many times lost because meaning doesn't translate well in saying alone. Case in point, how many times have you experienced a heated exchange between two people where one person eventually says, "that's not what I meant" and the other responds with, "well, that's what you said"?

Meaning is everything, which, brings a ton of validity to the ancient cliché, "it's not what you say; it's how you say it". Here, in North America, when it comes to love we are forced to rely on other things such as our tone of voice, emotion, and/or body language to aid us in conveying the correct meaning to our message so we increase the chances of it being received accurately. That's a lot of work which could have endured a much simpler process if more than one way of saying and conveying love had been developed from the start.

Take the Greeks, for example, who used four different words to describe love: **Eros, Storge, Phileo** and **Agape**. **Eros** describes a "romantic or sexual love" commonly shared by two people who are physically attracted to one another. Its purest form of expression is seen in a marriage between husband and wife. **Storge** was used to speak of "familial love". This type of love was commonly used to describe the love of a parent for a child. **Phileo** points to "brotherly love". It speaks of the warm affection shared between friends. **Agape** is known as a "self-sacrificing love". This was the love that God displayed when sending His only begotten Son to be the sacrifice for our sins. Some believe that *Agape* is the highest form of love that one can attain to because it describes and expresses the very nature of God Himself.

In the attempt to simplify our language, we've lost the flavor of love's dynamics. We've reduced it to a static, one-size-fits-all definition and the sacrifice for doing so has been the vastness of the treasure locked within. Re-calibrating ourselves

> THERE ARE TWO COMMON DENOMINATORS EXISTING BETWEEN EACH TYPE OF LOVE: LOVE MUST BE EXPRESSED AND LOVE MUST BE DESTINED.

to adopt, as the Greeks did, a multi-faceted view of love will not only expand our understanding, but will also release our *riches*. The customary, universalistic approach of our culture has been a bit misplaced due to a focus centered more on definition than expression. If you'll notice, there are two common denominators existing between each type of love: love must be expressed and love must be destined. It is an ACT motivated by an AIM. *Eros* is aroused through a passionate connection whose purpose is only fulfilled through romance. *Storge's* craving can only be satisfied through a parent in the presence of their child. *Phileo's* warmth is felt in the company of friends. *Agape's* benevolent supply is used when a sacrificial demand has been made. Any demonstration of love is a key that unlocks a greater treasure than simply the emotion it comes with; it opens the vault of a greater means. Without a reason, love becomes stagnant and soon lends itself and its hosts (me and you) to a dangerous state of idleness. More simply put, if love doesn't move it dies.

YOU'VE LOST THAT LOVING FEELING

This point is well-proven by the recent, upward trending statistics of failed marriages within our own country. The majority of divorce papers may read, "irreconcilable differences", but the truth is somewhere along the way love stopped moving. It usually sounds something like, "after we got married, he stopped doing the things he did while we were dating to win me over", or, "she stopped appreciating me like she used to". "The things she seemed to admire about me at one time now seems like the things she hates." No matter what cause is identified, you can rest assured that one or the other had a change of heart not because of irreconcilable differences, but because of inconsistent efforts.

Now you have another reason why I don't like love. It's hard. It requires something from me and that something usually looks like work. At some point, sustained love demands that emotion is replaced with decision, interaction takes precedence over inaction, and sacrifice is seen as a privilege, not a prison. These are the *rules* of everlasting love and if you desire a life that sustains and multiplies love you must play by the rules.

1. Emotion is replaced with decision: Many of us have encountered the intoxicating emotion of love. Needless to say, it's an extremely powerful feeling that everyone should experience at least once in their lifetime, however, it is beneficial to know ahead of time that it's temporary. Believing that emotion alone has the ability to sustain any relationship is to live under an illusion. At some point, the euphoric, physical vibration will wear off. This is the place where decision must take its stand. Love may be sparked through emotion, however, it will only be sustained through choice. This doesn't mean that feelings will become entirely obsolete or that they should be rejected when they arise; it just means that we proceed with the understanding that they work best as igniters, not sustainers.

2. Interaction takes precedence over inaction: *Love is an action*. I've heard this statement more times than I care to count and I agree with it to a certain extent. The issue with leaving it there is that it's incomplete. At the time of this writing, I am about six weeks away from celebrating my ten year anniversary of marriage. These ten years have taught me many things, but none truer than this: all actions are not created equal.

My wife is very much a show-me-you-love-me type of person and believes that telling holds validity only when preceded and proceeded with some act of service. For her, love doesn't stop at doing something for her, it's also doing it in a way that pleases her. She has taught me that love is not just any action, love is an interaction. It's loving in a way that communicates to her in the language she prefers and understands. Many have "lost that loving feeling" because they didn't allow interaction to take precedence over inaction.

Some have come to define inaction as simply lacking action. In my mind, inaction comes in two forms: lack and waste. The first is easy to identify and fix. Simply get your lazy butt of the couch and start doing something. The second is a little more difficult to detect and can cause extreme strain in relationships. Let me explain. When we first got married, my idea of cleaning the house was to wipe a few counters, take out the trash, and unload the dishwasher (obviously not all on the same day and certainly not every day). Early on, I would do one or the other as a way to "serve" (love) my wife. I would be excited for her to come home to an empty dishwasher or a clean counter and I had an image in my head of her walking through the door and praising me for all my "hard work" on cleaning the house. To this day, I have no idea how an unloaded dishwasher equaled a clean house in my mind, but it did. To my surprise, she either wouldn't notice at all or she would offer a courtesy thanks backed by advice on how to do it better next time. This would infuriate me. "I cleaned the house and this is the thanks I get?" I would say to myself. It took me years to realize that her advice was not a knock on my effort, it was a suggestion on how to love her better. The lesson? Wasted action is the same as inaction. I've often wondered what percentages of terminated relationships were due to wasted action. As funny as it is to tell this story at this stage of our journey, the anger for me was real just as the disappointment for her was real. Allowing interaction to take precedence over my wasted action has allowed me to become a better husband and has played a vital role in us growing closer together over the past ten years instead of farther apart. So, we know where I started minimizing my wasted motion, but where did the interaction occur? First, interaction is an action between two parts or partners. The interaction that occurred between myself and my wife came between her suggestion and my adjustment. The next time I cleaned the house I knew what her expectations were and I did my best to clean to that standard. Was it perfect? No. Was it done exactly as she would've done it? No. Did she notice that I tried? Yes. Did she feel more loved as a result? Yes. Interaction, therefore, is more than a house occupied by two people who have the occasional casual conversation simply because they live in the same space. It's the adjustment of accents to speak in the language that most resonates with the love the other person understands.

3. Sacrifice is seen as a privilege not a prison: *I, Chevis, take you, Keri, to be my lawfully wedded wife, to have and to hold, from this day forward, for better, for worse, for richer, for poorer, in sickness and in health, until death do us part.*

If marriage could be summed up into one word it would have to be "sacrifice". On the day of our ceremony, standing face to face with our partner, with tears in our eyes we read this part of our vows (or something similar to it) without a clue as to how sacrificial we will have to be if our parting goal truly is death. We think we know, but we have no idea. It doesn't take long before we're hit right between the eyes with this reality as we get ready to walk out the door to go play ball with the guys only to find out that she's scheduled dinner for you with herself and her parents. Uh oh! The first time it happens, it's not so bad. The second, third, and 30th time begins to take its toll until we soon find ourselves secretly feeling as if we're in a prison. Hence, the reason some refer to marriage as, "the ole' ball and chain". I've heard some say 'this is not what I signed up for'. My response is always, "Yes it is. Remember the vows?'

Signing up for any relationship is signing up for the sacrifices it's going to require to make it work. Therefore, we have two choices: We can keep viewing the *give and take* as a prison or we can condition ourselves to begin viewing them as a privilege. The view we choose will produce two entirely different outcomes. Those living with the prisoner mindset live under a self-imposed sentence. In other words, their thoughts will continuously be consumed by the *end* of their punishment as this marks the date of their departure. On the other hand, those who live with a privilege mindset view their sacrifice as an expression of new found freedoms instead of the exemption from old freedoms. Their thoughts are not centered on *"the end"* but on the *"to be continued"*.

ALL THE WRONG PLACES

As you can see, love is no easy task. We are all in a constant limbo between violation and acceptance when it comes to the "rules" of associations and connections concerning our personal and professional relationships. That burden multiplies in its level of difficulty when we attempt to do it outside of the prescribed relational formula that Jesus gave us which commands, "love your neighbor as yourself".

I'm going to make a very bold statement: I'd like to suggest that we consider the increasing trend of divorce is not as much about two people falling out of love with one another as it is about two people not, first, learning to love themselves.

Taken a step further, I also believe this theory should be taken as a serious starting place for bringing a solution to many, if not all, of the rising, negative social issues we face today. When I watch any act of destruction — a man beating his wife, a cop killing an unarmed person, an addiction to porn, alcohol, or drugs, a cheating spouse, a lying child, a slander of someone behind their back, a father leaving the home — I can't help but ask, "What does the person committing the act not like about himself or herself? What personal fear or insecurity is he or she dealing with that causes this kind of response?" In the Christian circle, we've chalked it up to a "sin nature". While this could be labeled as an attempt toward a solution, it's one that has proven to be redundantly ineffective as it rebels against the purpose of Jesus' death, robs us of self-control, and removes us from personal responsibility.

Reflecting on the destructive experiences from my past, I can honestly say at the core of their manifestation was always a corrupt self-view. Any fight I got into wasn't really about an anger toward the other person as much as it was about fighting the coward I hated within. Dating multiple girls at a time wasn't about a search for the right person, or even trying to be cool with "my boys". It was about a search for acceptance from the opposite sex in order to the fill the void that was left from an inability to accept myself. My experimentation with drugs and alcohol was really an experiment of creating multiple pathways to provide temporary relief from the negative thoughts and emotions that I harbored concerning me.

Every event I've just described reveals I desperately wanted to be someone I wasn't. I desperately wanted to change. The problem I had with the tactics I was using is that I was looking for it in all the wrong places. The change I was seeking was on the other side of a love for myself, which couldn't be found in a fight, or girls, or drugs, or alcohol. It could only be found through an encounter with Love Himself.

REFLECTION QUESTIONS

#1. Do you believe Jesus wants you to love yourself? If so, can you honestly say that you do? Why or why not?

#2. What are some of your initial reactions (emotional, mental, or otherwise) to the *"Forgotten Commandment"*? Why do you think those are your first responses?

#3. What are some potential "dangers in learning to love yourself? What are some "benefits"? In your opinion, is it worth the risk? What can you do to make sure you stay on the side of "benefit"?

#4. Do you agree or disagree that people's actions toward others are a reflection of how much they love or don't love themselves? Why or why not?

MEDITATION/APPLICATION

By far, one of the hardest things I've ever had to do was learn to love myself. On top of the many negative experiences I had before coming to Christ that told me I wasn't worth loving, I stepped into a church and teaching that measured the love of God by the sacrifice of self. *"None of me, God, all of you"* and *"I must decrease, You must increase"* were just a few of the staple prayers I'd hear the more mature believers praying and eventually adopted as my own. There was just one problem I kept running into: There was a time where He had "none of me" and He obviously didn't like it, proven by the fact that He created me. And, to top it off, He thought I was worth sending His only Son to die for. How could I keep seeing myself as unlovable or keep praying those types of prayers? Have you ever thought that maybe, just maybe, we've measure our love for Him using the wrong standards? If we are not the measuring stick, then what standards should we start using?

2

JESUS LOVES ME THIS I KNOW

"I Love You"

—GOD

Growing up my dad left when I was five or six years old, so, my mom was forced to try and "man" the reigns of responsibilities left by his absence. Included within the added weight of her other duties was becoming the only and primary provider of our home. Needless to say, she had to capture any and every "overtime" opportunity afforded to her by her job to make sure that our needs were met. This was on top of an already grueling eight, ten, or twelve hour schedule set by a swing-shift rotation. Some weeks she would work first shift meaning that she was required to be at work around 7 or 8 in the morning and was set to get off at 4 in the afternoon. Other weeks were a second-shift obligation that switched her to a schedule requiring her to arrive around 4pm and leave at midnight. And, worst of all, were the weeks she had to work third, better known as the "graveyard shift". During this rotation, she would go in at midnight and work until 8 in the morning. From my memories, weekends usually provided the best opportunity for overtime (obviously in the event that she wasn't already scheduled to be there).

My dad leaving combined with a very demanding job schedule didn't exactly create the best situation for us to consider going to church with any type of consistency. I went with friends here and there, but to make it a part of our family tradition was nearly impossible. Although I do remember a time around nine or ten years old where we began attending a Baptist church for about a year. Not real sure what happened that allowed my mom to take me, but I remember going. The memory will last with me forever. Not because I had some amazing Jesus encounter, but because the level of boredom I experienced in that year is simply unforgettable. I would have to wake up early on Sunday, get dressed in my "Sunday best", and go to Sunday school class to learn about some mystical Bible character or sing some cheesy children's church song.

As I've gotten older, I must admit what was boring to me then is attractive to me now. The best explanation I have for that is maturity can sometimes open our hearts to the depths of what or who was really behind a story or song. One such song that stands out to me is *"Jesus loves me — this I know"*. There are times where I catch myself singing it out of nowhere. I don't know why. Maybe its unsolicited visitation is just that, an unsolicited visitation, or maybe, just maybe, it's a needed reminder of where love begins.

SAYING AND SEEDING

I've spent a large majority of my Christian walk trying to live up to the classic clichés of church talk. Oddly enough, I've spent the same amount of time emotionally distraught over the lack of sustainability in my efforts. One such axiom in particular that has left me with more days of self-discontentment and disillusionment than I can count is *"You can't put God in a formula (or a box)"*. This usually came on the backside of me failing at some moral goal I had set for myself which would always propel me into a frantic search of scripture followed by an emergency "deliverance" phone call to an elder or a pastor in hopes that one of them could give me a systematic if-you-do-this-then-you-get-this solution. The dilemma I constantly ran into by taking this dual approach toward an answer was the supposed wise elder and the sacred scripture always seemed to be on opposite ends of the spectrum. One would assume that I'd just go with scripture since it is considered *sacred*, but the reality is I would ultimately undermine my own biblical findings because it seemed way too simple compared to the depths of revelation that would pour forth from the mouth of my "teacher". It's funny to think about now, but the content I'd receive from my closed-door deliverance session was so profound I thought to myself, "this has to be what I'm looking for because it's just too 'smooth' not to be right". There was only one problem. Although the information sounded good, was backed by an off-the-charts IQ, and deeply rooted in a solid theological education (proven by a wall covered with seminary degrees), I would immediately forget more than half of everything that was said as soon as I walked out the door. All of it was impressive, but, none of it was applicable. Usually somewhere within the conversation I would offer a few of my own discoveries only to hear something like, *"in God, rarely does A+B=C"*. In other words, "your answer is far too simple and systematic to be God". It took me a while to realize that much of today's theological sense doesn't always equal common sense. God Himself may not fit into a formula, however, He did a real good job of putting the entire world into one.

In the beginning the earth was created with three major issues that needed to be addressed: it was **formless, dark, and void (see Genesis 1:1-3)**. As you explore the Hebraic text for each of these words, you will discover the problems which inhabited the earth were much more intense than many of our English versions have been able to accurately express. Re-written to reveal the true magnitude of the world's crisis at that time, it would read "the earth was **confused, empty, and insignificant**". Otherwise stated, it lacked identity, worth, and purpose. We will spend more time unraveling each of these in later chapters. For now, I want us to turn on our focus to God's chosen solution for what He saw. It reads like this:

Then God said . . .

His solution was His saying and Jesus told us in Luke 8:11, *"The Seed is the Word of God"*. The Greek word for *seed* is *sperma* (where we get our English word, "sperm"). Like sperm, His word carries potential and that potential carries the need for process in order to see it realized. Most of us have held to the idea that as soon as God spoke, the thing He spoke about appeared immediately. Because He's God and "all things are possible" with Him, that's a difficult point to argue. However, I'd like to suggest, in light of our natural understanding of "seed(s)" (and Jesus calling the Word of God, "seed"), creation may not have happened as fast as we may believe (immediately) because seed doesn't sprout at the moment it is sown. It requires stages of maturation and progression unique to its nature. I believe, by speaking, he was actually planting within (impregnating) the thing he was speaking to its potential. Along with that potential came its "formula", or its predetermined path of development. The seed of an orange tree carries the potential of an orange grove. The seed of oak tree carries the potential of a forest. The seed of a human carries the potential of generations. As we all know potential doesn't guarantee actual. Potential, in any form, in anything, is subject to a certain process before we are able to see its manifestation. And, process is usually determined by location and/or timing. While an orange tree holds the potential for an orange grove, that potential will never be seen if planted in the frozen tundra. It's also true that an acorn holds within its DNA an oak tree and the oak tree a forest, still, the environmental factors below and above the surface must be conducive for us to see this demonstration in it fullness. Likewise, the potential of a strong, healthy, vibrant newborn baby needs the womb of its mother and a nine month gestation period to be fully realized. Contrary to much of the advice I have received over the years, everything, and I do mean everything, in our world derives from a formula, a set of governing principles if you will, expressed through the concept and character of seeds, which are:

SEED PRINCIPLE #1: SEEDS ALWAYS PRODUCE ACCORDING TO THEIR KIND

*Then God said, "Let the earth produce vegetation: seed-bearing plants and fruit trees on the earth bearing fruit with seed in it **according to their kinds.**" And it was so. The earth produced vegetation: seed-bearing plants **according to their kinds** and trees bearing fruit with seed in it **according to their kinds.** And God saw that it was good. Evening came and then morning: the third day* (Genesis 1:11-13).

An apple seed can only produce apples. A pear seed can only produce pears. Animals can only produce animals. And humans can only produce humans. It is true. We reap exactly what we sow, but sowing is not the origin of seed, *kind* is. The *kind* of thoughts, beliefs, and feelings we have concerning anything will determine the *kind* of words, actions, or results we get. Good thoughts sow good actions and reap good results. Bad thoughts sow bad actions and reap bad results. This is the life cycle of seeds and man.

SEED PRINCIPLE #2: SEEDS ALWAYS MULTIPLY

To every *"creeping thing"* — animals, insects, man, etc. — God gave the same "blessing": *Be fruitful and multiply.* (see Genesis 1:24-31) Another way He could have said this is "be like fruit and multiply". Fruit is a seen reality pointing to a greater unseen reality. It carries seed and seed carries the capacity of multiplication. From a literal perspective, seeds really do multiply. It's a part of their inherent God-given capacity. However, I believe it is within the figurative, metaphorical context of life's intended progression that we'll discover a world we never knew existed.

Unbeknownst to me at the time, the lesson of "seed multiplication" in life and man began in my English classes coming through school. I don't recall the exact grade, but I do remember learning about comparative and superlative adjectives. Comparative adjectives compare two things. Superlative adjectives compare more than two things. Here are a few examples that will jog your memory and may even give you a few flashbacks of the extreme boredom you may have experienced in your English classes (hang with me I promise we are going somewhere with this):

Old	Older	Oldest
Young	Younger	Youngest
Bad	Worse	Worst
Good	Better	Best

The Bible taught me that seed multiplies. My English classes taught me *how* seed multiplies. Seeds, like comparative and superlative adjectives, begin in one form, but end in another. The final form is always a multiplied version of the original. As a part of God's perfect plan, He placed within everything's beginning a **better** ending. Perhaps this is why

He said, *though your beginning was **small**, your latter days will be very **great** (Job 8:7, Haggai 2:9)*

THE LAW AND ORDER OF LOVE

What does all this have to do with the unsolicited visitations of the children's church song from my past? Some would identify it as a being nothing beyond a simple reminder that "Jesus loves me". Although the thought alone does bring a level of emotional security, my personal conviction is that it's meant to be a reminder of where He intends His love to go and grow. Like seed, love holds the potential of multiplication — of becoming a better version of itself. Also like seed, it must submit to a unique process of development — a certain law and order, before its absolute best versions can be fully realized.

The law and order of love governs and protects the probabilities of its potential (multiplication). If followed, love will increase. If violated, it will die. In His conversation with the "expert", Jesus revealed what is referred to as *"The Greatest Commandments"* (Mark 12-35-40). Explore them a little deeper and you'll find the Greek word "entole", which can also mean "order". More specifically, it means *"to command, emphasizing the end-objective, i.e. reaching the purpose, consummation, or end result of an order — i.e. as envisioning how or where it ends up"*. What Jesus gave us was His vision of how/where He intended the "The Greatest Orders (Commandments)" to end up. He was giving us a picture of the finished product of love after it has deposited and transformed into its multiplied effects — its "great, greater, and greatest" **kinds**.

You see, loving others is the multiplied form of loving yourself. Loving God is the multiplied form of loving others. However, we would be operating amiss if we didn't remember that all "greater" versions (multiplied forms) point to the reality of their much "smaller" beginnings (as seeds). Attaining to the highest forms of love — the love of God — is the ultimate pursuit. It is the "Greatest" Commandment and the most glorious ending. Nevertheless, we cannot get there by using some hidden bypass or by "despising the day of small things". We must go through the right stages of process remembering that to every *greatest* there was first a *great* and *greater*.

I John 4:19-21 says, "*We love because he first loved us. Whoever claims to love God yet hates a brother or sister is a liar. For whoever does not love their brother and sister, whom they have seen, cannot love God, whom they have not seen. And he has given us this command: Anyone who loves God must also love their brother and sister.*

If we were to take this portion of scripture and merge it with that of the two greatest commandments, *Love the Lord your God with all your heart, mind, soul, and strength. And, Love your neighbor as yourself,* it would read something like, "**You can't love God without loving others. And you'll only love others to the measure that you love yourself. And loving yourself begins with God loving you.**

God Loves Us (GOOD)	We Love Ourselves (GREAT)	We Love Others (GREATER)	We Love God (GREATEST)

Contrary to traditional beliefs, the Christian life doesn't begin with us loving God; it begins with God loving us. More simply stated, His love is the "beginning of a work" (see Zechariah 4:10). It is the seed whose next step of development is not a love for God, but is instead a love for oneself.

TRULY BEING "LIKE HIM"

It has been said and passionately taught that the entire pursuit of our Christian lives is to be "like God" — to walk, talk, and act as much like Him as possible. However, most of our customary aim in doing so has been guided by a checklist of

Do's and *Don'ts* with the latter outweighing the former 10 to 1 in most cases. *Thou shalt not* has become the overarching theme of righteousness and the gauge of success in our obedience to it has been determined more by what we avoid or hate than what we embrace or love. For example, the standard of how much we love God has commonly been measured by how much we hate the world, hate the devil, hate sin, and, worst of all, hate ourselves. The fact is, God loves us so much that He sent His Son to die for us (John 3:16). If we truly believe that the ultimate pursuit of our lives is to obey God and become "like Him" shouldn't that resemblance also include loving who and what He loves?

Understanding the law and order of love is not as much about submitting to a list of rules as it is about stewarding a process of development. It is a means to a critically important end. Allowing the Love of God to lead you to loving yourself not only ensures your arrival at loving Him, but also allows you to see yourself as He sees you. Until you learn to see yourself through the eyes of God, who is love, you will never be able to know who you truly are. And if you don't know who you are, then you won't know what you're worth or why you're here. These three elements are the reason you and I live — it's the reason we breathe and the reason He came. This is why we must receive it just as Jesus gave it, both as a command and a commission.

REFLECTION QUESTIONS

#1. Do you *really* believe that Jesus loves you?

#2. Seeing that another word for "commandment" is "order" (defined by a "vision of how and where it ends up"), how does this change the way you've interpreted the Greatest Commandments and/or love?

#3. Does God give love with the seed in mind — with the expectation of multiplication? In order, what are the multiplied forms of love — where does God intend for it to "end up"?

#4. Comparing Matthew 22:37-39 and I John 4:19-21, does this alter how you've traditionally understood the Greatest Commandments?

#5. Can we be like God without loving who and what He loves? Do you agree or disagree that this means we should learn to love ourselves?

MEDITATION/APPLICATION

If you take I John 4:19-21 and merge it with that of the two greatest commandments (Love the Lord your God with all your heart, mind, soul, and strength. And, Love your neighbor as yourself) it could read something like, **"You can't love God without loving others. And you'll only love others to the measure that you love yourself. And loving yourself begins with God loving you.** Does this begin to bring "things" into their proper perspective for you? Are you beginning to see the intended "flow" and "order" of love? How does this change the way you've been living and how will it change how you live (and love) moving forward?

3

LAST WORDS

"Just try to leave a lasting impression."

—ROD COLEMAN

*T*he first impression is the lasting impression. For many years, psychologist have studied and confirmed the validity of this argument. They have determined that in as little as one-tenth of a second we form hundreds of opinions about a person, place, or thing. That is both staggering and concerning.

It's staggering because it reveals a small part of just how powerful our brains can be. Literally, in less than a second, a profile is built in our mind's eye based on the picture presented to us in any given moment. This is not to assume that the profile is always accurate or even fair as we know it constructs the idiosyncratic image in our heads based on many factors that include but are not limited to cultural and physical influences. For example, the parents of a two year old toddler see an unfamiliar dog in the neighborhood that resembles a pit bull and automatically sense "danger" based on the story portrayed about "those" types of dogs while watching the late-night news last week. The child who grew up in poverty encounters a rich person for the first-time and without any formal introduction being made quickly stereotypes him or her as greedy or hard working depending on what they've been taught. The pastor who pulls up to church in a Rolls Royce . . . do I really need to finish the sentence? You get the point. First impressions can be accurate or inaccurate since they are, most times, formulated as final conclusions under the influence of unquestioned opinions rooted in our most dominant social, environmental, or cultural persuasions.

These impressions are extremely powerful and totally inevitable which also makes them very concerning. Another study reveals, *"It takes 20 additional interactions to fix a bad initial impression"*. What took one tenth of second to formulate takes 20 additional interactions to eradicate. Although it can be completely unjustified, the impression will still be made. So, what do we do? We can . . .

• ADAPT

The common approach to making this truth work in our favor has been to ADAPT to it. Without knowing it, many of us are taught from an early age the art of making a solid first impression by our parents who place constant pressure on us to have and display good manners. They teach us to eat with our mouths closed, to say "yes sir" and "no sir", "yes ma'am" and "no ma'am", to be reverent in church services, and quiet at funerals. As we progress through life, we also learn the way we dress and the way we walk and talk has a massive impact on a dad allowing us to date his daughter or an employer hiring us for a job. The bottom line is this: *first impressions matter*. Whether we want to be stereotyped or not, we will be. With that said, I'm in complete agreement with Paul's adaptation technique revealed in his letter to the Corinthians:

I have become all things to all men that I might save some
(I Corinthians 9:19-23).

Paul understood the power of adaptation — how to leverage life to work for him in order that he might *"win some"*. I
suggest we follow his lead if we want others to give and receive
positive assessments concerning our character. If we know that
first impressions hold that much power — that people will
subconsciously assemble opinions about us in seconds then
we must remain conscious enough and humble enough by
putting our best foot forward at all times.

• ADOPT

First impressions may be lasting, but they may not always be
reliable if left to act alone as the sole influencer of our judg-
ments. In the processes of preserving (accepting, adapting) our
old, yet effective ideas, we can and should also be partnering
(introducing, adopting) with some new ones. We must become
open-minded to making space for co-habiting stimuluses of
analysis in reaching our conclusions. Think about this! What
if we used reverse psychology? What if we "tricked" ourselves?
What if we could get ourselves to draw no lasting conclusions
until all evidence has been presented — the evidence of the
first impression and the evidence of the last? Since hearing
about the research and findings of the power within the first
impression, I have always questioned and meditated on the
potential power of the last? Does it or can it have an influence
on our final rulings?

A WILL OF WORDS

Not to get strange, but I've always had a weird infatuation
with people's final moments. Particularly, their final words
in those moments. These words give us a final impression of

what they were thinking after all has been said and done. We are able, in some cases, to know if they loved the life they lived or if they regretted it, if they became all they dreamed of becoming, accomplished all they desired to accomplished, or if they are going to the grave with some unfinished business. It's as if their words become a will of sorts to those living after them. Whether we know them personally or not, we feel connected to them in that moment as we tune ourselves into being the hopeful recipients of an inheritance locked within their final utterances.

LEONARDO DA VINCI: *"I have offended God and mankind for doing so little with my life"*

Da Vinci is known to most as a famous painter. A deeper look into his life reveals so much more. He was, in fact, a true Renaissance man gifted and successful in many areas. He was an inventor, a scientist, a painter, an architect, an engineer, a musician (as a performer and a composer), able to sing and compose songs spontaneously, a noted anatomist, a geologist, a geometer, a mathematician, a sculptor, a physicist and astronomer, a Roman Catholic, a vegetarian and so much more. Perhaps the most bizarre part of the words he offered with his last breath is that he did so in the arms of King Francis, the King of France, which was the highest honor one could have accorded in those days as the King was considered divine. To them, it was the same as dying in the arms of a god.

It's very difficult not to become somewhat fearful at the possibility of living a long life only to arrive at death feeling as if it meant nothing. How can a man so gifted, so accomplished, and whose legacy lives with us more than 500 years later die feeling as if he did "so little with his life"? Was he just being hard on himself or was there really more he should have and could have done? There's probably not a real way of gaining an accurate answer and most responses to these questions, including my own, will be based in total assumption, but, one thing we can be 100% sure of from Da Vinci's story is that it's possible to live an accomplished life apart from a fulfilled life.

Achievement and fulfillment are not the same thing. The first has been referred to as a science — a skill that can be learned or a system that can be applied to produce a guaranteed result. For instance, Da Vinci knew the science of painting masterpieces. He knew the way he should position the canvas, how he should hold the brush, what corner of the canvas to start on, and how to choose the right combination of colors. Although the *Last Supper, the Mona Lisa, and the Vitruvian Man* produced a different visual end, the skills and system for producing that end were the same.

Da Vinci was a master in the Science of Achievement. He knew how to do many things and how to do them well, however, it's clear that he didn't know himself and this is why his last words couldn't have come from a fulfilled man.

Fulfillment is called an art because it's different for everyone. What one person thinks is beautiful, the other does not. Therefore, to live a fulfilled life — a life whose last breath is one of satisfaction and contentment — demands that you "know thyself and to thine own self be true".

As great as his works were, it's obvious they were not what brought him gratification. What that was for him we will never know, but we can know for ourselves. Da Vinci's greatness as an artist can't be denied as proven by the immortal impact of his work so many years later, still, it's worth considering that his greatest heritage to us may not be from his brush, but from his words. Because he dared to admit dissatisfaction in his final moments, we all benefit from a new perspective so that we don't repeat the same. As Tony Robbins often says, *"success without fulfillment is the ultimate failure"*. We should strive to live a skilled life as well as a fulfilled life as both are essential elements to a complete life.

NATHAN HALE: *"I only regret that I have but one life to lose for my country"*

Nathan Hale and his words are legendary. In nearly every American History class across our nation, as students begin to learn about *The Revolutionary War*, this man's story is told and his final declaration quoted. And rightfully so. His personal sacrifice, bravery, firm resolve in the face of death, and passion for his country are all worthy reasons of placing him among our nation's archive of heroes.

After graduating from Yale (in two years) in 1773, Hale began his career as a teacher. Two years later, as the War for Independence heated up, he decided to enroll in the armed forces where he would be commissioned as a captain in the Continental Army. He served in Boston and New York, where he would end up volunteering himself to go behind enemy lines as a spy (an act punishable by death) to gather intelligence and report on British movements. After a week of being disguised as a Dutch school master, on September 21, 1776, he was captured and immediately sentenced to death. The following day at 11:00am Nathan Hale was hanged. Before doing so, he was allowed to give a final speech that ended with the indelible final words: *"I only regret that I have but one life to lose for my country"*.

Most would agree that the ultimate goal of life is to leave with no regrets. Hale gives us hope that it's possible. In his final moments before death, with his life flashing before his eyes, the 21-year old only regretted that he didn't have

IN THE WORDS OF WINSTON CHURCHILL, *"WE MAKE A LIVING BY WHAT WE GET, BUT WE MAKE A LIFE BY WHAT WE GIVE".*

another life to lose for his country. In essence, he wished he could live again to die again for a worthy cause. One would think a man so young would be saddened over the many experiences — marriage, parenting, career, etc.- he'd be missing out on by not living longer., but that wasn't case.

Hale's inheritance to us is a living, breathing definition of a meaningful life — that it has nothing to do with how old one is or how much one has experienced; it is all about how much one has given. In the words of Winston Churchill, *"we make a living by what we get, but we make a life by what we give"*.

STEVE JOBS: *Oh wow! Oh wow! Oh wow!*

Modern society is no stranger to Steve Jobs. Most of us alive today get to say we shared the same planet with, arguably, the greatest inventor the world has ever known. He was the co-founding visionary of *Apple* who helped usher in the era of personal computers and was also responsible for leading a cultural transformation in the way that music, movies, and mobile communications were experienced. Having mastered digital technology in conjunction with learning how to capitalize on his intuitive marketing sense, Jobs had ultimately come to define the personal computer industry along with an array of digital consumer and entertainment businesses centered on the Internet. His ability to tap into his own resourcefulness afforded him the good fortune of amassing a personal net worth of $8.3 billion.

To say that he was an accomplished individual would almost feel like a devaluing of his successes. This man could have anything he wanted when he wanted it. He could walk into any store, expensive or not, and buy whatever he desired. Heck, he could buy the entire store and even the entire franchise of stores if he felt the urge. It's an extremely hard concept to grasp, but Jobs had absolutely no restraints on his life . . . except one: he was human.

On October 5, 2011, Jobs passed away at 56 years old in his own home in Palo Alto, California from respiratory arrest following a long battle with pancreatic cancer (7 years). Details of his final moments were told by his sister, Mona Simpson, who approved the New York Times to publish the following eulogy which she delivered at his memorial service:

> *"His tone was affectionate, dear, loving, but like someone whose luggage was already strapped onto the vehicle, who was already on the beginning of his journey, even as he was sorry, truly deeply sorry, to be leaving us," she writes.*
>
> *When she arrived, she found Jobs surrounded by his family — "he looked into his children's eyes as if he couldn't unlock his gaze," — and managing to hang on to consciousness she said.*
>
> *However, he began to deteriorate. "His breathing changed. It became severe, deliberate, purposeful. I could feel him counting his steps again, pushing farther than before. This is what I learned: he was working at this, too. Death didn't happen to Steve, he achieved it."*
>
> *After making it through one final night, wrote Simpson, her brother began to slip away. "His breath indicated an arduous journey, some steep path, altitude. He seemed to be climbing.*
>
> *"But with that will, that work ethic, that strength, there was also sweet Steve's capacity for wonderment, the artist's belief in the ideal, the still more beautiful later.*
>
> *"Steve's final words, hours earlier, were monosyllables, repeated three times.*
>
> *"Before embarking, he'd looked at his sister Patty, then for a long time at his children, then at his life's partner, Laurene, and then over their shoulders past them.*
>
> **"Steve's final words were: 'Oh wow. Oh wow. Oh wow.'"**

What Jobs saw as he looked over their shoulders is unknown. All we know is what he saw made a man who had attained to life's greatest heights, who undoubtedly was able to see parts of the earth's beauty that very few may ever see, and whose memory lives on in the hands, on the desks, and in the homes of millions today, say, *"Oh wow. Oh wow. Oh wow"*. The mystery within these words leaves us with the impression that there is a beauty that exists at and beyond death that nothing on this planet can compare too. So the conclusion, or better yet, the inheritance, is that death is not an event to fear, rather, it is an event to look forward to as we pass from one glory to a higher and more beautiful glory. It is not a tragedy; it is a beauty.

WHO, WHAT, HOW

Some last words disturb us, as in the case of Leonardo Da Vinci. Others inspire us, as in the story of the great patriot and hero, Nathan Hale. Others still are an enigma to us, as in the death of Steve Jobs. Then, there are those that leave us with an assignment — a call to a work whose completion rest on the shoulders of those standing close enough to hear it — as in the departing words of Jesus Christ.

After Jesus' resurrection, He made 11 additional appearances to his disciples and followers at various times. All are important and contain some type of revelatory value, yet, none stand out quite like his final appearance recorded in Matthew account because it was here that He offered what we have deemed *The Great Commission*.

As far as we know, this was the very last time the disciples would get to see Him on this side of eternity, which also meant, it would be the very last message they would receive from Him as well. His words, therefore, had to be precise, direct, and intentional. This wasn't the place or time for "rabbit trails", misplaced thought in delivery, wasteful theory, or impressive one-liners. It was a place of commissioning.

Think about the gravity of this moment! Standing in the tension of His work stopping or continuing, becoming a pile of trash or becoming a portion of treasure, was a group of very young men who had already proven the fickleness of their faith while he was with Him. Now, they would be asked to carry on into *greater works* (John 14:12-14) without Him (without His physical presence that is). What amazes me is that He never showed any hesitation in authorizing them as leaders of a coming revolution whom He commanded to move forward with the following assignment as their mission:

> *"All authority has been given to Me in heaven and on earth. Go therefore and make disciples of all the nations, baptizing them in the name of the Father and the Son and the Holy Spirit, teaching them to observe all that I commanded you; and lo, I am with you always, even to the end of the age."* (Matthew 28:18-20)

While I'm amazed by his willingness to trust them in spite of their past failures, I'm more intrigued by what He commissioned them with. These were Jesus' last words. This was His final impression. He could've said anything and I'm sure He had an abundance of assignments to choose from, but this is the one that made the cut. It's almost as if He was saying, *"If you forget everything I've taught you or said to you, don't forget this."* The question, then, becomes why? Because of this, I paused to take a deeper look, to explore more of the meaning behind the message, more of what was really on His mind, and more of what the *Great Commission* was really about. And, in the heart of that commission which says, *"Teach them to observe everything I've commanded you"*, I offer you my observations.

Commission is defined by one source as "the act of passing a responsibility to someone else". Another source defines it as the "authority to act for, on behalf of, or in place of another". And, yet other interpretations describe it as "a group of people entrusted by a government or other official body to do something". Regardless if we choose believe it is the actual "act of passing responsibility", the *responsibility* itself, or those "entrusted with the responsibility", it is clear that a commission must have three elements to exist: **the mission, the strategy, and the soldiers.**

A mission tells *what* is to be accomplished. The strategy reveals *how* it is to be accomplished. The soldiers are *who* will accomplish it. Every commission therefore contains a mission, every mission requires a strategy, and every strategy needs a soldier. Any missing piece will result in a failed assignment. With that, let's unpack each of these in their own respective light.

#1. <u>WHO</u> — THE SOLDIERS

"All authority has been given to Me in heaven and on earth. Go therefore . . ."

During His time on earth, Jesus held the esteem of supreme authority — a responsibility delegated to Him by His Father. According to our military ranking system, He would've been considered a General — the highest ranking military officer in our armed forces (except for the Navy, which would've made Him an admiral). He acknowledged His position by saying,

"All authority has been given to Me in heaven and on earth".

In other words, you don't get any higher than this and the responsibility doesn't get any greater than this. Aware that the end of His earthly reign (rank and position) was drawing near, He saw that a promotion was in order and a new generation of Generals would need to be "knighted" if His work were to continue. It only made sense that the next-in-line would be those that He spent the majority of His time developing, equipping, and teaching. After all, they knew Him. They knew His plans, His attitude, His methods, and His leadership better than anyone else, therefore, He offered them the promotion along with the delegation to *"Go, therefore"*.

The disciples received the first pass of the kingdom baton, but it didn't end with them. This relay has continued from one era to the next until it has reached the current generation of soldiers — you and me. Is it possible that the "weight" we feel on the earth is not as much about the mess we are surrounded by as it is the mission we've been assigned to? Could it be that our internal tension is not meant to push us away from the world, rather, is meant to pull us toward it? What if, in fact, the problems we see are to be perceived as invitations to solve them? No matter how we pose the question, the message is clear: We have been called "to a time such as this" and commissioned to a world such as this (see Esther 4:14). It's time to stop running, stop surrendering, and start invading. It's time to "GO".

#2. <u>WHAT — THE MISSION</u>

". . . and make disciples of all the nations . . ."

If I were to ask you, "what is God really after?" Most of you would answer, "The salvation of souls". That's how the greater majority of us have been taught to view the mission of God, as a rescue mission, where He is seeking to deliver us from a lost, dying, and hopeless world. Clearly, God's mission is not to remove us from the world. It is to send us into it. Jesus prayed on behalf of his "followers" in John 17:15-18 saying,

> *"**My prayer is not that you take them out of the world** but that you protect them from the evil one. They are not of the world, even as I am not of it. Sanctify them by the truth;*

your word is truth. **Just as you sent me into the world, so I also send them into the world."**

That's quite different from what we've been told isn't it? This is why I make the case to you that we've been playing the game entirely too small. We've made disciples *in* nations, however, we've yet to make disciples *of* nations. While we have succeeded at increasing the number of "raised hand confessions" of Christ in our services, we have also managed to decrease the size of our impact on the world at large (proven by the increasing statistics of divorce, crime rate, poverty, etc. in the societies we live in) and the result has been none other than an incomplete mission.

Completing the mission demands that we change the way we think. We must think bigger. **We must understand that we were not saved to be rescued, we were saved to be enlisted**. We were not only saved to go to heaven; we were saved to bring heaven. Out of His grace, He comes to the current generation as He did with the previous asking *"Who will go for Me? Whom shall I send?"*

Here I am, Lord, Send Me.

#3. <u>HOW — THE STRATEGY</u>

"... baptizing them in the name of the Father and the Son and the Holy Spirit, teaching them to observe all that I commanded you; and lo, I am with you always, even to the end of the age."

To consider that we have been saved to "take" nations is exciting. I think most would also agree it can also feel a bit overwhelming and impossible. How does one disciple an entire nation? This is a legitimate question and the answer to the fulfillment of this mission is the same as it is with any and all other missions: there must be a strategy — a specific set of plans and methods for determining the actions needed to accomplish the overall chief aim. Without a strategy, the mission means nothing. A clear destination without a specific direction is to be lost in a familiar place. Herein lies the ultimate frustration. Knowing what needs to be done, but lacking the additional knowledge of how to do it has been the hindrance and eventual demise of many great assignments throughout history. Winston Churchill said it best: *He who fails to plan is planning to fail.*

A carpenter by trade, Jesus understood the value of plans (blueprint) to the accomplishment of a purpose (finished product). Because of this, He would not dare offer or authorize any of us with such a massive task like *"making disciples of all nations"* without also offering the blueprint for its completion which is *"baptizing them in the name of the Father and the Son and the Holy Spirit, teaching them to observe all that I commanded you".*

Over the years, we have only scratched the surface of the "drawings" we've been given. This is not to say the generations before us made a mistake in their interpretations as they were simply living and teaching from the revelation that was given them for their day. This is a new day, however, and a new generation. And, God is ready to update the blueprint. For this reason, I write this book — to reveal more of the strategic details, to reach beyond the surface in order to bring an updated revelation for our present day so that we can be *confident of this, that he who began a good work in you will carry it on to completion until the day of Christ Jesus (Philippians 1:6).*

The most essential part in the design of any project is the inclusion of its foundation. However, we must remember that it is still just a part and not the whole. Home builders are fully aware of how foolish it would be to be hired (commissioned) to construct a home (fulfill a mission) and consider it to be complete immediately after the foundation was laid. When it comes to building homes, that's an obvious statement. In fact, you don't have to be a professional home builder to know just how ridiculous that would be. We know that foundations make our homes stable, but they don't make them livable. What may not be so obvious, though, is how closely this resembles the way we treat many of our Biblical interpretations, such as *the Great Commission.*

TRADING GREAT FOR GOOD

When the Commission originally began to emerge in its importance, it was rightfully founded on a literal interpretation and application. For example, when we were commanded to *"baptize in the name of"* each person in the trinity, we responded by searching for any source of water we could — creeks, lakes, rivers, pools, oceans — and proceeded to dunk the masses while quoting, "I baptize you in the name of the Father, the Son, and the Holy Spirit". The issue that eventually arose is that we never built anything on top of the foundation, therefore, it has never truly served its greatest purpose: offering strength to a structure. We took the commission and turned it into a tradition and have been found guilty of "making the word (commissioning) of God of no effect" (Mark 7:13 KJV — parenthesis mine added) by doing so. The foundation of the literal settled a long time ago and has been more than ready to serve the purpose for which it was laid, but the builders (you and me) settled with it accepting an inferior trade-off by swapping the Great Commission of *"nations"* for the Good Commission of *"individuals".*

To be honest with you, it makes me extremely uncomfortable to promote this. Then again, I realize what's happening. New wine (an updated revelation) is being poured into old wineskins (traditional thoughts, emotions, and attitudes) and we keep cracking under the pressure. There is more to this strategy than what we have implemented thus far. To find it, we must be willing to climb out of the comfort of our baptismal pools into the discomfort of our armor embracing the commission as one that commands us to *Go Ye* instead *Come Ye* or *Stay Ye*. We must be willing to reach beyond the safety of the *literal* into the risks of the *figurative*. We must be willing to get off the start so that we can finish. Make no mistake. If Jesus needed to be baptized in water then so do we. And, we must also be like Jesus in that He understood and pursued another kind of baptism — one that would not only "fulfill all righteousness", but would also "fulfill the whole assignment" (see Matthew 3:15).

As we've already revealed, the word *"baptism"* has roots in both the literal and figurative. While so much revelation resides in the figurative, it can be dangerous if left to act alone. It makes a beautiful structure, but a terrible foundation. This is why the literal had to come first: to serve as a foundational platform that we could build on and understand from.

The Greek word for baptism is "baptize", which means "to repeatedly dip, immerse, submerge, or, metaphorically, overwhelm". With that said, a literal baptism is one that "dips, immerses, or submerges in water". It is from this picture that we are able to more accurately embrace the baptism Jesus spoke of in *the Great Commission* and more clearly interpret its strategy, thereby, positioning ourselves to move forward into the long overdue next phase of our assignment.

The prescribed baptism would not only be a literal baptism in water; it would also would also be a figurative baptism in "name". Again, reaching the beyond the traditional translation we've been given will allow us to capture the magnitude of what He was saying and what we would be receiving.

In the Greek, the word for name is *"Onoma"*, meaning, "name, authority, cause". Specifically as it relates to this particular passage it means "to do a thing; by one's command and authority; acting on his behalf, promoting his cause". When bringing it back to its purest form, our assignment could read,

*"Go, therefore, and make disciples of all nations. **immersing** them in the **authority/cause** of the Father, and of the Son, and of the Holy Spirit."*

What exactly does that look like and what does it mean? It's an immersion under three distinct *causes* that provide answers to the three most dominate questions throughout the existence of man. These questions are:

1. WHO AM I?
2. WHAT AM I WORTH?
3. WHY AM I HERE?

WHO AM I? AUTHORITY AND CAUSE OF THE FATHER — BAPTISM IN IDENTITY

Fathers play many roles in the lives of their children. These can include anything from being the provider of their most basic needs (such as food, clothing, and shelter), to being the protector of their physical, mental, and emotional well-being, to being the preparers of their inheritances, beliefs, values, attitudes, perspectives, paradigms, and so on. As vital as each of these paternal functions are in their own right, they are still subsidiary tasks working toward the accomplishment of one main objective: the development of identity.

The ultimate cause of any Father is they have been made the preeminent authorities over the identity of their children. They hold the answer to the question of "Who Am I". While we will explore each of these baptisms individually in the subsequent chapters of the book, understand for now that the first baptism we must undergo is the BAPTISM OF IDENTITY.

WHAT AM I WORTH? AUTHORITY AND CAUSE OF THE SON — BAPTISM IN INHERITANCE

"The Son" alluded to in the Great Commission is Jesus. Discovering the type of baptism we are to undergo means that we must look to His life, in view of His *authority/cause*, to find our treasure. Jesus' primary cause for coming to earth was to advance the Kingdom of His Father. How would he do this? As a Son. *"Son"* reveals not only who He is connected to, but also what He was equipped with. Many believe that he came *as* the Savior of the World. He *became* the Savior of the world, however, He did not come *as* the Savior of the world. He came as a Son equipped with salvation. Others promote that He was sent as a Healer. Once again, He came as a Son equipped with healing to display the nature of the Father. This misinterpretation of who He was is nothing new. At one point Jesus asked the disciples,

> *"Who do men say that I am?" They said, "Some say John the Baptist, others say Elijah, and still others say you are one of the prophets". "But who do you say that I am?" He asked. Peter said, "You are Christ, **Son** of the living God". Jesus replied . . ." (Matthew 16:13-20; Emphasis mine added)*

Notice! Jesus only *replied* to being a Son. Everyone around Him in those days was trying to find an accurate context to put Him in order to describe the *acts* — miracles, healing, resurrection of the dead, casting out demons, cleansing lepers, forgiving people of sins, etc. — they saw Him perform on a daily basis. As great as their guesses were, they all fell short of the only comparison that Jesus saw as being worthy enough to respond to: *Son.*

We have all been found guilty of defining Him according to what He was *sent with* instead of what He was *sent as*. What's the point? He was sent *as* a Son *with* an inheritance. The writer of Hebrews proves this point, writing:

*Long ago God spoke to the fathers by the prophets at differ-
ent times and in different ways. In these last days, **He has
spoken to us by His Son. God has appointed Him heir
of all things** and made the universe through Him. The Son
is the radiance of God's glory and the exact expression of His
nature, sustaining all things by His powerful word. After
making purification for sins, He sat down at the right hand
of the Majesty on high. **So, He became higher in rank than
the angels, just as the name (Son) He inherited is superior to theirs** (Hebrews 1:1-3; underlines, highlights, and
parenthesis are mine).*

Everything He demonstrated on the earth — miracles,
healing, signs, wonders, teaching, authority, casting out
demons, ruining funeral processions, and the like — pointed
to the inheritance He carried within Him from His Father.
All inheritances have value and point to worth. The baptism
in the Son, then, is a BAPTISM OF INHERITANCE. It
points to what we carry, what we have to offer, and, most of
all, provides an answer to the question of *"What Am I Worth."*

WHY AM I HERE? AUTHORITY AND CAUSE OF THE HOLY SPIRIT — BAPTISM IN INFLUENCE

*Gathering them together, He commanded them not to leave
Jerusalem, but to wait for the what the Father had promised, "Which," He said, "you heard of from Me; for John
baptized with water, but you will be baptized with the Holy
Spirit not many days from now . . . **you will receive power
when the Holy Spirit has come upon you; and you shall
be My witnesses** both in Jerusalem, and in all Judea and
Samaria, and even to the remotest part of the earth (Acts
1:4,5,8 NASB; highlights are mine added).*

The Holy Spirit comes to give us power to accomplish a
purpose. In other words, it is a BAPTISM OF INFLUENCE

answering the question of *"Why am I Here"*. While it is my personal belief that the most important question that needs answering is 'Who am I', I am not naïve to the fact that the answer humanity craves the most is "Why Am I Here". Each of us have an instinctive, undeniable, irresistible hunger toward our reason for existing and rightfully so. Everything on planet earth, whether it has life in it or not, was created for a purpose. Birds were created to fly. Fish were created to swim. Roadways were created for travel, cars were created for transportation, phones were created for communication, plates were created to hold food, couches were made to sit on, and homes were made to live in. Literally, nothing exists without a reason. Even the nastiest insects in the world, such as cockroaches and maggots, were created for a unique function. Perhaps this is why the late Myles Munroe was famous for repeatedly saying, *"The greatest tragedy in life is not death, but life without purpose"*. Purposelessness works against our most inherent design. Jesus was fully aware of this when He said *"Go, baptize the nations in the name of the Holy Spirit"*. He was saying, "be a repeated reminder to them that they were born to complete a specific assignment. Immerse them in the truth that the very breath in their lungs is a sign that their life contains something that their generation needs".

WHEN TITLES MATTER

The final point of emphasis that we can't miss concerning the names set forth in the Great Commission is not just the *authority or cause* they carry, but also the specific titles they hold: **Father, Son, and Holy Spirit**. The truth is God has been referred to by us and has even referred to Himself according to many other names outside of *Father* (72 in total to be exact), such as

Adonai: *Lord/Master*	Yahweh: *Lord/Jehovah*
Jehovah Nissi: *The Lord My Banner*	Jehovah Rah: *The Lord My Shepherd*
Jehovah Rapha: The Lord My Healer	Jehovah Shalom: *the Lord Our Peace*

Jesus has also been dubbed with additional names, other than *Son*, like

Wonderful Counselor	Mighty God
Prince of Peace	The Second Adam
Author and Finisher of our Faith	Alpha and Omega

Finally, the Holy Spirit has followed this same pattern of supplementary references being called,

Comforter	Counselor
Guide	Advocate
Spirit of Wisdom	Spirit of Grace

As you can well see, there were no lack of names to choose from when determining the type of baptisms we were to be commissioned by and were to commission with. *Father, Son, and Holy Spirit* were chosen intentionally because God wanted us to be baptized into the context of family. We were not to become servants of a Master, or subjects of a King. We were to become sons and daughters of a Father, co-heirs with a big Brother, and ambassadors to a world of orphans predestined for adoption.

This brings us back to where we started — love. Within the context of family is love and love is the key that unlocks the treasure of our identity, our worth, and our purpose. Until we accept the love of God as permission to love ourselves, we, nor the world around us, will ever really know who we truly are, or experience the gift that we carry within us, or be made richer by the purpose we were created to accomplish. That is why I write this book — to immerse you in the discovery of your identity, to reveal to you the value of your inheritance, and to authorize you into the greatness of your influence.

REFLECTION QUESTIONS

#1. Does the figurative interpretation of baptism change the way you view the Great Commission? How about your role in it? What new revelation, personally and/or corporately, is starting to emerge as you embrace this new-found revelation?

#2. What are some practical steps we can take with where we are right now, as individuals and as a group, to begin to immerse the world in the *"cause"* of the *Father, Son, and Holy Spirit*?

#3. Are you feeling more confident about the call to love yourself? Do you see the connection and influence it has on the commission we've been assigned to?

MEDITATION/APPLICATION

Only ask, and I will give you the nations as your inheritance, the whole earth as your possession (Psalm 2:8 NLT).

Is it really possible to make disciples, not just **in** all nations, but **of** all nations? To be quite honest, this mandate excites and overwhelms me at the same time. Really, how do we disciple an entire nation? Admittedly, I've yet to reach a full answer, but, I have reached an answer. We must start small. It's easy to see a massive call and feel that you have to do something massive in order to bring a satisfactory response. I want to encourage you that's not the case. In Zechariah 4:10, the Spirit of the Lord said, *"Do not despise these small beginnings, for the LORD rejoices to see the work begin, to see the plumb line in Zerubbabel's hand (NLT)."* All God wants to see is that we've picked the call, even the smallest piece, and are doing are best to make it a reality. About three or four years ago, with the encouragement of Bill Johnson and Bethel Church in Redding, California, I decided to "adopt a nation" that I could pray and intercede for. While I don't believe this is the ultimate assignment, I'm showing that I want more by placing the "plumb line" in my hand. What nation or nations can you adopt? Are there any other "small beginnings" you can think of besides prayer and intercession so that we can create momentum in fulfilling the assignment we've been given?

PART I

IDENTITY
WHO AM I?

"Knowing yourself is the beginning of all wisdom"

—ARISTOTLE

4

LOST AND FOUND

"If I want to be free, I've got to be me.
Now, I better know who me is."

—BILL GOVE

*A*dam, where are you? This was the question God pre-sented by God as He walked through the garden "in the cool of the day" after Adam and Eve fell (Genesis 3:1-9). The perplexing part of the way He asks it is He makes it seem as if He really didn't know **where** Adam was. If what David said about Him is true, this couldn't be the case.

> *O LORD, you have examined my heart*
> *and know everything about me.*
> *You know when I sit down or stand up.*
> *You know my thoughts even when I'm far away.*
> *You see me when I travel*
> *and when I rest at home.*
> *You know everything I do.*
> *You know what I am going to say*
> *even before I say it, LORD.*
> *You go before me and follow me.*

You place your hand of blessing on my head.
Such knowledge is too wonderful for me,
too great for me to understand!

I can never escape from your Spirit!
I can never get away from your presence!
If I go up to heaven, you are there;
if I go down to the grave, you are there.
If I ride the wings of the morning,
if I dwell by the farthest oceans,
even there your hand will guide me,
and your strength will support me.
I could ask the darkness to hide me
and the light around me to become night—
but even in darkness I cannot hide from you.
To you the night shines as bright as day.
Darkness and light are the same to you (Psalm 139:1-12).

God is omniscient and omnipresent — He "knows" everything and is "everywhere at all times" — proving that He knew exactly *where* Adam was and the exact time to call out to him so that he could hear Him. His question, then, was not a question of geography. It was a question of identity. When He asked, *"Adam, where are you"*, He was really asking, *"where is the man I created you to be"*?

MANKIND, WHERE ARE YOU?

Adam's name literally means "mankind" revealing that he was created as the prototype for every man and woman destined to come after him. Therefore, when God looked at Adam, He didn't just see one man, He saw all men. So, when God called out to him in the garden, He was calling out to "mankind" as a whole, not a single individual. How do we know this? Eve was with Adam when he fell. In fact, if you read the story, she was actually the one who engaged in the initial conversation with the serpent which eventually led them to succumb to the temptation (Genesis 3:1-7). We could argue that the bulk of blame for their disobedience rested more on her shoulders than his. However, after their "eyes were opened", both of them hid together in the same place: "among the trees of the garden". God, in His search, called out only to (Adam) because His interest was not in bringing condemnation to the guilty, it was in bringing restoration to the entity.

Eve came from Adam (Genesis 2:22). She was "taken from him" (His rib) just like we all have been taken from him. By calling for Adam, God was also calling to Eve, along with the entire species that he carried within him.

As soon as God released the statement, *"Mankind (Adam), where are you"*, an indelible subconscious echo has existed deep within the crevasses of every subsequent soul since, crying back, "Who Am I". You see, man's greatest loss as a result of giving into the temptation was not over the territory he

> GOD, IN HIS SEARCH, CALLED OUT ONLY TO (ADAM) BECAUSE HIS INTEREST WAS NOT IN BRINGING CONDEMNATION TO THE GUILTY, IT WAS IN BRINGING RESTORATION TO THE ENTITY.

was given to "cultivate and keep" (Genesis 2:15), it was over his identity. The serpent's craftiness was revealed in his ability to take what man already had an answer to and make him question it.

> *The serpent said to the woman, "Did God really say, 'You can't eat from the tree in the garden?'" The woman said to the serpent, "about the tree in the middle of the garden", God said, "you must not eat it or touch it, or you will die." "No, you will not die," the serpent said to the woman. "In fact, God knows that when you eat it your eyes will be opened and **you will be like God**, knowing good and evil"* (Genesis 3:1-4: emphasis mine).

Here's the deception. They were already "like" God (see Genesis 1:26), but the serpent was able to successfully entice them into turning their answer into a question — in shifting their "I am" to "Am I" and the rest is history.

Ever since this moment, mankind has been dominated by this question. Am I smart enough? Am I strong enough? Am I tall enough? Am I big enough? Am I handsome enough or pretty enough? Am I good enough? AM. I. ENOUGH? When you boil it all down, that's what we're asking isn't it? We are seeking to be enough signifying that we all feel a certain void deep within ourselves that causes us to ask, search, inquire, and explore. Our problem is that we don't realize what our search is really about. We think it's another book to increase our intelligence, or another degree to prove our competency, or another surgery to enhance or take away our physical imperfections, or another spouse who we think can better satisfy our love language, or more money, a bigger house, a nicer car to show we are successful. These things are not what we are looking for. They are not what the hole in our soul is seeking. As Solomon expressed through one of his sarcasm's in the book of Ecclesiastes:

> *"Everything is wearisome beyond description. No matter how much we see, we are never satisfied. No matter how much we hear, we are not content* (Ecclesiastes 1:8).

In the same vein, we could also say, *"No matter how much we acquire, we will not be pleased"*. It is only when we realize that our quest is not about the *"enough"*, it is about the *"I"*, that we will obtain true fulfillment.

BARRENNESS OF BEING

While the vacuum within us doesn't commonly lend itself to producing a positive state of mind or emotion, we can still find a measure of encouragement in it as God has made it the source to lead us to a long withheld revelation of our beings.

Barrenness is nothing new to God. Most of us are familiar with the unimpressive, hollow description of earth's beginning:

> *In the beginning, God created the heavens and the earth. The earth was **without form (Hebrew: confused)** and **void (Hebrew: empty)**, and **darkness (Hebrew: lack importance/purpose)** hovered over the face of the deep, and the Spirit of God was hovering over the waters* (Genesis 1:1,2; emphasis mine).

What we have not been so familiar with is God's solution for it. You can tell from the Hebraic translations in the previous verse what the earth lacked: identity. God looked at it, didn't like it, and decided to bring a solution to the problem. What may surprise you is what He chose to solve it with. We know that He used His words because verse 3 tells us,

> *Then God said, "Let there be light and there was light".* *(Genesis 1:3)*

However, it's not the words that I want to re-emphasize to you, it's the *what*, or better yet, *who* the words contained. Those immediate words contained an identity. They were not as much about releasing a function as they were about releasing a "being". How do we know that? While all of Genesis 1 reveals His creation, it is within that initial statement out of His mouth that we discover,

> *He **(The Son) is** the image of the invisible God, the firstborn of all creation. For **by Him** all things were created, both in the heavens and on earth, visible and invisible, whether thrones or dominions or rulers or authorities—**all things have been created through Him** and for Him. **He is** before*

*all things, and **in Him** all things hold together* (Colossians 1:16,17 NASB).

Of course, it doesn't just come out and say all of that, but it is there. Take a look . . .

#1. THEN GOD SAID . . . BE

Hundreds, if not thousands of books have been written on the power of words using this very verse. Most that I've read lead me to believe that the majority are true in their content, however, they always seem to make the same error in their context in that they separate the spoken word from the One speaking. John 1:1 clearly says,

> *"In the beginning was the Word, and the Word was with God, **and the Word was God**. He was in the beginning with God. All things came into **being** through Him, and apart from Him nothing came into **being** that has come into **being**."*

When God spoke to the earth, He wasn't just offering a *saying*, He was offering a *being* and that *being* was Himself. We can't continue to miss this. So, it really is true that "He is the firstborn of all creation" because He is His word and His word is Him.

Also notice that *"All things"* did not *"come into **doing** through Him"*. *'All things came into **being***'. An honest mistake, still, a mistake nonetheless and one that reveals our true lack in understanding of the creative process is when we think life comes from the words we speak instead of the identity they contain. It is correct that the earth found its form and function through what was said, but function (doing) is always the result of being. Before light could "do" what light does (shine), it had to possess the exact internal chemistry (identity) first. It could not give what it was not. The same is true for all created things. A fish cannot do what a bird does because it is not a bird. It doesn't carry the same internal make-up of "being". An animal will not survive trying to do what a plant does because it is not a plant. A snake cannot live at the altitude of eagles because it hasn't been built with the same "being". Even within the same species this is true. I cannot do what you can do and you cannot do what I can do because our *being* profiles commonly referred to as our DNA are different. If we could strip life down to its purest essence we see that it is all about being. God said, "Let there BE" and we are all a result of that. We were spoken into BEING by the SUPREME BEING.

#2. LET THERE BE

The case we've just built on God's identity being wrapped up in His spoken word is justified with the opening phrase out of His mouth! Think about this! Anytime God speaks it serves us to turn our attention in that direction and seek to understand what He is saying. However, this particular phrase is special because it not just any set of words, it is the **VERY FIRST WORDS** He ever released. For that reason, we tune in a little more, pause a little longer, and dig a little deeper to unveil the true impact of His earliest utterance.

It's important that we reemphasize God did not say "let there DO". He said "let there BE". Again, for something to do, it must first be. And, for something to be, it must embody a being. *Let there be* did exactly that. It was more than a phrase, it was a person. While it is translated into a three-worded expression, it is actually a single Hebrew word called, *Hayah*. This is not the only place it shows up. Later, when God spoke to Moses through the burning bush calling him to become the deliverer of His people, Moses responded to God,

> *Behold, I am going to the sons of Israel, and I will say to them, 'The God of your fathers has sent me to you.' Now they may say to me, 'What is His name?' What shall I say to them?" God said to Moses, "I AM WHO I AM"; and He said, "Thus you shall say to the sons of Israel, 'I AM has sent me to you* (Exodus 3:13-14 NASB; emphasis mine).

"*I Am*" is the exact same Hebrew word (hayah) as "*Let there be*". By replacing the phrase in God's originating statement to earth it would read, "*Then God said, I AM. . . .*"

The secret to the creative process is this: creation does not come from the Creator, creation is the Creator. His words are not an extension of Him, His words are Him. In fact, one translation records that just before God asked for Adam in the garden that Adam, "heard the voice of the Lord God walking in the garden (Genesis 3:8 KJV)". How does a voice walk? It doesn't. The revelation is He is His word and His word is Him. His walk is His talk and His talk is His walk. They are impossible to separate because they are one in the same. God was saying to everything, "*Let there be . . . ME*".

#3. LIGHT

Jesus spoke to the people and said, "I am the Light of the World" (John 8:12). Did you catch it? *I AM. . . . THE LIGHT OF THE WORLD.* What was the first thing God created? Light. Is it possible that He was really saying "I Am (Let there be) Jesus (Light)"? Now it makes even more sense that "*The Son was the firstborn of all creation and by Him and through Him all things were created*" doesn't it? Light, therefore, not only carries an added layer of evidence that He gave Himself to the earth before He gave the earth its functions; it also tells us that He gave the earth its solution before it had its problems.

Man fell and a whole heap of issues came as a result. Thankfully, "the last Adam", who is Jesus, who is the solution, existed before the "first Adam". "*Jesus came to seek and save that which was lost.*" What was lost? Adam (Mankind). Recall that God didn't ask, "*dominion, where are you?*" Or, "*rule, where are you?*" Or, "*Fruitfulness, where are you?*" Or, "*increase, where are you?*" He asked, "Adam (Mankind) where are you?" God wasn't seeking any of the things he "blessed" man with — dominion, rule, fruitfulness, and increase — He was seeking man. These were all important to why man was created, but they were still the effect of his being. Therefore, the greatest loss in the garden was not the garden, it was the gardener.

Yes, we were created to have dominion, to rule, to subdue, to be fruitful, and to increase all over the earth as most popular messages promote, yet, the function was not the primary focus of restoration. If we will restore the identity, the function will automatically follow. That's what Jesus came to do — to clothe himself in the lost identity (Adam) in order that it may become the found identity. He came, not to give the answer, but to **be** the answer.

We, mankind, are different and unique in so many ways from one individual to the next. We are different in the color of our skin, our nationalities, our genders, our interests, our tastes of food and music, our political preferences, and in our careers, callings, desires, and dreams that we have in life. WE.ARE.DIFFERENT. And, it is by these differences that we come to define ourselves forgetting that they point to the reality that we are all connected as the expressed models of Adam by the same search and drawn by the same barrenness of being that came as the result of our forefather's blunder which is revealed by the same intuitive question of WHO AM I.

JESUS IS THE ANSWER

The search for and question of identity has dominated humanity since the beginning of time and will continue its dominance until the end of time. Adam made the question available through his sin. God made the answer available through His Son. Apart from "the Light of the World", we will never truly *see* who we really are. We will keep defaulting to the same inferior conclusions and confusions as everyone else defining ourselves by the color of our skin saying, "I am Caucasian, African American, or Hispanic". Or, by where we are from saying, "I am an American, or I am a Mexican, or I am a Colombian". Or, by our religion saying, "I am a Christian, or I am a Muslim, or I am a Buddhist". Or, by the distinctions within those religions called *denominations* where we, as members, attach our identity to being a "Baptist, Methodist, Pentecostal, or Seventh-Day Adventist". Deepening our confusion, we will say we are our political preferences declaring, "I am a democrat or I am a republican". Some of us will even pledge the allegiance of our identities to our titles in the workplace saying, "I am a forklift operator, doctor, lawyer, or pastor." All provide *an* answer, but none provide *the* answer. JESUS. IS. THE. ANSWER.

REFLECTION QUESTIONS

#1. Do you ever feel confused, empty, or unimportant? For those who answered, "Yes". When you feel that way the most — where are you, who are you around, and what are you doing? Identifying who, what, where, and when will help you to identify the position of your focus and as a result your identity.

#2. *Before light could "do" what light does — shine — it had to possess the exact internal chemistry (identity) first. It could not give what it was not.* Have you ever tried to be someone or something you're not? How did that feel when you did it? Are you now ready to "be" yourself? What are some steps you can begin taking in order to do that?

#3. Jesus is the Light of the world (John 8:12) and has made you the light of the world (Matthew 5:14-16). What does it look like to be the "light of the world"? How can you begin to live in that identity?

MEDITATION/APPLICATION:

"I am" and "Let there be" are the same Hebrew word: *Hayah.* Therefore, when God said, "Let there be Light", it could be translated as, "I am Jesus", meaning, the plan for salvation was set in place before sin, not after it. How does the change the way you've always viewed the "sin" and "salvation" relationship? Because of this, can you now see how God's plans were always "good" for you?

5

I AM IN THE *I AM*

"I was lookin' for love in all the wrong places . . ."

—JOHNNY LEE (LOOKING FOR LOVE)

*T*here is not a more vital question we will ask ourselves than *Who Am I*. There is also no greater frustration to have to endure than searching for the answer in all the wrong places or faces. I know many of you are just like me. You have spent the vast majority of your life in an inferior pursuit, defining yourself by inferior people, places, and things, only to make the successful, yet, disappointing arrival knowing that you've fallen miserably short. Down deep, you know there's more to you than what you've been. You've just not been able to tap into it. It's not like you haven't been diligent. You've looked everywhere and you've looked for a very long time. You've looked for yourself in sports, but when sports came to an end, the all-too-familiar void appeared again. You've looked for yourself in popular social circles, conformed yourself to them by dressing, walking, and talking like those that everybody admires only to get home alone and realize that you don't admire yourself because you've "acted" like them for so long that you don't know who *you* are. All you know is when you look in the mirror, the person looking back at you feels more like stranger than anything else. You've looked for yourself in your career, worked your way to the top of your company, have plaques on the wall as reminders of your production, yet there's still an emptiness inside of you that causes you to realize no level of accomplishment is big enough to fill the hole within you. You've looked, man, have you looked. We could dedicate an entire chapter to all the people, places, and things you've looked to and in. I want you to be encouraged. Your search may have been to no avail thus far, however, it has not been in vain. The promise still stands that if you, *"keep on asking, you'll be given what you ask for. Keep on seeking, and you will find. Keep on knocking, and the door will be opened to you (Matthew 7:7)"*. Like Thomas Edison who finally got it right after his 10,000[th] attempt with the light bulb, you've found 9,999 ways not to discover yourself. Every attempt discarded has brought you closer to this moment. The moment where the deepest cry of your heart, to know it's true self, is finally satisfied.

WHO AM I IS IN THE I AM

The answer to *Who Am I* is not in my interests, my gifts, my talents, or my successes. *Who Am I* is in the I Am. Peter, formerly known as Simon would agree.

> *When Jesus came into the district of Caesarea Philippi, He was asking His disciples, "Who do people say that the Son of Man is?" And they said, "Some say* John the Baptist; and others, Elijah; but still others, Jeremiah, or one of the prophets." He said to them, *"But who do you say that I am?"* Simon Peter answered, *"You are the Christ, the Son of the living God." And Jesus said to him, "Blessed are you,*

Simon Barjona, because flesh and blood did not reveal this
to you, but My Father who is in heaven. "I also say to you
that you are Peter, and upon this rock I will build My
church; *and the gates of Hades will not overpower it. "I will*
give you the keys of the kingdom of heaven; and whatever you
bind on earth shall have been bound in heaven, and what-
ever you loose on earth shall have been loosed in heaven."
Then He warned the disciples that they should tell no one that
He was the Christ (Matthew 16:13-20).

The revelation of Jesus as "Christ, the Son" brought Simon
the revelation of himself as "Peter, the Rock". This was the whole
point of the question — to reveal Peter. He wasn't asking them
because He was extremely concerned about who they thought
He was. He, personally, already knew who He was and, that's
why He had absolutely no response, good or bad, to any of
their comparisons. He only responded to "Christ, the Son"
and it wasn't with a simple, "yes, you got it". Nor was it with a
"go tell the world what I've shown you". After all, *"He warned*
the disciples that they should tell no one that He was the Christ
(Matthew 16:20)." His reaction carried something, or, more
accurately, someone within it. That someone was "Peter". By
seeing Jesus, Simon saw himself. What does this reveal to us?

#1. HE DOESN'T COME TO GIVE YOU A NEW IDENTITY, HE COMES TO EXPOSE YOU TO YOUR ORIGINAL ONE — HIS PURPOSE CONTAINS OUR PERSON.

Many have called Peter's moment an upgrade. It's treated as
if Jesus came to put something on him that he didn't already
possess. The exact opposite is true. He didn't come to upgrade
him. He came to unveil him. He didn't come to put the
identity of Peter *on* Simon, He came to draw the identity of
Peter *out of* Simon. What this tells us is that Peter was always
in Simon, but, for whatever reason, somewhere along life's

journey, an inferior trade-off occurred and he began living as a "reed" (Greek word for Simon) when he was really created to be "a rock" (Greek word for Peter). Christ came and, for a lack of better words, said, "I am here to build a church, but I need a firm foundation — a rock — to do so. Peter, you are that foundation (rock)".

In the purpose of Jesus was the person of Peter. Like Simon, we too will find our person in His purpose. When God revealed to Simon that Jesus was 'Christ, the Son', He was revealing His purpose. "Christ" literally means "Anointed One" and anointing always points to the endowment of a unique ability for the accomplishment of an assignment. The assignment here is "Son of God".

Jesus was anointed to be the Son of God, which carried a heavy responsibility that would require something "extra" — the anointing — to complete it. As "the Son", He came to reveal the love of the Father by offering himself as the sacrifice for our sins. In our modern language, he came to bring us salvation. The work of salvation, then, is not as much about where you go when you die as it is about who you are while you live.

> THE WORK OF SALVATION, THEN, IS NOT AS MUCH ABOUT WHERE YOU GO WHEN YOU DIE AS IT IS ABOUT WHO YOU ARE WHILE YOU LIVE.

He comes to save you from who you've been, or the identity you've expressed, so that you can become who He created you to be, your original identity. He comes to introduce you to yourself.

#2. HE DOES NOT CALL YOU, HE REVEALS YOU. AND, WITHIN THAT REVEALING IS YOUR CALLING.

This thought echoes the idea in the previous chapter that "*If we will restore the identity, the function will automatically follow.*"

You don't have to force the sun to shine. The sun shines because it is the sun. You don't have to strain to get the moon to come out at night. It comes out at night because it is the moon. You don't have to teach a fish how to swim. They swim because they are fish. You don't have to tell a bird to fly. A bird flies because it is a bird. In the same way, you don't have to instruct "a rock" on how to be firm foundation. It is a firm foundation because it is a rock. Notice when Jesus said, *you are Peter, and upon this rock I will build My church; and the gates of Hades will not overpower it. "I will give you the keys of the kingdom of heaven; and whatever you bind on earth shall have been bound in heaven, and whatever you loose on earth shall have been loosed in heaven",* He never offered him a class on how to be a rock, or step-by-step instructions on handling the gates of hell, or even told him what doors the keys went to. He simply said, "You are Peter", and that was enough. Having the work of Christ built on him, being an immovable force to the gates of hell, carrying the keys of the kingdom to bind and loose was to Peter what swimming is to a fish and what shining is to the sun: the natural expression of his heavenly identity. These were not things he would have to strain to do. All he had to do was live as Peter, not Simon, and the byproduct would happen naturally. Therefore, He does not come to call us, He comes to reveal us and within that revealing is our calling.

#3. OUR IDENTITY IS GOD'S *TOP* PRIORITY:

When my wife and I first got married, we had just graduated from college and were starting out with the first jobs of our professional careers. Needless to say, we were like most college grads who thought our degrees were going to be a fast-pass straight into the promised land of wealth. That is until we ran face first into the reality check of a combined income of a little more than $40,000 per year (enough to pay our mortgage and power bill. Meaning, we had to learn the art of bumming off of the in-laws for food every now and then).

Like most men who desire to prove themselves as good providers (and whose immature pride refused to allow his income to be the lesser of the two), I sought for and found another way to make money. I joined a network marketing company.

During my time with this company, there were weekly conference calls made available to us that offered live trainings from top leaders in the business on the "in's" and "outs" of what we needed to do to be successful. I never missed a call and can honestly say they all brought value on some level, but there is one in particular that I have never forgotten. The leader on this particular day was the #1 income earner. While I can't say I remember any of the business building techniques he shared, I do remember a statement he made that hit me like a ton of bricks leaving an indelible mark on memory forever. He said, *"Advancing to the next level is not about the money. It's not even about hitting the next rank and the feeling of accomplishment that comes with it as a result. It's about who you have to become to get there."* Although I'm no longer with this company, I have a huge amount of respect for this man because he was willing to teach us newbies the importance of prioritizing our person above our pursuits — that if we would focus on the *"who"* then the *"how, what, and when"* would work itself out.

I've come to believe that this man's training was inspired by God (for me at least) because it made me aware of who I needed to become above what I wanted to have. It helped me see that everything begins and ends with identity and that our identity is God's top priority. Throughout the pages of scripture, we see this story playing out as God visited man. These visitations were never without motives. Each time He showed up, promises would be released as expressions, or should I say, invitations of His purpose. Before they could be fulfilled, the person called to carry them would need to be dealt with.

For some, God would change their name (a symbol of their identity) just as He did with Abram, *the father of multitudes*, who became Abraham, *the father of Nations*. Or, like he did with Jacob, *who wrestled with God* and received the name Israel as a blessing. For others, their identity was dealt with through a change in their self-perception as with Moses who said, "*Who am I that Pharaoh should listen to me?*", or Gideon who asked, "*How can I save Israel? My clan is the weakest in Manasseh and I am the least in my family?*" Then there are those whose encounters exposed the inferior, sinful parts of their nature like Balaam who said, "*I have sinned. I did not realize you were standing in the road to oppose me*" or Isaiah who declared, "*Woe is* me! For I am undone; because I *am* a man of unclean lips, and I dwell in the midst of a people of unclean lips: for mine eyes have seen the King, the LORD of hosts." The fulfillment of any and every promise is subject to the person or persons carrying them. In the words of the late Myles Munroe, "Your destiny is chosen by God, but its fulfillment will be decided by you."

By stepping into His promises, we are stepping into His process and that is where our true person is found. What the leader said is true: it's not as much about the accomplishment of a goal, or the fulfillment of a promise, or the apprehension of a dream as it is about *who* we become in the process. So, I ask you just as Jesus asked the disciples, "*And what do you benefit if you gain the whole world but lose your own soul (identity)? Is anything (rank, position, title, accomplishment) worth more than your soul (identity)?*" (Matthew 16:26 NLT: Parenthesis mine added).

REFLECTION QUESTIONS

#1. Have you ever felt there's more to your life than what you're currently experiencing? Why do you think you feel that way?

#2. Peter had a revelation of Jesus and, in turn, received a revelation of himself. Is there a time where you've had a similar experience? What was the outcome? Did that one moment tell you everything you needed and wanted to know about yourself?

#3. What are some things we can do to receive a greater and deeper revelation of Jesus?

MEDITATION/APPLICATION:

Peter was living as a "reed" when he was created to be a "rock".

"Peter" (the rock) was always in "Simon" (the reed). It's not clear why he was living this way, but I think it's safe to assume that someone or something — a life experience — convinced him of it. He's certainly not alone is he? We can all attest to a similar moment in our lives where we realized we were living far below the person God created us to be. What I'd like to draw your attention (and meditation) to, however, is what happened AFTER the revelation. Although it was an exciting moment for him, it still didn't remove the need for process. In other words, "Simon" had to learn to live as "Peter" just like you will have to learn to live as your true self. Facing the inevitable reality that some days will be better than others, what can you do stay encouraged in the process? On the days that "Simon" seems to getting the better of "Peter", how can you avoid "beating yourself up" and get back on track?

6

SOUL FOOD

"I am not what you see; I am what He breathed"

(THE SOUL OF GOD)

lthough identity has proven to be the most prevalent and desperate search among mankind, its discovery has also proven to be the most elusive to find. The greatest and brightest minds in history, from philosophers to theologians to inventers to teachers, have all weighed in and their conclusions have still left us wanting, waiting, and seeking. Even today, our foremost catalytic thought leaders and best communicators show no fear in their attempts to provide an answer, but it doesn't take long before the uncertainty in their voice and the uncharacteristic shakiness of their delivery exposes that they too are as unclear as the common man as to where to begin when it comes to the question of self. While most of the concerted efforts haven't produced much in terms of a definite answer, they still provide us with the ever-so valuable information of "where not to look" inching us closer to the treasure we seek.

PLENTY IN NOTHING

We don't always think of our inconclusive evidence as having much value, but it does. And, sometimes, more so than its counterpart. If you and I were to go on a vacation together 15 hours away from a designated starting place, doesn't it serve us just as much to know which roads we should not take if we wish to have a safe and successful arrival at our destination? When taking a test, doesn't the process of elimination require that we know the wrong choices as well as the right choices in the pursuit of passing? Isn't maintaining peace in relationships the result of knowing what buttons not to push in addition to what buttons to push?

This is the ebb and flow of learning, a partnership if you will, between what is known and what is unknown. It is no different when it comes to defining our identities. Knowing who we are not is critical to knowing who we are. Booker T. Washington said it best: *"Start where you are with what you have, knowing that what you have is plenty enough"*. We are a fortunate generation because we don't have to start at ground zero — that's already been done by those who have explored before us. We don't have to be the creators of new ideas and theories. We are inheriting hundreds, if not thousands, of years of information. Whether or not it's inadequate, inferior, or wrong is not the point. The point is it's still information. The greatest mistake we could make is to throw it all away forcing ourselves to re-create new ideas instead of innovating former ones. What we have may not be a satisfactory place to settle, nevertheless, it is *plenty enough* to keep us progressing forward. And so we begin.

I AM NOT WHAT YOU SEE, I AM WHAT HE BREATHED: *The Soul of God*

And God formed man from the dust of the ground and breathed into his nostrils the breath of life, and man became a living soul. (Genesis 2:7)

Without a doubt, the body is an amazing creation in and of itself. Each part was fashioned with such precision and detail that we have yet to fully unveil its depth in 6,000 years of examination and existence. The brain alone has over 100 billion nerve cells. A human ear contains about 24,000 fibers. The human eye has 110 — 130 million receptors to perceive light. Our nose can remember 50,000 different scents. We have been given 206 bones, over 600 muscles, and 230 movable and semi-movable joints. The human liver performs 500 different functions. There are over 300,000,000 capillaries in our lungs and if stretched out tip to tip they would reach approximately the distance from Atlanta to Los Angeles. On average, a person's head has 100,000 to 150,000 hairs. The entire body is made up of 50 — 70 trillion cells, all of which die and regenerate every so often, meaning we literally become a new person multiple times over throughout the course of our lives. In a 24 hour period, the blood in our body travels 12,000 miles — that's four times the width of North America. An adult is made up of around 7,000,000,000,000,000,000 ,000,000,000 (7 octillion) atoms. And these examples don't even begin to scratch the surface of just how "fearfully and wonderfully made" our bodies really are. With such inexhaustible features and functions, it's no wonder the earliest identity theorists and some modern day theorists lean towards it being the most logical way to find ourselves. However, we are not our bodies. We live in our bodies, but that is not who we are. According to Genesis 2:7, the body and everything it was made of — the atoms, the cells, the lungs, the brain, the various systems — had no 'life' until God breathed a soul into it. So, I am a soul, but not just any soul. **I AM THE SOUL OF GOD**.

Whether or not God has a soul has been and will continue to be a heavily debated topic. The point here is that I am not what I see, I am what He breathed. If you can't handle that you are the soul of God, then let's say you are the breath of God. He literally took what was inside of Him and breathed it into us and we came alive. Every inhale and exhale serves as a constant reminder that we live from the inside-out — that we possess an invisible inner man that is superior to the visible outer man. The reality which surrounds us is always the offspring of the dominate reality within us. Like the body, the soul came with some amazing features, with some specific characteristics, that as we begin to discover what those are, will unveil more of the person we were created to be and unleash more of the power locked within us.

Regardless of where you look, the Hebrew language or the Greek, the baseline definition of the soul is the same. Generally speaking, it has been defined as the *"mind"* and *"emotions"*. More specifically, it is described as *"the psyche, desires, appetites, emotions, and passions"*. Either way, we arrive at three major conclusions. The first is we have an inner man. The second is our inner man, like our outer man, is the summation of some smaller individual parts that make up the whole. The third is these individual parts contain intricate aspects of our identity that reveal themselves through the often overlooked and rejected conduit of feelings.

FEELING IT

Desires, appetites, emotions, passions. The soul was made to feel. More intensely and accurately stated, the soul was made to crave. And it is within the details of those cravings that we are more able to readily divulge more of who we really are. Over the years, our feelings have taken on a bad rap and for legitimate reasons. We have all, at some point or another, been misled by them. We could each testify of an event where we allowed our emotions to get the best of us and have been found guilty of reacting in less-than-desirable ways to that event or the people in them. We've all allowed passion to outrun wisdom, anger to replace forgiveness, and hate to reign over love. Because of the pain that came back through these experiences, we have chosen to adopt a belief and teaching that promotes our feelings as inherently bad and unable to be trusted. We say things like, "it is better to walk in faith than emotions", or "don't be so emotional", or "your feelings will mislead you; they can't be trusted". We've persuaded ourselves that emotions and faith don't mix and we've even went as far as to make feelings out to be faith's worst enemy. That sounds good on the surface and preaches good on Sunday until you realize that Jesus was, on many occasions, moved FIRST by emotion ('compassion') before displaying any measure of faith for miracles, healing, signs, and wonders (see Matthew 15:32, Matthew 9:36, Matthew 14:14, Mark 6:34, Mark 8:2-3, Luke 19:41-42).

The bottom line is this: we will never be able to get rid of or ignore our feelings because they are literally the "stuff" our souls are made of. Removing them would be to remove the soul altogether. Therefore, our emotions are from God. They were not given to hurt us, they were given to help us. For this reason, we must put an end to the worthless pursuit of rejecting them and begin the more worthy pursuit of accepting them as an irremovable part of our beings and educating ourselves on how to leverage them to work for us instead of against us.

Much of the disorientation we have concerning their influence on our lives is due to the fact that we don't understand how to guide them and this leads us to become guided by them. With the correct knowledge that places them in their proper order, feelings become incredibly beneficial assets to our intrapersonal and interpersonal lives — they protect instead of destroy, connect instead of divide, encourage instead of discourage, reveal instead of conceal, and motivate instead of stagnate. Apart from that knowledge, it becomes quickly apparent that feelings are a double-edged sword. They can heal or they can kill, evoke positive responses or negative reactions, instigate good or bad behavior, and trigger tears of sadness or shouts of joy. Actor Jonatan Martensson said it beautifully: *"Feelings are much like waves, we can't stop them from coming, but we can decide which ones to surf"*. With that, Martensson reveals the secret to having them cut on our behalf rather than cutting us in half: it is making them subject to our decisions, not our decisions subject to them.

Feelings, in and of themselves, are nothing more than vibratory signals of communication that our bodies sense when our perceptions are drawing or have drawn a certain conclusion about an experience we are having. For example, let's say our spouse usually arrives home at 5:00pm, but one night he or she doesn't walk through the door at the precise time they normally would. At first, we *think*, "no big deal". Then, 6:00pm rolls around, we send a text, get no response, and **worry** begins to set in. 6:30 and still no spouse. Our worry has turned into a mild panic. Our minds are racing with every speculation imaginable — "what if he or she has been a wreck", "what if they are cheating on me", "maybe I did something or said something wrong last night during our argument and he or she has decided to run away". The clock strikes 7:00pm, we stand at the front door with it open, looking out to the empty street trying our hardest to hold onto the last shred of hope we have. By now, we are nothing short of an emotional wreck. What began as worry that transitioned into panic has also transformed itself into anger, fear, guilt, and depression. Finally, we see the headlights of the car turn onto the road and we recognize it's them. We are a mix between angry enough to kill them and ecstatic enough to hug them until we kill them.

Stepping out of the car they say, "Hey babe." We respond with fake calmness, "Where have you been?" As they open the trunk and start grabbing bags of food, they remind us, "don't you remember when I told you last night that I was going to the grocery store after work?" And, we lie and say "oh, yes". In that span of two hours, we took a ride on the proverbial roller coaster of vibration called emotions. To say they are influential would be a massive understatement. Here's the lesson to all of it. Emotions alone can do nothing but vibrate (send signals) and nothing in life (emotions included) has any meaning except the meaning you give it. It's only those feelings that we give meaning to through our decisions and actions that become empowered to have an effect in, on, and around our lives. And, as we've just shown and often experience, some emotions serve us and some do not which is why God didn't leave them to act alone.

The "breath" that went into making us a "living soul" is a Hebrew word called "*Neshamah*" — defined as "divine inspiration and intellect". Within the same soul, the ability to feel was accompanied by the capacity to think. Recall the New Testament, or Greek translation for soul! It is "*psuche*", or psyche — it's your mind. The mind is not the brain. When we reduce it to being just the brain, we separate our thinking and our feeling because we know our feelings don't exist in our brain. They do, however, exist in the same mind (soul). The thinking faculty of the mind has been called "the conscious, or intelligent mind". The feeling part of the mind has been called "the subconscious, or emotional (inspired) mind". Either one can become superior as it's really not about one *above* another. It's about one *with* the other. Feelings balance thinking and thinking balances feelings. Too much feeling and we become impulsive. Too much thinking and we become idle.

Up to this point, we've spent a considerable amount of time unpacking the emotional part of us. Unpacking the intellectual part of us is as simple as understanding this is

the segment of our souls where conscious reasoning, processing, deliberating, and deciding takes place. This is the part of
us that contains the needed "processing" capabilities to help
us decide between which apples we eat and which apples
we don't — which "tastes (appetites)" we satisfy and which
"tastes" we neglect.

AN ACQUIRED TASTE

Learning to exercise our reason helps to clear up some of the
psychological cloudiness that have surrounded us due to an
unbalanced state of life where feelings have been allowed to
reign supreme. Not only can we settle much of the confusion
surrounding our emotions, but we can also unearth more
of our identity through them by tapping into the reasoning
part of our souls and distinguishing between which of our
'appetites' are *acquired* and which are *intuitive*.

Evil is an *acquired taste* passed down to us from our fore-
fathers. It is not who we are. It may be what we express at
times and it may be how we are perceived by those around us
as a result, but down deep it is a learned behavior operating
under a false identity. If you'll recall, evil was introduced
through the fall as we have already learned when Adam and
Eve partook of the tree of the knowledge of good and evil (see
Genesis 3:22). Previous to that, Adam's soul was dominated
by one craving and one choice: good. As soon as Adam sunk
his teeth into the apple, there was an immediate conflict
in his inner man because the soul now had to deal with an
unfamiliar, opposing 'desire'. It was thrust into the tension
of choosing between its newly acquired tastes (evil) and its
original intuitive tastes (good). For way too long, we have
lived in a state of disarray because we haven't been able to
distinguish between the authentic and the fake. Anger, shame,
guilt, condemnation, hate, and the like are all acquired tastes.
None of them are natural to us, which is why we experience a

certain conviction within ourselves when doing them. We've lived with them for so long that the "feeling" of conviction has worn off and we have concluded they are natural when, in fact, they are not. Just as if you tell a lie long enough you'll eventually start believing it, the same rings true that if you live a lie long enough you'll start believing it too. The greater danger, however, with living a lie is you not only start believing in the lie itself, you also start believing that lie is who you are. There's only one way to properly deal with any lie: knowing the truth (see John 8:32) and deciding to follow the truth (see Matthew 16:24). The truth is our original, God-given, God-designed inner man was constructed with an instinctive taste for four things which were revealed immediately after man received his soul (see Genesis 2:7). He was given . . .

1. **A WORK TO ACCOMPLISH** — *INFLUENCE* *(Genesis 2:8,15)*
2. **A WILL TO EXERCISE** — *INTENTION (Genesis 2:16)*
3. **A WORLD TO CO-CREATE** — *INVENTION* *(Genesis 2:19)*
4. **A WIFE TO LOVE**– *INTIMACY (Genesis 2:20)*

A WORK TO ACCOMPLISH — *INFLUENCE*

Have you ever heard someone say, "I felt so alive when I did 'that'?" What about you? Have you ever had a moment where you "came alive" doing something — where you went into a timeless awareness that you felt you could've done whatever you were doing for the rest of your life without ever getting tired of doing it? It felt so effortless didn't it? There was a certain flow to it, a rhythm you seemed to be 'dancing' to, yet, there wasn't any music being played. Or, maybe there was depending on what that moment was for you as some of you experienced it while singing or playing an instrument. Others experienced it while on a mission trip to a distant country somewhere. Then, there were others who spoke in front of a crowd of people for the first time, or taught in a classroom, or coached a sport, or started a business. No matter how short or long the moment was, you felt like a different person. Every cell of your being seemed to wake up all at once and connect you to the present in a way that you've never been connected before. You were 100% fully engaged, fully focused, fully interested, and fully alive. Your confidence soared to heights you never dreamed it could go, your energy became contagious to everyone around you, your thoughts were crystal clear, and your delivery was flawless. Once it was over, you became mildly upset, depressed even because you didn't want to leave "the moment". Stepping back into life as usual made everything, even your so-called greatest accomplishments, seem average at best. You've been haunted by the frustration that was left by that experience. You've burned with the hope that one day, sooner rather than later, you could do it again. "Just one more time" has been your prayer. What you have failed to realize is that experience was meant to be more than a moment for you. THAT EXPERIENCE WAS YOU. **The residual effect that has caused so much frustration was never meant to lead you to depression, it was meant to lead you to an obsession**. It was meant to draw you into unveiling more of who you really are.

The world and everything in it is the result of words — God said, and there was. However, when it came to Adam, God interrupted this flow. Man is not the result of **_word_**, he is the result of **_work_**. He was created through being made, not spoken (see Genesis 1:26). To be "created" means that God took *something from nothing* and brought it into manifestation. To be "made" means that He took *something from something* that already existed'. Man was created in the image of God and made from the dust of the ground. Here's where things start to get interesting. The ground wasn't just some random spot on the earth's new surface, it was actually a representation of the garden he would be called to "cultivate and keep" (Genesis 2:15). So, mankind does not come *for* work, he comes *from* work. This is why there seems to be an unshakable bent in us to find our calling. In the deepest recesses of our beings, we sense we are not here by mistake. We know the breath in our lungs is for more than just giving us oxygen to sustain life for another day of existence; it points to a greater purpose that we were born to live — an influence we were meant to have.

When you find your "work", you will find a part of yourself in it because you were taken from it. The question is how do you find it? We will answer this in greater detail in part III of this book entitled, 'Why Am I Here'. For now, realize that it's extremely important you follow God's example by making your purpose a priority in your life. God is a God of purpose. Nothing was created without it. Even the most meaningless things surrounding you right now wreak of purpose. And, in that same vein, God showed just how important purpose was to Adam's soul by giving him, before anything else, a garden — a work to accomplish. To offer you a clue of where to begin your search, realize that it is not outside of you, it is within you. It starts with tuning into the frequency of your desires, appetites, emotions, and passions — it starts by learning to live from your feelings.

A WILL TO EXERCISE — *INTENTION*

> *"You are fettered," said Scrooge, trembling. "Tell me why?"*
> *"I wear the chain I forged in life," replied the Ghost. "I made it link by link, and yard by yard; I girded it on of my own free will, and of my own free will I wore it."*
>
> —Charles Dickens, A Christmas Carol

Free will. It can imprison you and it can set you free. It can make you and it can break you. It can cause you to lose control and it can put you in control. It is everywhere, in every moment, at all times. Nothing can separate you from it. There's no height it can't reach, no depth it can't transcend, no darkness it can't find you in, no land too distant for it, no speed too fast for it, no road that's unfamiliar to it, and no moment it hasn't experienced. When you wake up in the morning, it's there, buried comfortably under the covers with you whispering, "Do we get up now or wait a few more minutes?" When you drive to work, it catches a ride with you asking, "Which route are we taking today — the shortest or most scenic?" When you take your lunch break, it asks, "What are we eating? Fast food or healthy?" When you go exercise, it's the partner in your head saying, "Should we stop here or keep going?" When you lay down at night, it asks, "What time are we doing it all again tomorrow?" It's impossible to have a day go by without it, an hour it doesn't effect, a minute that doesn't need it, or a second that's not shaped by it. You can't ignore it, you can't outrun it, and you can't hide from it because IT IS YOU.

You don't just have a will, you are a will. And, more specifically, you are God's will. Remember, your soul and all that it craves is a reflection of His soul and all that it craves. He took from what was in Him and breathed it into you. Therefore, your ability to choose is not a revelation of some gift or tool that God gave you; it's a reflection of His identity in you. To be the will of God means you are THE CHOSEN OF GOD — you are His preference.

Science has proven that at conception, a healthy man releases 200-500 million sperm. Of the 500 million, only 200 million ever reach the egg to even have a shot at fertilization. Out of those 200 million at your own conception, do you want to guess which one made it? YOU. Do you know what that means? You faced a one in 500 million chance of making it and you did it. You overcame the immediate 300 in 500 million chance of death, but once again you beat the odds.

You had to be the strongest, the fastest, the smartest, and the most persistent — and you were. Give no mind to what your parents have told you or what others may believe about you. YOU. ARE. NOT. AN ACCIDENT. You may not have been planned, but you were preferred and you were purposed. Within you is the very DNA of acceptance. This is why it feels so unnatural and tiresome for you to work for acceptance. You were made to work from it because it is who you are.

In the book, *Harry Potter and the Chamber of Secrets*, JK Rowling writes, *"It is our choices, Harry, that show what we truly are, far more than our abilities."* Free will, or choice, does exactly that — it "shows what we truly are". The forbidden tree — the tree of the knowledge of good and evil — was never about temptation; it was about an introduction: the introduction of man to Himself. It wasn't put there to be the cause of his fall, it was put there to be the cause of his freedom. It was meant to serve as a reminder of what was in man and free him into the liberty or becoming all that God designed him to be. So, the next time you have to make a choice, no matter how great or small, let it serve as a reminder of who you are — THE CHOSEN, PREFERRED, AND ACCEPTED OF GOD.

A WORLD TO CO-CREATE — *INVENTION*

> *Mind is the Master power that moulds and makes,*
> *And Man is Mind, and evermore he takes*
> *The tool of thought, and, shaping what he wills,*
> *Brings forth a thousand joys, a thousand ills: —*
> *He thinks in secret, and it comes to pass:*
> *Environment is but his looking-glass.*

—James Allen, As a Man Thinketh

> *I am the master of my fate,*
> *I am the captain of my soul.*

—William Ernest Henley, Invictus

Environment's matter. That statement could be taken one of two ways: as a statement emphasizing the importance of your surroundings or as a statement pointing to the substance or substances that your surroundings are made of. In either case, both are true. Environments do matter and environments are constructed by matter.

There's a long-standing debate that has caused confusion in many people, including myself. That is the argument over which statement holds the greater truth, thereby, creating the greater probability for change: *Our environments influence us **versus** we influence our environments.* One group contends that we are totally influenced by our surroundings, so, the change we seek is on the other side of removing ourselves from negative settings. Another group appeals that the exact opposite is true — that your environments change when you do. They argue there's no need to leave the setting you're in, instead, you can simply change the setting within and you will obtain the natural by-product of a transformed life. The controversy of these comparisons will never be settled by clinging to or arguing from an *either/or* perspective. Clarity can only be gained when we consider it to be a *both/and* reality of living.

We possess *both* the potential to be influenced by our environments *and* the potential to influence our environments. The key is learning how to leverage the "potentials". But, what is that potential? Matter. Just as James Allen revealed to us, "Environments are but man's looking-glass". They are the external reflection of an internal reality. The entire material world which we can see is a mirror for the "matter" world within us which we can't see. It's what Allen calls, 'the Mind'. The rub sets in when we begin to realize that sometimes the reflection we see is not our own. This is the purest definition of what it looks like to live under the influence of an environment. It means you're living in a world "molded" by the "matter" of someone else's mind. It means you've allowed their thinking and will to shape your world. Have you ever questioned why there's such a natural rebellion in you toward someone else controlling you? It's because you were not created to be controlled, you were created to be in control — the "master of your own fate", "captain of your own soul", and creator of your own world.

This point is proven in Genesis 2:19,20 that says, '*Out of the ground the LORD God formed every beast of the field and every bird of the sky, **and brought them** to the man to see what he would call them; and whatever the man called a living creature, that was its name. The man gave names to all the cattle, and to the birds of the sky, and to every beast of the field.* Adam was given the privilege and power to literally "name" the environment that he would live in. As God brought the animals to him, "whatever" he thought, or imagined, they should be "called", "that was its name". The interesting part of the story is God never argued with any of his replies. In fact, He never questioned Adam at all. He simply trusted in the sound that his soul was offering and welcomed the creativity of His newly delegated authority over earth.

> CREATING IS NOT A SKILL WE'VE BEEN INVITED TO LEARN, IT'S AN IDENTITY WE'VE BEEN CALLED TO EXPRESS.

It's easy to miss, but Adam's participation in the creative process set a new standard — the standard that He would never again bring anything into manifestation apart from a man or woman to co-create with. Creating is not a skill we've been invited to learn, it's an identity we've been called to express. But how does it work? Michaelangelo said, *"I saw the angel in the marble and carved until I set him free".* The unique revelation of this statement is the exact same marble in the hands of another sculptor had the ability to produce a very different image. While Michaelangelo saw an angel, Leonardo Da Vinci might have seen the Mona Lisa, and Picasso might have seen a goat. The real magic was not in the chemistry of the marble, it was in the chemistry of its makers mind. Much like the great sculptors of times past, we too, have been given a blank canvas: Earth (see Psalm 115:16). And it will become "whatever" we say because creativity is our identity. So, we must learn to use the tools of that identity — our imagination, our intention, and our inspiration — to "carve until we set free" the picture we see.

A WOMAN TO LOVE — *INTIMACY*

"Our souls crave intimacy"

—Erwin Raphael McManus

Even with a work to accomplish, a will to obey, and a world to co-create, man's soul still wasn't complete without a woman to love. Our souls MUST have intimacy. For most of us, especially the male species, when we think about intimacy our thoughts become centered on sex. While sex could qualify as an expression of intimacy, it is not the only expression — it is possible to have intimacy without sex and sex without intimacy. Shana Schutte gives a brilliant explanation of our point in an article she wrote on intimacy, saying:

> *Real intimacy is not found just by merging bodies in sex. When Jesus said, "and the two shall become one . . ." I can't help but think that He meant more than just the physical. After all, how many couples go to bed at night, share their bodies, but not their hearts? Undoubtedly, many of these people would say they are very lonely. Why? Because just as a garden hose is not the source of water, but only an expression, or vehicle for it, so sex is not the source of intimacy, but an outlet (or expression of) it. No matter how hard you try, if real emotional and spiritual intimacy does not exist before sex, it most certainly won't after.*

I couldn't agree more. Our souls crave an intimacy with depth and meaning. It desires to do more than share the body it abides in. It also wants to share the heart it gives life to and the mind it makes. The soul experiences fullness when it gives itself in full. If it is only allowed to express itself through the physical and is detached from the spiritual, emotional, and mental, it will remain empty. Many have ran and are continuing to run on an "empty tank", or with an "empty soul", because they've not yet learned to embrace an expanded definition (God's definition) of intimacy. One whose foundation doesn't begin with contact, but with companionship (**a close, affectionate connection built through the attraction of similarities and the acceptance of differences**). This is the balance of intimacy that God intended for us — where strengths and weaknesses don't become a breeding ground for competition, but completion, where "birds of a feather can flock together" and "opposites can attract" all in the same social space. This was the motivation for Eve's creation and a part of the intended example of relational dynamics that she and Adam were made to portray.

Eve was given to Adam to be his . . .

• **<u>Company</u>:** *It is not good for man to be alone. (Genesis 2:18)*

Our soul's greatest enemy is isolation. Much like our bodies need water, our souls need company. We should not and cannot live without it. While it is healthy to have some 'me' time at certain junctures in life, living with just 'me' for sustained periods of time is an extremely dangerous place. It not only makes me selfish (see Proverbs 18:1), it also makes me vulnerable to distorted perspectives about the "outside world" and will leave me vacant of discovering who I am.

I know this because I experienced it first-hand. If you'll recall, I grew up as an only child with a Mom who worked a lot of hours to provide. I started staying by myself on some days/nights because she trying to save money and suitable baby-sitters came with a cost. Alone. Just me, myself, and I. Nobody to answer to, no parent to obey, and no lock on the pantry with all the sweets. Now, to a 10 year old child, this would sound like a dream come true and if I'm being honest it was fun. It made me feel like an adult and gave me a sense of personal satisfaction knowing that I was able to do what very, very few of my other 10 year old friends could or would do. Sure, there were times I was scared to death, especially when Mama worked the night shift, but, in the morning, when the monsters outside the window had vanished and the ones under my bed decided not to come out, I stepped out of bed with a massive amount of pride about my accomplishments. I managed to keep myself fed (canned ravioli, ramen noodles with cheese, and little Debbie cakes) without burning our apartment complex down, the house clean (because I was playing way too many video games on my Sega Genesis), and even brushed my teeth before bed (I'm counting the morning brushing of course). Unbeknownst to me, there were other 'accomplishments' as well. I also managed to answer my own questions about life, draw my own conclusions about the drunk guy beating his wife in the apartment beside us, figure out why in the world that man and woman were naked together on the tape my 15 year old friend put in the VCR, and even learned that taking lumber from a house being built on the other side of the woods to construct my 'underground play-house' was called 'stealing'. I've often said, 'I wouldn't change a thing about how I grew up because it was all a part of making me who I am today. It taught me many valuable lessons that have served me as I've become a man, a dad, a husband, and a business owner.' However, as I've had some time to think about that statement within the framework of 'self-discovery', there is one thing I would change: the perspective I gained on "individuality" and "community" and how those were meant to work together.

Individualities are the aggregate of qualities — the gifts and talents we possess, the personality traits we express, and the hobbies we like best — that distinguish us one from another. Another definition says it is "the interests of the individual as distinguished from the interests of the community". Herein lies the misinterpretation that has caused many to exalt independency above interdependency and to segregate the one from the many. While God did make us individuals with unique individualities, they were never meant to separate us from the context of community, but to distinguish (highlight) us within it. In other words, what we were given was to set us apart amongst others, not from them. The goal of individuality has never been and will never be isolation, it is integration. My uniqueness, my gifts and talents, my passions and desires — those things that make me different from you are not for my own personal benefit, they are for yours. What I have and what I don't have, what I am good at and what I am not good at, my strengths and my weaknesses are ALL a part of God's grand design. Had He made me good at everything then I wouldn't need you would I? So what did He do? He placed the missing pieces of my identity in you and the missing pieces of your identity in me. He made us to need each other, to need a group, to need a community, to need company. He made us to be a complement.

- **Complement:** *I will make a helper as his complement. (Genesis 2:18)*

Perhaps this may come off somewhat strong, but its truth cannot remain hidden. When I detach myself from engaging in a community of people, I am literally robbing them of not only my presence as the answer to their aloneness, but also of my complementary attributes as a help to their deficiencies. I carry something within me the community needs and they carry something in them that I need. Again, we can't make this statement enough: God created our strengths as well as our weaknesses, our sufficiency as well our deficiencies, our plenty as well as our lack, our dexterity as well as our inadequacy — it is ALL from God and it is ALL for a purpose. When Eve's time had come to make her debut on earth, it is recorded that,

> *The Lord God caused a deep sleep to fall upon the man, and he slept; then He took one of his ribs and closed up the flesh at that place. The Lord God fashioned into a woman the rib which He had taken from the man, and brought her to the man* (Genesis 2:21,22 NASB).

It was NOT Adam's strength that brought him into contact with the greatest blessing of his life, it was his defect. She was the perfect fit to his missing piece. She was his help and she was his complement.

As his *helper*, she became the protector of his promise, the assistance to his aptitudes, and the support to his strengths. As his complement, she became the stability to his inability, the good to his bad, and the completion to his incompletion. Without her, Adam could've never successfully fulfilled his work on earth. Neither would he have ever truly discovered who he was. She was in him and he was in her which is why he said,

> *This is now bone of my bones, and flesh of my flesh; She shall be called Woman, because she was taken out of Man. For this reason a man shall leave his father and mother, and be joined to his wife, and they shall become one flesh (ONE IDENTITY ENTITY).* (Genesis 2:23, 24 NASB; parenthesis is mine added).

The secret to your identity is in your community. It is there that you will find the "foot" that fits (complements) the "glass slipper" you carry.

- **<u>Confidence</u>:** *Adam and Eve were both naked, and they felt no shame (Genesis 2:25)*

There is no greater place of vulnerability than being naked. The mere thought of it causes a level of anxiety in some of us. Even so, the standard of relationship offered by Adam and Eve that we are to pursue **<u>for</u>** us and provide **<u>from</u>** us is one where we can be naked and "feel no shame".

My daughter, Avery, is a little over three years old at the time of this writing. Every day I am more and more amazed at what she teaches me. So much so, that sometimes I wonder who the teacher and the student really is in our relationship. Out of all the lessons that I have taken from her, the one of self-confidence stands out the most. I'm not sure why. Maybe it's because the memories of my own childhood are filled with such extreme insecurity that I constantly monitor that in her to make sure I am reassuring her in every way possible so that her story doesn't become a repeat of my own. Or, maybe it's because strength and courage are such irresistible, magnetic attributes that it's impossible not to notice. Whichever it is, it's clear that she is totally unashamed of who she is and proves it by her willingness to get naked anywhere and everywhere (a fact I'm sure many parents can relate to). While her mother and I do our best to guide in the ways of public decency, I can't help but to love and envy the purity of her shameless-ness. She doesn't do what I do. She doesn't care about what her stomach looks like, or what the person next to her is thinking about how she is shaped, or whether or not she has the perfect tan. Equally as true and more to be envied, if one of her little buddies is around and decides to strip down, she has no judgment about him/her either. To me, that is a perfect representation of heaven's view on relationship: a place where our "nakedness" doesn't become a source for critique and condemnation, but instead, becomes a display of confidence as a result of the comfort and certainty I have in my spouse/ partners/friends and that they have in me.

In conclusion, it's beneficial to recognize there is literal nakedness — as I just described about my daughter. And, there is also figurative nakedness. The figurative is where I want to turn your attention to. How many of your relation-ships right now are you totally exposed in? Meaning, they know every single part of who you are– your imperfections and your perfections, your flaws and your flawlessness, your blemishes and your beauty. How many of your relationships provide that level of confidence? How many of your relation-ships do you provide that level of confidence to? Bill Johnson, Pastor of Bethel Church, in Redding, California emphasizes the importance of honor in relationships and delivers, what I believe, is the perfect description of what God had in mind for the intimate connections of our lives saying, *"A culture of honor is celebrating who a person is without stumbling over who they are not."* Is someone able to, figuratively, get undressed in front of you without you "stumbling over who or what they are not"? Are you able to celebrate who they are without becoming jealous and coveting what they are that you are not? Your connection to others and their connection to you should provide confidence springing from a trust that neither of you will judged, only accepted, in each other's presence. If it does not, then you have every right to question the value of it, as well as, the benefit of moving forward in it.

WALKING WITH A LIMP

So many people move throughout life with a limp. If you look at their physical bodies you won't notice it because it's not external, it's internal. The have a soul limp due to a dysfunc-tion, or amputation of, one or more of its four parts. Let me reemphasize that the soul is like the body. When one part is out of place, or missing altogether, then the natural by-product of a handicap will occur. And because the soul is directly connected to the identity, a crisis is born. The human race at large has been and continues to be affected by the pandemic of an "identity crisis". We simply don't know who we are and the societies we live in are left to suffer the consequences. Crime rates continue to rise, gang participation is becoming more of the common answer for those looking to belong, drugs and alcohol are being found in younger and younger hands as the preferred sources of fun and/or pain numbing solutions, divorce rates are steadily growing, governmental leaders are choosing corruption over character to maintain status and position, church pastors are killing themselves, and the list goes on. Such is the result of the greatest plague history has ever seen — The Plague of Identity Ignorance.

The issue in providing a cure hasn't been a lack of effort. Nor has it been a lack of courage in attempts. We have boldly gone into some of the worst neighborhoods on the planet, covered the graffiti on the walls with fresh paint, witnessed to and prayed for the individuals who live there, only to discover that when we left, the fresh paint was covered over, not with graffiti this time, but with the blood of the one we prayed for shot by the one we witnessed to. We have spent an incredible amount of time and money traveling to the most poverty-stricken, hell-ridden nations of the world, 'knighted' pastors within those nations, planted them in churches, and the return on our investment has been yet another 'service' with three worship songs at the beginning, followed by the passing of the tithe and offering buckets and a 30 minute sermon in the middle, and a call for salvation at the end. When we saw that wasn't working, we adjusted. We increased the intensity by going back into the neighborhood and painting the school walls along with the community recreation center and even added a Monday night intercessory prayer service for those nations we are committed to supporting. We even went out and got a new mortgage on a bigger building to house more of the "hurting". Still, the trend on the negative statistics in our societies continue to point due north. All of this effort and courage and we haven't even come close to immunity. Why? Because we've painted structures and prayed for salvation, but we've not understood, and, consequently, have not reached the souls. Our first lesson is this: **societies are a reflection of their citizens and citizens are a reflection of their soul**. The answer we seek for the change we desire is a whole soul. *Beloved, I wish above all things that you may prosper and be in good health, even as your soul prospers (III John 1:2).*

REFLECTION QUESTIONS

#1. Have you been guilty of suppressing your emotions? Now that you've discovered they were put within you by God and actually make up a part of your identity, how can you begin to allowing them to flow?

#2. Your soul was built with four cravings: a work to accomplish, a will to exercise, a world to co-create, and a woman (or man if you're a woman) to love. Have you starved any specific part more than the others? If so, which area(s)? Why do you think that is? What steps can you take to begin feeding it?

#3. Why do you think with all of the efforts to bring change, the negative statistics still rise? Is there anything different we can do? If so, what and how?

MEDITATION/APPLICATION

The prosperous soul is a full soul. In my experience, everyone has a part of their soul that's hungry. For me, it was the relational part. It is something I really have to work at not neglecting. And, honestly, it hasn't been because I don't want or like relationship. For me, I grew up as an only child in a single parent home with a mom who had to work a lot. By default, I was forced to stay by myself, feed myself, and take care of myself when she did. The inevitable result was I grew up being 'ok' with being alone and even comfortable in smaller group settings or isolated settings. However, the Bible says, "It is not good for man to be alone" and "A man who isolates himself seeks his own desires; he rages against all sound judgment" (see Genesis 2:18 and Proverbs 18:1). Is there an area that's deficient for you — that you have to really work at? What have you done or what can you do to begin filling it? What predetermined choice(s) do you need to make now so that when you start to step outside of your comfort zone you don't retreat?

7

ONCE UPON A TIME

"I am not who or what "they" say; I am who and what He scripted"

(THE STORY OF GOD)

I believe in the *Big Bang Theory*. WAIT!!! Before you close the book and throw it away to be burned, let me explain. I don't believe in it as it is commonly presented, I believe in it as it is heavenly presented. In simple terms, The *Big Bang Theory* explains how the universe expanded (evolved) from a single point. It promotes that 13.7 billion years ago that all matter, energy, and light were compacted into an indefinitely dense point and emerged rapidly from this point forming the universe. As you dive deeper into this theory and its supporting suggestions, there's a lot on the periphery that I can't find a basis for siding with, however, the core thought of a "single point of origin" (God) from which things evolved is a place that offers enough solidity to which I can anchor my belief. Not only that, it also becomes a place of discovery unveiling another important piece of our identities.

INCEPTION

From the traditional Christian perspective, when it comes to "the beginning", the spoken word usually takes precedence as the "single point of origin" by which all things were created. And, for good reason. We are simply drawing our conclusions based on the face value of what we've read or have been taught: "God said, 'let there be . . . and there was'". Because of this, we have given and continue to give an immense amount of focus to words and the "power of life and death" they possess (see Proverbs 18:21). What may come as a surprise to you, however, is that the world was not the result of the word, the word was the result of the world. Genesis 1:1-3 reveals:

> *"In the beginning God created the heavens and the earth, the earth was without form and void and darkness covered the face of deep; the spirit of God was hovering over the waters. **THEN** God said, Let there be".*

What came first — the word or the world? "Then" is the dividing line that provides the answer: *The heavens and* the *earth (the world)* came first. Without a doubt, the spoken word was a critical part of the creative process that shouldn't be left out, but it is inaccurate to continue to credit it with being the inaugurator of creation. As a natural effect of this revelation, the next question becomes, "if the spoken word is no longer to be considered the primary commencer of the heavens and earth, then what is"?

John 1:1 provides an answer:

> *"In the beginning was **the Word**, and **the Word** was with God, and **the Word** was God."*

"Word" in the Greek is 'logos' — defined as "a word, uttered by a living voice, embodying a conception or idea".

Another definition offers a slightly different spin: 'a word, being the expression of a thought'.

Re-written it could read,

"*In the beginning was an* **Idea/Thought (Jesus)**, *and the* **Idea/Thought** *was with God, and the* **Idea/Thought** *was God*" (Emphasis mine).

Creation began in the mind of God. It was *compacted into an indefinitely dense point* of mental impression called "thought" or "idea". Look around you right now! Anything you see which has found tangible form on this physical plane called Earth, whether it has life in it or not, originated, first, in the non-physical plane, through the intangible form of cerebral impulses called ideas. For this reason, it could be argued that ideas are the most powerful force on the planet because absolutely nothing and no one exists without them. Think with me for a moment! Before there was light, there was the idea of light. Before there was the sun, moon, and stars, there was the idea of the sun, moon, and stars. Before there was an office desk, there was the idea of an office desk. Before there was a chair, there was the idea of a chair. Before there was a car, there was the idea of a car. Before there was a business, there was the idea of a business. And, most importantly, before there was me and you, there was the idea of me and you.

Just recently, I watched a popular movie from 2010 for the first time called *"Inception"* (AN ABSOLUTE MUST SEE). In it, Dom Cobb, played by Leonardo DiCaprio, is a unique kind of "thief" that specializes in the dangerous art of extraction: stealing secrets from the subconscious during dream state when the mind is at its most vulnerable. This rare ability has made him a much sought-after item in the emerging new world of corporate espionage, but has also made him an international fugitive and costs him everything he has ever loved — wife, children, and normalcy. Cobb has accepted these things as life sentences of fate and misfortune until he is offered a chance at redemption. One final job holds the potential of giving him his life back if he can accomplish what has been deemed as a most impossible task: *Inception*. Cobb and his team of specialists would not be asked to pull off the perfect heist, rather, they would be asked to do the exact opposite: to plant an idea, instead of steal one. The reason Cobb accepted the seemingly impossible task is because he fully understood the power of ideas to transcend the impossible saying, "an idea is like a virus, resilient, highly contagious. Once an idea has taken hold of the brain, it's almost impossible to eradicate."

Much like the task of inception that Dom Cobb was asked to complete, some would deem it "impossible" for God to be infected with a virus of any kind. Nevertheless, even God Himself couldn't shake the ideas in his own mind. Eradication from it would only be found through the creation of it (more on this later in the section on purpose).

Famous horror author, Stephen King, has been quoted as saying, *"Sometimes stories cry out to be told in such loud voices that you write them just to shut them up."* That's what makes ideas so contagious: the stories they carry. There was a story crying out so loud in the heart of God that His only relief would come from telling it. That story was the story of me and and the story of you. The psalmist David echoed this reality as he penned the words, *"Your eyes have seen my unformed substance; and in your book were all written the days that were ordained for me, when as yet there was not one of them. (Psalm 139:16 NASB)"*.

God was infected with the "resilient, highly contagious idea" of you. And, within the idea of you was the identity of you. Another way to say it, using the context of stories, within the story of you was the character of you. With that, another truth about who we are and who we are not is revealed.

I AM NOT WHO/WHAT 'THEY' SAY; I AM WHO/WHAT HE SCRIPTED

The Story of God

Heaven has a book with your name on it. That's an overwhelming thought isn't it? That God actually took the time to think through the intricate, detailed elements of your story — the character you would play as well as those you would come in contact with and be surrounded by, the various external and internal settings you would move in and out of, the conflicts and climaxes you would face, and the resolutions you would bring and become. An amazing thought indeed that leaves us with a sense of awe and wonder about ourselves, however, the harsh reality remains that a story scripted is much different than a story acted.

A story written does not guarantee that it will be story lived. If you were able to take a sneak peek into the hardcopy edition of "You", you would

A STORY SCRIPTED IS MUCH DIFFERENT THAN A STORY ACTED.

inevitably find that your story has already been completed. Yet, for so many, their book has yet to even be opened. But why? While the book of "You" may be similar to the traditional novels that we see on bookshelves today in that it contains a plot structure — a clear beginning, middle, and end — it is vastly different in the structure's playout. Case in point!

THE BEGINNING: EVERY STORY HAS A BEGINNING, BUT NOT ALL STORIES BEGIN.

Your book doesn't sit on an easily accessible shelf for anyone to pull down and flip through its pages. It is locked in one of the "many rooms" in the mansion of God's heart (see John 14:2) and reserved for your eyes only. The key to access the room and open the book is in your hand. For your story to begin, three things are an absolute must: **your authorization, your participation, and your evasion.**

#1. <u>YOUR AUTHORIZATION</u> — THE COMMENCEMENT OF YOUR STORY IS IN THE COMMITMENT OF YOU.

There's an interesting conversation in the Bible between a man named Nicodemus and Jesus. Nicodemus was referred to as a "Pharisee, a leader of the Jews". To be considered a Pharisee meant that he had dedicated himself to the intense study, disciplines, and promotion of the pharisaical way of life, which was built from the law — a list of rules and regulations laid out by Moses in order to be considered holy and qualified. In other words, Nicodemus was living the story of a Pharisee. Jesus, considered a rebel by most of the pharisaical brotherhood, stepped on the scene with a new model, or story, called, "the Kingdom" and began to violate much of what they considered to be important.

Now, it's unclear as to why Nicodemus came to him. Many assumptions have been made and most all sound good, but where I want to turn your focus toward is the statement that Jesus gave him as it reveals the path to stepping into and starting God's story for our lives: *Truly, Truly I tell you, no one can see the kingdom of God unless he is born again.* Stated otherwise, no one can open the book that God has written about their lives unless he or she is born again.

To be born again marks the end of one story and the beginning of another. It means that we are literally born again into a new narrative. So, your story starts with your birth, although it's not your first birth, it's your second — the birth of your commitment. Unlike our first, it's the birth where we get to choose.

When you choose God, when you say "yes" to Him, you

are saying 'yes' to Him as not only the Savior of your soul, but also as the Author of your story (Hebrews 12:1,2). The fact is your "yes" serves as the required signature needed to guarantee you eternal life *after* death as well as grant Him the needed permission to unveil to you the pre-scripted narrative of your life *before* death.

Some believe Nicodemus was drawn by the miracles Jesus displayed. Others believe He was drawn to the authority He spoke with because Nicodemus was "Israel's teacher" and like all ambitious people, he wanted to increase his impact. I believe these things resonated with something much deeper within him. In fact, I believe this is *the thing* that draws each us — our original, God-written story. We may not recognize it in the moment, yet, something somewhere becomes the impetus that ignites a hope, a wish, a dream, or an image of a another life in our mind's eye and suddenly we find ourselves entertaining the idea of what we see possibly being who we really are.

My junior year of high school there was a poster on the wall close to my desk that had a picture of two paths in the middle of the woods with the last part of a poem by Robert Frost written on it: *Two roads diverged in a wood, and I — I took the one less traveled by, and that has made all the difference.* There are not many English classes I can say I looked forward to attending. This one was different. It wasn't because I enjoyed the subject; it was because of that poem. Whenever I read it, something inside of me would come alive. I've spent years searching for a language to accurately express what I really mean by that, but it was like a part of my imagination that I now call "my real story" was set free and reaching out to me — almost like it was offering an invitation. I would envision myself as a father opposite of the one I had — present in the home as a provider, protector, and preparer. I would dream of a marriage that never ends — one that was healthy and whole, where we loved each other and endured no matter what. I pictured myself in a career that did more than just make money to put food on the table, rather, it is one that also came with a massive amount of impact, influence, and income. A smile that was genuine — I saw that too. Everyone around me was happy; I was happy. While I am not brave enough to say I was having an out of body experience, I am confident enough to say that it wasn't a present body experience either. Visions, images, and dreams would run wild in my thoughts as I faded away into this world of ultimate possibility.

It felt so real and over the years I've come to realize that's because it was. It was my life — my God-designed life, my pre-scripted story-reaching out to me, inviting me to step in. While many of the details were left out, I sensed the new path (the new story) leading to the new me would require a new commitment from me.

#2. <u>YOUR PARTICIPATION</u> — IT'S POSSIBLE TO BE THE MAIN CHARACTER IN YOUR OWN STORY AND NEVER BECOME THE LEADING ACTOR.

Somewhere along the way a belief was introduced and accepted that "God will do everything for us" if we will just accept Him. While He does promise to live *in* us and *through* us, He never said anything about living *for* us. It's not because He can't, it's because He won't. God is not interested in a dictatorship. He is interested in a partnership. As referenced previously, Myles Munroe once said, "Your destiny is chosen by God, but its fulfillment is decided by you." Stated otherwise, in light of our context: your destiny is your untold story and it is subject to your decision to get involved — to merge the premise of the character with the participation of the actor in order that the written word may become the lived truth.

John 1:1-3,14 reads: *In the beginning was the Word, and the Word was with God, and the Word was God. He was in the beginning with God. All things, came into being through Him, and apart from Him nothing came into being that has come into being. In Him was life, and the life was the light of men. The Light shines in the darkness, and the darkness did not comprehend it.*

And the word became flesh and dwelt among and we saw His glory, glory as of the only begotten from the Father, full of grace and truth.

Every story has a beginning, but not all stories begin. The story of Jesus was written *"in the beginning"*. He was the chosen character created to embody the entire world's 'being', to carry "life" within Him that was to be the "light of men", and to hold the high esteem of being the "only begotten of the Father". However, the character and all of His characteristics meant nothing unless "the word became flesh" — unless the character found an actor to bring it to life. And that's exactly what happened. Jesus became the living actor of His story. Not only did we benefit from all the gifts of His participation — *being, life, and light* — we also benefited from the example He set. **The example that every written word seeks to become living flesh and does so when the main character recognizes that he or she must also become the leading actor.**

#3. <u>YOUR EVASION</u>: YOU *START* LIVING THE STORY OF "YOU" WHEN YOU *STOP* LIVING THE STORY OF "THEY".

You are already living a story. The question is whose story is it? Ashamedly, I have to confess that I have lived the story of "they" for the greater part of my life. In fact, "they" have controlled everything about me — my values, my beliefs, and my self-perception — for way longer than I like to admit. The vast majority of my existence has been dedicated to the pursuit of trying to live up to who "they" said I should be or to who I thought "they" wanted me to be.

"They" come in all shapes and sizes. And, so do their stories. Sometimes we know who "they" are. A father, like mine who walks out on his family leaving them with the story that "you are not important or wanted". A teacher that tells his or her student, "you're not smart enough to be in this class". A coach who says, "You're not good enough to play on that level". A cheating spouse who blames you for their actions saying, "You're not fulfilling enough". A pastor who says, "You're full of the devil and if you keeping doing what you're doing God is going to take everything from you."

Other times, we have no idea who "they" are. They are nobody — just a set of ideologies that have been passed from one person to the next until their limited and lifeless story has reached you and me. Their former name has long been forgotten and replaced by the new name of "they". I know you are well aware of this group as we've all heard the ever-so dangerous preceding setup of "you know what 'they' say", followed by a usually negative story.

It's insane really — how easy it is to be influenced by and remember the story of easily forgettable people. Yet, we still find ourselves being daily bombarded by and submitting to their thoughts, opinions, and ideas. We can't deny their stories can sound convincing, especially, when spoken with the level of conviction and passion they are usually spoken with. However, "they" are never a good place to attach our identity to because the ideas of "they" will always be inferior to the ideas of Him. Even so, this is the tension we often find ourselves in. The tug-o-war of stories: the story of "they" versus the story of Him. The report of a qualified expert concerning your health versus the more qualified report of God. The opinions about your reputation from those who knew you before Christ versus the truth of the word about your reputation since accepting Him. The story of an earthly father's abandonment versus the story of a heavenly Father's acceptance.

The truth is there will never be a moment in our lives where a story is not presenting itself. The one we choose to lean into is the one we will live and become. With that, I ask you, "Whose report will you believe?" You start living the story of "You" when you stop living the story of "they". What is *YOUR* story?

THE MIDDLE: EVERY STORY HAS A CHARACTER AND EVERY CHARACTER HAS A CONFLICT.

The Middle is a fitting way to describe the meat of our existence. This is a place of great tension where the bulk of our lives are lived out. It's the place where we enter into the climax of our narrative — where we as the principal character meet with the conflict we were created to resolve.

Truth be told none of us like conflict. The word in and of itself throws off an unwelcoming vibe doesn't it? We despise it even more when communicators like myself bring its reality to the surface. We know that we will have to face it and we know that there's no such thing as life without it, but we don't like anticipating it. However, conflict is not an entirely bad thing, especially, when you understand the *why* behind it — the reason it was written into YOUR story.

Donald Miller wrote in an excerpt from his blog called, *"Storyline"*

> *Every character must go through conflict. Far from being a bad thing, conflict in story is a necessity. In America we live in a culture that avoids conflict but we do so to our own detriment. Conflict fills a story with meaning and beauty. Not only this, but conflict gives value to that which we are trying to attain. And conflict is the only way a character actually changes. There is no character development without conflict. So when we choose our ambitions, they should be difficult and we should anticipate and even welcome conflict.*

Customary fiction authors understand the importance of Miller's message to the overall meaning of their novels. They know that without a climax — a conflict for the character to resolve — the story is dead because it won't be engaging to the readers. Why? Because they must have something to connect to and nothing on the planet bonds humanity quite like the struggle.

The same holds true for our own stories. They would be dead, boring, uninteresting, and unengaging without something to undergo and overcome. This is why we must change our thinking when it comes to the trials we face by remembering who the Author of our lives is and what He is like. He is only and always good and has worked (written) all things together according to His goodness (see Romans 8:28). As a result, we must view the challenges that we face through this lens — the lens of "good". When it comes to the conflicts set forth in each of our stories, two paradigms must never leave our thinking: We are built *for* it and we are built *from* it.

#1. <u>BUILT *FOR* IT</u>: GOD DIDN'T CREATE THE CONFLICT FOR YOU; HE MADE YOU FOR THE CONFLICT.

Although every story must have a character and every character will have conflict, no two stories, characters, or conflicts are exactly the same. They will most certainly possess similarities, but they will never be identical. For example, there are many who have a story like mine of growing up fatherless, yet, each of our testimonies of how it impacted us, what it was like, and how we overcame (if we have overcome) will sound drastically different from one another. For me, I would tell you about the extreme insecurity and lack of self-confidence that came from it — how I didn't like anything about myself (the size or shape of my hands, my height or weight, the way my body was built, my hair color, my shoe size, etc.). Or, you would hear about the way I desperately wanted to be the athletic superstar or the president of my class but was never able to achieve it because I simply didn't believe I could. Another may tell you about the anger and violence it produced in them — how they grew up getting into trouble, were in and out of detention centers, and eventually joined a gang. Others still would recall the feeling of rejection, or being unwanted, which eventually led them to having sex early and often with many different partners because it brought satisfaction, although temporary, to their deepest craving for love and acceptance. I'd like to suggest to you that the diversity of our testimonies — the unique account of how our settings have affected us is a sign of what we've been called to resolve. It is a path to our own unique destiny. Perhaps we should say it like this: our problems reveal our purpose. It's no accident that my own fatherless account is dominated by low self-esteem and I'm now writing a book about it. I'm doing it because I changed the way I viewed my story. I stopped believing that God created my problems for me and started believing that He created me for my problems. I've realized that's why any and every character exists: he/she has been built for (as the solution to) his/her own unique conflict.

Do you want to know why Superman was created to be *"faster than a speeding bullet, more powerful than a locomotive, able to leap tall buildings in a single bound"* The same reason The Amazing Spiderman could *"spin a web any size"*, Captain America had the strength to *"throw his mighty shield"*, the Incredible Hulk possessed *"the power of a bull"*, and why Iron Man had *"amazing armor"*. It's also the same reason why you were given your strengths and abilities too. Each character was uniquely made for the conflict of their storyline. If insecurity has been your greatest nemesis, it's because you have the goods that no one else has to beat it. The same holds true for the enemy of violence or rejection. You see, as "Amazing" as Spiderman was, he couldn't do what Superman could do, therefore, he couldn't beat who Superman could beat and vice versa. As "Incredible" as you may think your own living heroes are, as "Powerful" as they may seem to you, they can't do what you can do and can't beat what you can beat because they were fashioned with the necessary "equipment" to resolve the struggle of their own plots. Not only should this bring us out of being paralyzed by the pains of our past, it should also help us realize that confronting your pain will bring you to your purpose. Again, Superman wasn't written into Spiderman's narrative. If Spiderman hadn't of stepped up, the "enemy" would remain, and, here's the even tougher reality: that enemy would've went on to wreak havoc in the cities and on the citizens that he was meant to protect and set free. NYC and its inhabitants were safer because Spiderman embraced his conflict as his call and lived as if there were NO PLAN B's (more on this is the section on Purpose).

#2. BUILT *FROM* IT: CONFLICT FROM THE OUTSIDE REVEALS CHARACTER ON THE INSIDE.

Your character is in your conflict. I fully believe that you don't know who a person really is until you've been close enough to watch them endure some challenges. Going a little further into an even deeper conviction, I believe you can't fully know who YOU are apart from adversity. Albert Einstein famously said, "Adversity introduces a man to himself". I'd like to suggest that Einstein may have been capturing the reason that God would allow conflict into each of our stories — so that He could introduce us to ourselves. An unfortunate reality, however, is most never step into the God-given character of their heavenly stories because most spend their time running from, ignoring, and avoiding their conflicts. Never quite grasping the fact that conflict from the outside reveal character on the inside.

As I grow older, I find myself leaning more and more towards the possibility of the global identity crisis which surrounds us being more the result of cowardice than con-fusion. The majority of us would rather flee than fight. At first glance, it seems easier, but my own personal experience has proven it is not. Fleeing — living knowing that you're a coward — is hard. Fighting — waking up to the reality of a battle everyday of your life — is also hard. Either way, a hard choice will have to be made. How do I know? I've done both. One conceals while the others reveals.

Some people have asked me if I could go back and change the way I grew up — if I could somehow place my father back in the home, back in my life, and back in my story — would I do it? Every single time, especially with age, there's usually a long pause followed by, "I don't think I would change a thing". This response usually leaves them with a perplexed look on their face. I've yet to come to a confident conclusion as to why that feels like the right response. Maybe it's because I've lived this way for so long it's difficult to imagine anything different. Or, it could be there's some strong subconscious connection I've made to it being a futile consideration since that is the very thing I wanted more than anything else in my childhood and I simply never got it. Or, perhaps I've realized I wouldn't be who I am today — the character — and I most likely wouldn't have the present story I have apart from his absence. There's a chance I may not have the wife I have or the daughter I have and that in itself is enough for me to live with no regrets. I've not always been able to say this, but I am so thankful for every conflict that I chose to embrace and face. It forced to me learn, to adapt, and to grow. It showed me that I'm stronger, more durable, and more capable than I would have ever given myself credit for. And, it will do the same for you when you simply decide to fight instead of flee, when you choose to challenge your challenges, and when you allow the conflict of your story to do what it was designed to do: introduce you to yourself.

THE END: GOD'S STORY DOESN'T END, IT EXTENDS.

There's one remaining contrast between stories written in Heaven and those written on earth and it's this: the stories in and of Heaven don't end, they extend. Ecclesiastes 3:11 tells us that *"God has set eternity in the hearts of men"*. That means we carry a script in our hearts that was written with an eternal pen by an eternal Author from an eternal perspective. With that said, eternity has to become more to us than an after-life destination; it must also become a present-life obligation of recognizing and accepting the responsibility of stewardship over a narrative that is . . .

#1. <u>IMMORTAL</u> — OUR STORY WILL OUTLIVE OUR BODY.

Our bodies are not immortal; the stories they carry are. Without a doubt, all flesh will eventually cease to exist, however, the end of our physical presence does not spell the end of our story's presence.

We've been on the right track with our view of death. It is not to be seen as a conclusion, rather, it is to be viewed as a graduation — a turning of the page into a "new chapter" of existence where we become a *new person* living in a *new location*. This is the perspective of eternity we are most familiar with — one where we leave earth and enter heaven — but it is only half of the eternal equation penned for us by God. He designed our after-life to come in two forms and settings**: our soul in heaven and our story on earth**. Peter said it best:

> *For you have been born again, not of perishable seed, but of imperishable, through the living and enduring word of God* **(STORY OF GOD)**. *For, all flesh* **(THE BODY)** *is like grass, and all its glory like the flowers of the field; the grass withers and the flowers, but the Word of the Lord stands forever (I Peter 1:23-25 BSB).*

While we may move on from our bodies, we will live on through our stories — in the memories of those that loved us, in the generosity we expressed from the least to the greatest, in the impact of our fulfilled purposes, and in the legacy of the sons and daughters that live beyond us. He made our stories immortal because He made our stories . . .

#2. <u>GENERATIONAL</u> — OUR STORY DOESN'T CONCLUDE BECAUSE IT INCLUDES.

In the book of Joel, God opens the "final chapter" of each of our stories to us in what He calls "the last days" revealing where his focus was when writing it and where our focus should be when living it. In it, He says, *"In the last days, I will pour out My Spirit on all flesh. Your sons and your daughters will prophesy. Your old men will dream dreams and your young men will see visions (Joel 2:28)".* Sons and daughters as well as old men and young men point to a generationally connected storyline. Prophesy, dreams, and visions point to a future — one we will see and experience with our own eyes (visions) and the other we will not (dreams). Through marrying the concept of generations with the concept of dreams and visions, He makes it incredibly clear that the final chapters of "all flesh" is to be on the future of the generations that will come after them. He is beckoning to "all flesh" (that's us) to wake up to the realization that we are both individuals and generational and that the end of our earthly story should never be centered on the fear or potential pain of dying. Rather, it should be on the promise and priority of continuing.

Just recently, it snowed here in Georgia where we live and it was a day I'll never forget. First, we were fortunate to be in a transition period of moving and are currently living in the pool house at my in-laws while searching for our next home. Trust me when I tell you, if there is any place on earth where you want to be snowed in it is at my in-laws. They live in the mountains so you can imagine the size of the hills you're able to sled on. A massive 100 yard slope with the added weight of my 33lb three –year old daughter on my back equals a lot of speed and a real fun time (until you have to walk back up the hill 500 more times because you're in the stage of parenting where anything exhilarating leads to a huge smile and the broken-record request of "I want to do it again, Daddy"). Don't get me wrong, I was happy to do it again — anything to make my girl smile or hear her laugh is worth it. It didn't take long, however, until her little legs got tired from the multiple hikes. Do you want to guess what happened? That's right. I had to carry her back to the top many, many, many more times because her legs got tired, but her desire to "do it again" did not (funny how that happens).

On one of our much slower walks back up the hill, I came across the second unforgettable part of my day: the lesson that God placed in the outline of our footprints from one our previous journey's to the top. It was a visual lesson on the passage in Joel we just mentioned that I was unusually wise enough to snap a few pictures of for you:

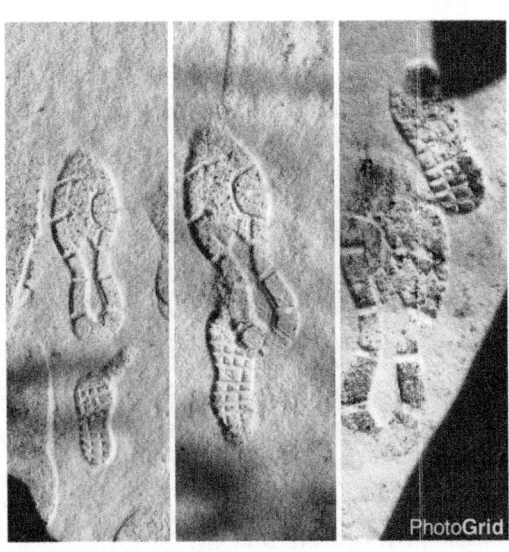

The picture of the bigger footprint is obviously mine and the picture with the smaller footprint is my daughter's. Here's the lesson on how the end of our stories were designed to overlap with the future of our succeeding generations. From left to right:

PIC #1: FOLLOW: They walk *behind* our footsteps
PIC #2: MERGE: They walk *in* our footsteps
PIC #3: EXCEED: They walk *beyond* our footsteps

We start out by doing everything *for* them, ultimately, setting the example of how life should be done. Then, we move into doing things *with* them — still teaching while allowing them the freedom to make some of their own choices. Here, we know that some of those choices will lead to favorable outcomes which we will celebrate and others will lead to mistakes which we will need to remediate. In either case, their steps are merging with ours because we are aware of a life that will be lived without us and beyond us. Finally, we will reach the phase where their stories, along with their steps, reach past our own. This is where the ceiling of our life becomes the floor of theirs. They still carry the story of what we did "for" them and "with" them, but they are void of our physical presence, and we, or I should say our narrative, now lives *in* them.

We are not living just for ourselves. We are living for the generations that will come after us. This is why dreams and visions are so vital and why we must give ourselves permission

> DREAMS AND VISIONS ARE NOT SELFISH. THEY ARE THE UNTOLD STORIES OF FUTURE GENERATIONS SEEKING TO BE TOLD.

to see, desire, and pursue the future appealing to us in our minds and hearts, because, contrary to most thinking and teachings, dreams and visions are not selfish. They are the untold stories of future generations seeking to be told.

As a final point of emphasis, I'd like to give you a few last "food for thought" items that will hopefully seal the deal for you concerning our point. Notice that dreams are connected to "old men" and visions are connected to "young men". What would be the need for the old to dream? Aren't they the ones closest to death? The answer is YES. My interpretation is that their dreams are not for their eyes — they are images of a future story that the dreamers eyes may not get to see. So, why dream? Because they are dreaming on behalf of another generation: "the young". Visions, connected to the 'young' — aka: those with plenty of life left in them — are images of a future story that the visionaries' eyes will have the privilege of seeing, living, and experiencing. Putting it all together, I believe that the 'dreams' of the 'old men' are meant to become the 'vision' of the 'young men'. This is what happened with David and Solomon in the Bible. David had a 'dream' to build a temple for God, but God had a different plan for David and revelation for us. For those of you that may not know, Solomon was David's son and it was at his dedication that Solomon gave this account concerning the temple:

> *Now it was in the* **heart** *(the dream) of my father David to build a house for the name of the LORD, the God of Israel, but the LORD said to my father David, "Because it was in your heart to build a house for My name, you did well that it was in your heart. Nevertheless* **you shall not build the house, but your son** *(a future generation)* **who will be born to you, he shall build the house for My name".** *Now the LORD has fulfilled His word which He spoke; for I have risen in the place of my father David and sit on the throne of Israel, as the LORD promised, and have built the house for the name of the LORD, the God of Israel. There I have set the ark in which is the covenant of the LORD, which He made with the sons of Israel.* (II Chronicles 6:7-11 NASB- parenthesis and emphasis mine added).

David's dream became Solomon's vision and revealed that some things we see in our hearts are for a generations — a time and a people that our eyes will never see. And it is through this generational passing of the torch that we are able to live a story that outlives us — one that is eternal, meaningful, and . . .

#3. <u>HISTORICAL</u> — HE WILL MAKE HISTORY *THROUGH* US WHEN WE EMBRACE HIS-STORY*FOR* US.

One of the most familiar and inspirational lives in all of history is Martin Luther King, Jr. His legacy will forever mark him as one of the greatest reformers to have ever walked the earth. The willingness he had to step out as a hated minority, looking demons of prejudice in the eyes while intentionally placing himself in front of hostile crowds and becoming the voice of equality makes him, without a doubt, the epitome of courage. His unwavering fight for freedom is no less than impressive as it paved the way for a culture we now call normal. The only real way to bring honor to his life is to make sure his story is never forgotten. Regardless of color or ancestral background, we ALL have been greatly impacted by his fight. MLK, Jr. wasn't a literal soldier. Figuratively, however, we would be hard pressed to find another individual — past, present, or future — who more closely resembled one. He waged violent wars on the battlegrounds of injustice against the enemy of racism with the weapon of his dream. Although he died without personally experiencing the fulfillment of his heart's cry, his fight doesn't fall on empty ground of wishful thinking, nor is it still a prisoner of "one day". We are the "one day" of his dream — a living testament of heirs representing the accuracy of what he so artistically painted a word picture of during his monumental *"I have a dream"* speech on August 28, 1963.

As brave as MLK, Jr. was, as inspiring as his pursuit for equality was, as legendary as his speech was and still is, the fact remains that "one day" would've never happened without him picking up the dream of those who lived before him and without future generations picking up his. That's how history is made — many generations reaching toward a common pursuit. Although it is commonly viewed as a story of the past, what causes uncommon events and/or person(s) to be recorded on the pages of historical significance is that present and future generations choose to become the manifested reality of their predecessor's unfulfilled dreams. They accept that they are part of their ancestor's stories and their ancestor's stories are a part of theirs. Had it not been for Rosa Parks and her refusal to move to the back of the bus, MLK may have never had the meeting in his church to protest on her behalf, which many attribute to being the igniter of the civil rights movement. Had it not been for the collective efforts of those who continued to march in protests and fight for equality even after MLK died, segregation may have never been done away with. Furthermore, if these men and women had not responded to HIS-STORY in their hearts, whether they knew it was God or not, then history would have never been made.

God seeks to make history through us as well. And, He will when we embrace HIS-STORY for us. Becoming that story requires that we learn how He writes and speaks. In his book, *"Dreaming with God"*, Bill Johnson writes:

> *The beauty of His will is lost for the purpose who does not know the language of the Spirit. It is vital to learn how He speaks. His first language is not English. In fact, it would be safe to say it's not Hebrew either. While He uses the language of men to communicate with us, He is more inclined to speak through a myriad of other methods.*

He then goes on and calls those other methods "languages of the Spirit". Once such method he reveals is "the language of Dreams". This is what MLK was able to catch — that *"his-story"* wasn't written, nor could it be read in letter; it was written and could only be read through his *"dream"*. HIS-STORY for is still waiting to be read and told through you. So I ask you, what is your dream?

REFLECTION QUESTIONS:

#1. Before you were born, God wrote a book about your life. What "chapter" do you sense that you're in or leaving?

#2. *Every story has a beginning, but not every story begins.* Have you authorized your story to begin? Are you participating in it or have you been waiting on "life" to give it all to you or God to do it all "for" you?

#3. *The story of '"you" begins when you stop living the story of "they".* Have you been trying to live someone else's story? If so, why? Where did you start to believe that yours wasn't good enough?

#4. Have you ever considered your conflicts as a good thing — as a way to identify your calling and develop your "character"? How will this change your approach to life moving forward? Can you name some conflicts in the past that ultimately turned out to help you in some way?

#5. Your story is given with the generations in mind. Limiting yours also limits theirs. Does this give you added motivation to embrace all your story contains — hardships included — so that the generations can live in the fullness of theirs? Have you seen this dynamic played out in your life, good or bad?

MEDITATION AND APPLICATION

MLK "caught" that his story wasn't written, nor could it be read in "letter"; it was written and could only be read through "dreams". Dreams are the language of the Spirit. We are able to read the story of our lives by "reading" the dreams of our hearts. Take some time to identify what your heart is saying. And, go the extra step by writing out a one-page description of what you see. Let's call it your, "I have a dream speech". Start it by writing, "I have a dream that one day" and proceed by giving it as much detail as possible. Don't feel overwhelmed or confused. Do the best you can. You can always update it along the way, but for now, it's important for you to know what God has written about you and how He intends to make *His-story* through you.

8

MY FATHER?

"I am not who birthed me; I am who made me"

(THE SON OF GOD)

When you look at Jesus' life on earth, there are many reasons that can be listed on *why* he came: to destroy the works of the devil, advance the kingdom of God, be the Savior of the world, heal the sick, raise the dead, cast out demons, and cleanse lepers. Each of these and many others would undoubtedly make it onto a final ballot concerning His overarching purpose for leaving heaven and coming to earth, but, only one makes sense as the unanimous, stand-alone winner: **He came to reveal the Father**.

As a twelve year old boy, He set the precedence of why He chose to remove His robe of glory and replace it with human flesh by saying to His parents (who were frantically searching for him after realizing they had left him behind at the "Feast of Passover"), *Why is it that you were looking for me? Did you not know that I had to be in My Father's house (Luke 2:41-52)?*

Later, He also taught His disciples to pray beginning with *"Our Father"*. Then, giving an account to the miracles He displayed, He would say things like,

> *Do you not believe that I am in the Father and the Father is in Me? The words I say to you, I do not speak on My own. Instead, it is the Father dwelling in Me, carrying out His work. Believe Me that I am in the Father and The Father is in Me — or at least believe because of the works themselves* (John 14:10,11 BSB).

Even after death, preparing to make His last appearance on earth and eternal departure to heaven, He passes the baton to His disciples with the following marching orders: *"Peace be with you. As the Father has sent Me, so also I am sending you (John 20:21)"*. As glorious as the miracles were, as jaw-dropping as his wisdom was, as amazing as His teachings were, and as extraordinary as His sacrifice still is, it was and continues to be the result of this one primary pursuit: to reveal a loving Father to an orphaned planet *(Deut. 31:6; Hebrews 13:5)*.

FROM BASTARDOM TO KINGDOM

Early in my journey I learned that one of the greatest benefits to a fatherless child giving their lives to Christ is they enter into a Kingdom family that has a Father who is ALWAYS and will forever be present — who promises to "never leave us, nor forsake us *(Deut. 31:6; Hebrews 13:5)"*. I also learned for that same fatherless child, often times, their greatest benefit can also turn out to be their greatest challenge.

Moving from life without a father to life with a Father felt good in conversation, consideration, and meditation, however, its application proved to be much, much harder than I anticipated. You would think an abandoned child would dive head-first into an opportunity for a father-son relationship. Trust me. It's not that simple. While the void in many abandoned hearts (and identity) cry out day and night for adoption, we still find ourselves in a posture of resistance when the opportunity actually presents itself. Some have referred to this guarded stance as "rebellion" and, more specifically, "rebellion towards authority". The problem with the "some" who hold to this belief and promote it is they are wrong. THEY. ARE. DEAD. WRONG. We are not rebelling. We are confused. While an abandoned dynamic leaves us with more negatives than positives, it's still familiar territory to us. Sure, our circumstances may appear to be unfortunate to many of the outside labelers, but they are not to us. This is what we call "normal" because this is all we have ever known. Therefore, if we look unsettled when presented with the possibility of a life with a Father — a life without absence — it's because we are. We have no past experience to give us a frame of reference for how to deal with the moment of change we're being thrusted into. We are in a transition — moving from something old to something new — and we honestly don't know if we're doing it right. Lance Wallnau defines transition as, *"the polite word that Christians use to describe a state where they're going through hell, but they're convinced God is in it"*. Then, further describing it as, *"the process of working out the aftermath of a change that occurred in moment of time — a process of acclimating the head and heart to the new reality brought about by a change in your life"*. This is the part the labelers are not aware of. They are catching us in the transition — in the middle of a process where we are attempting to work out the aftermath of the greatest identity-alteration we have ever had to endure: the shift from being a slave of bastardom to being a Son in the Kingdom.

I'll never forget the request I made to God about five or six years ago during prayer: *God, you call me your son and you call yourself, 'My Father'. That sounds good to me, but, I have no idea what it's supposed to look like. Would you please teach me how to be your son — a son to a Father?* At first, I was stunned by my own request. It was almost like someone else was asking it for me. It was my voice that offered the petition, still, I can confidently say it wasn't my mind or even my desire that inspired it. The best way to explain it is it was as if God used my mouth to pray His prayer — the one He wanted to hear the most from me and the one He wanted the most for me.

After the daze started to wear off, I became somewhat angry with myself that I hadn't asked sooner. At the time, I had been a Christian for more than 10 years and had put in plenty of requests by then (mostly selfish) and it never hit me that this was the most perfect petition that I could ever lay before His feet. Really, if the bulk of your prayer life is going to be selfish you might as well make sure it has some type of quality and substance right?

Here's the deal: I'm a son to a single mom who never allowed a man into the house until I was 17 years old. I'd like to tell you it was because I asked her not to date anyone because I secretly hoped that she and my dad would get back together. I'm almost 100% certain that wasn't the main reason. Although I've never asked her "why", I feel I could narrow the answer down to a one of two options. She either didn't want to love again and risk being hurt or she didn't want to expose me to the "wrong" kind of man — perhaps one that was abusive or would abandon us again. Or, maybe it was a little bit of both. The point is there was no father-figure . . . at all . . . at any point during my childhood. There were male-figures such as older friends, uncles, coaches, teachers, and eventually pastors, but no direct paternal influences. What all this means is that I knew how to be a son to a mother but not to a father. So, God knew what He was doing the day He forced the words out of my mouth, "teach me how to be Your son — a son to a Father".

What came next? Well, I am living the "next" right now . . . six or seven years later. This wasn't the type of request that would be granted in one sitting or in a few words to satisfy the intellectual part of my being. No, this was an answer, or, perhaps, an invitation to a process of learning, adapting, learning, and adapting some more.

The education and, better yet, experience I've received since the day God hijacked my prayer has been nothing short of amazing and I'm going to share them with you. Before I do, there's something I want you to know. By no means do I believe my list is an exhaustive list of what we can know about Him as "our Father". It's simply a "God-as-my-Father" point of view and it's continually being updated. Yours may be different. In fact, I know yours will be different because He becomes the kind of Father that each one of us needs, revealing Himself uniquely to every individual so that each individual's uniqueness can be revealed to them. I encourage you to use what He has taught me and embrace it as your own if it resonates with you, but please don't allow it to limit what He wants to show you personally — the part of Himself and, in turn, the part of yourself that He reserved just for the two of you. With that said, this brings me to the foundation of all the lessons I've learned thus far:

I AM NOT WHO BIRTHED ME, I AM WHO MADE ME (THE SON OF GOD)

This lesson can be either music to your ears or offensive to your soul, depending on whether or not you had supportive parents who were present in your life or non-supportive parents who were absent. A further explanation of what this really means should awaken the hearts of the abandoned and settle the hearts of the offended. It is not meant to be demeaning in any way toward those who raised you; it is meant to bring an awareness to where you've attached your identity. No matter if you had a great mother and father or a terrible mother and father, the moment you connect your identity to either of them is to choose where you will level-off in life, and, even worse, it is to choose where you place the limitations on the generations that will come after you.

The deepest pain of my life is not the day my dad left. The deepest pain of my life is the day I realized that I allowed my identity (as "Son") to leave with him. As it is with most voids, they don't remain vacant. I soon replaced the empty hole of "son" with "bastard", "unwanted", "unloved", "rejected", "stupid", "ugly", "average", and many other inferior labels of identification. Obviously, this message, "*I am not who birthed me, I am who made me*", was incredibly freeing news to me. As I matured and crossed over into adulthood, thoughts of marriage, parenting, and future generations consumed my mind. The anticipation of the images that I saw of my likely future brought a momentary measure of hope and excitement. Long term, however, it would eventually be outweighed by a larger measure of anxiety, worry, and fear. Although I deeply desired to be called "son", to become a catalyst of change for my generations and have a family of my own, I was deeply terrified that I would somehow end up sabotaging it in some way. I was scared that I would end up divorced or abandoning them because that's what my father did and I reasoned that since I came *from* him then that was the inevitable, uncontrollable outcome of my life. Thankfully, I didn't know what I didn't know and God showed me over time that who we come *through* is vastly different than who we come *from*.

You and I were produced in the belly of God's imagination long (see Genesis 1:26-28) before we were reproduced *through* our parents. What this tells us is we were His offspring before we were theirs and that is where our identity lies. Ephesians 1:5 says, "*He predestined us to adoption as sons through Jesus Christ to Himself, according to the kind intention of his will*". See! We never stopped being "sons and daughters"; we simply stopped believing we were.

Our personal restoration and our process of recovery begins with our own personal responsibility. Leaving was my father's fault. There's no part of that decision that I should take on myself. However, my identity leaving with Him was mine and it is my responsibility to reclaim it. How? You **_MUST_** go to the one you forfeited it to.

REVELATION VS RECONCILATION

As encouraging as it was to be enlightened to my real identity, it was just as discouraging to discover that there's a major difference between enlightenment and recovery. Knowing that you are God's son doesn't automatically put you back into that role; it simply lets you know what's available. Herein lies many of our irritations. Too many times we mistake revelation for reconciliation and they are not the same thing. Revelation is an invitation to reconciliation — a required starting place — but enlightenment without enactment is to be a king standing in the presence of a taunting giant and never put on the "armor" (the identity) or exercise the authority you've been given to take him out, ultimately, taking possession of what's truly yours anyway. It is to hind behind the title of your promise or promotion hoping the giant will either be frightened by his own sudden personal revelation of who you are or get tired and leave. THIS. WILL. NEVER. HAPPEN. A promise is not enough. A prophetic word is not enough. A title is not enough. A revelation is not enough. Total reconciliation — death of the giant you fear most and recovery of the identity you want most– will only come when personal revelation meets personal participation. We are going to have to put on the armor and get in the fight. Without a doubt, it will be uncomfortable and we will be afraid, but we engage remembering that if we *"do the thing we fear the most then the death of fear is certain (Mark Twain).*

9

RECLAIMING SONSHIP

"I am not who birthed me; I am who made me"

(THE SON OF GOD)

What I desired most (to get my identity as "son" back) was in the hands of who and what I feared most (a confrontation with the one who abandoned me). At this point, I think it's fair to my dad to make it clear that my fear wasn't driven by a thought that he would be abusive toward me because he's never given me a reason to think that way. Rather, my fear was more the effect of knowing that I'd be entering into unfamiliar territory, fighting with weapons that I hadn't used before, and, therefore, couldn't explain their purpose to anyone — such as my father — even if my life depended on it. Oddly enough, my life did depend on it and there weren't very many options available outside of take the risk and go. I had to take the chance. I figured if I failed I could live with knowing that at least I tried. I had to give myself an opportunity see what was on the other side of the offer that God was putting before me. So I went. And,

I'm still going day-by-day walking out what I've called, "The Three Steps to Reclaiming Sonship":

STEP #1: FORGIVE — *RELEASE THE PRISONER*

To be entirely honest with you, I was tempted to find another topic to write about — one that sounded much sexier, that would feel much less redundant, or that would motivate you with a take-over-world kind of response. Then, it became apparent to me that the sexiness would eventually wear off, redundancy would once again set in, and the newfound motivation would be short lived as I'd be attempting to encourage you with a lie because it wouldn't be the actual process that has allowed me to move from slave to son.

At face-value, according to how we've taught it and understood it, forgiveness can feel like an extremely repetitious and boring task as it has been (and remains) the ancient "first-step" in nearly every born-again believers sanctification process. However, as we resist being anesthetized by a familiarity-breeds-contempt attitude, we will awaken to a form of forgiveness that offers far more than what we've traditionally accepted.

Forgiveness is far more than a logical first-step to clean up our act. Fully understood, it becomes a supernatural weapon of warfare capable of pulling down the strongest of strongholds and setting free all that is imprisoned within. Before we go there, let's go over some of the basics concerning forgiveness so that we can make sure the "footing" underneath the structure we're going to add on top is firm.

• FORGIVENESS IS PART OF THE "HOUSE RULES"

A point revealed by Matthew, who wrote,

> *For if you forgive others for their transgressions, your heavenly Father will also forgive you. But if you do not forgive others, then your Father will not forgive you (Matthew 6:14,15).*

Forgiveness is a non-negotiable with our heavenly Father. To lay aside the clothes of a slave and put on the robe of a son means that we must act accordingly — according to the robe we wear (aka: the identity we carry) and according to the "rules of the house" we live in.

On more than one occasion growing up, I remember hearing my mom say (especially during my more rebellious years), "if you're going to live in this house, you're going to abide by these rules". She was saying, "You're my son and I love you, but there a standards to living here that you must follow". It's no different living as a son in the "house (kingdom) of God". There are rules we must live by and one of those happens to be forgiveness. It's an odd rule, but a rule nonetheless that says: ***You can't enter the house without forgiveness and you can't be forgiven without forgiving***.

Suddenly, it all started to become gut-wrenchingly clear to me that it's possible (and unfortunately common) to stand outside of the door knocking and begging "father please forgive me, please let me in" and be deaf to the voice coming back from the other side with the answer to access: "you must first go and forgive those who have 'trespassed' against you" (see Matthew 5:16).

You can imagine the internal tension I began to feel as I was confronted with this "rule". I knew exactly what it meant. If I wanted to live in the house owned and operated by my heavenly Father I had to forgive the transgressions of my earthly father.

What are transgressions? The Greek says it means, "to fall away after being close-beside'. That's an eerily accurate way to describe the "act committed" by my dad isn't it? He "fell away from" (rejected, abandoned, left) his role and call to stand "close-beside" me. In spite of my anger, or how unfair I thought the rules were, or the pain I felt from his choice to leave, these were the guidelines and if I wanted to move beyond the doorsteps of the house to occupying a room within then I had to comply.

• FORGIVENESS RELEASES THEM FROM THEIR PENALTY AND OUR PERSON FROM THEM

Our Father makes the same promise to each of His children: "everything I have is yours" (see Luke 15:31). And, we will receive "everything" once we do *the* thing that He requires: FORGIVE. In short, forgiveness means to "release or discharge". It is literally to remove a person from the sentence of their guilty verdict, to liberate them from serving the remaining time for the crime they committed, and to wipe their slate clean from the responsibility of all charges placed on them.

The truth is my dad underwent an unfair trial concerning his crime of abandonment as he was forced to stand before a court of one — ME. I was the judge and the jury of his case and I made sure that he got the maximum sentence (Life) for his wrong doing. I didn't just want him to pay. I wanted to him pay an inordinate, insurmountable price. I didn't just want him to feel guilty. I wanted to bury him under an immovable weight of regret and condemnation. I wanted him to hurt as much as I was hurting and, most times, I wanted him to hurt more. And, I was doing a heck of a job at being the harshest, most unrelenting, and unforgiving judge I could be until Jesus stepped into my life.

One would assume "stepping in" might look more like an emergency intervention where He would remove me from my "position" of authority, especially considering how contrary it is to His own, but, He didn't. In fact, He did the exact opposite by leaving me in the magistrate's seat as the supreme judiciary power over my father's case and even enlarged the authority I had there saying *"if you forgive anyone's sins, their sins are forgiven; if you do not forgive them, they are not forgiven (John 20:23"*. Condemnation and acquittal was now a part of my repertoire. And, it came with an ever-so subtle "catch": *Forgive and your sins will be forgiven.*

Suddenly, I was not only the presiding arbitrator over my dad's life. I was also my own. The measure I used toward him would be the measure I'd be using on myself (see Matthew 7:2). Passing out verdicts of condemnation wasn't so hard when it just about his life. It's funny what happens to the certainty of your judicatory decisions, however, when you realize there will be a direct impact on your own life in return. The expansion of my jurisdiction gave me the right to exercise a new form of magistracy called forgiveness, however, there was one setback to the promotion — I didn't know how. All of my expertise and experience lied within the only ruling I had ever permitted myself to use: GUILTY!

Learning to how to forgive wasn't easy. It meant embracing discomfort, doing things in a way I've never done them before, "judging" in a way I've never had to judge before, and sifting through the well-intentioned, yet, limited definitions of those who had attempted to walk the path of pardon before me. One such interpretation was that "forgiveness is not for them, it's for you". That's an extremely dangerous and inaccurate definition. Its absurdity is unveiled to the highest degree when we view it with Jesus as the backdrop.

What if I came to you and said, "When Jesus comes to forgive, He's not really doing it for us; He is doing it for Himself"? Doesn't make very much sense does it? Wouldn't it make us question if we are truly forgiven or not? Considering it from this angle is enough to evoke a sarcastic laugh or a disappointed shaking of our heads, yet, this has become the accepted interpretation of absolution we hold amongst one another.

Forgiveness is for both the offender and the offended. For the offender, it releases them from the penalty of their wrong. This is the perspective we are most familiar with and have previously explained. Still there exists another part of the equation that totally blew my mind. For the offended, when we choose to bravely pardon, we are not just releasing the offender from his or her penalty; we are also releasing our "person" from it as well. Earlier I made a statement: *The deepest pain of my life is not the day my dad left; the deepest pain of my life is the day I realized I allowed my identity to leave with him.* This was "the day" I was referring to — the day I learned the dual nature and reward of forgiveness. For years, I thought by placing my dad in an unpardonable prison for his offenses against me and my mom that I would be protecting us somehow. What I didn't discern was that by imprisoning him I was also imprisoning myself since I gave myself to him. No wonder I couldn't figure who I was. "I" was with him . . . in the prison that I sentenced him to. Little did I know, by exercising the courage to set him free would mean setting "me" (my person/identity) free as well.

• FORGIVENESS IS NOT FINAL NOR DOES IT GUARANTEE YOU WILL FORGET

I really wish I could tell you that forgiveness is a once-and-for-all event. It is not. Forgiveness is NEVER final and it certainly NEVER guarantees you will forget. Without a doubt, the freedom I experienced from its application was incredibly exciting. And, the new home and new identity I found myself adjusting to was a fit I could get used to. Still, they came with some fine print that read something like the conversation between Jesus and one of his disciples concerning this very topic: "*How often should I forgive someone who sins against me? Seven Times? 'No, not seven times', Jesus replied, 'but, seventy times seven'*" (Matthew 18:21,22).

One thing was becoming painfully clear: whatever it took to get me in the house, it would take "seventy times" that to keep me there. The initial act of forgiving in and of itself required so much convincing, so much processing, and so much work that a consideration of adding anything too it, much less a lifetime commitment, was ludicrous. Regardless of how unbearable it seemed or how preposterous I thought it was, I was beginning to realize that a lifetime commitment is exactly what I signed up for — a choice that I'd have to make every single day for the rest of my life. And, sometimes, most notably on the tougher days where his "trespasses" and their effects seemed to haunt me a little more, I'd have to forgive him every few minutes.

Personally, I wanted to release my dad, but I only wanted to do it once and be done with it. I wanted to move on with my life and allow him to move on with his forgetting any of it ever happened. That's just not how it works. A lifestyle of forgiveness is not one that lends itself to a lid or offers divine amnesia. Instead, it is one that makes the commitment that says, "when the memory of the transgressions come, I will forgive as many times as is necessary until I am no controlled by its effects."

STEP #2: REDEEM — *RESTORE THE PAST*

I once heard Lance Wallnau facetiously, yet, accurately refer to God as "not just Jehovah Rophe or Jehovah Nissi, but also Jehovah Sneaky." It's true. He loves to "trick" us. Before we go any further, let us keep in mind that He does so as a good, loving, and righteous Father who only has our best interests at heart. It's kind of like the game of hide-and-seek that I play with my three and a half year old daughter. While I do hide from her, it is with a careful intent, positioning, and antici-pation of being found, not remaining hidden. I will duck behind the sofa and deliberately leave a part of my body out in the open so that she will see it and be able to "find" me. When she does, the exposure rarely looks like a tag-your-it kind of discovery. It usually ends with her tackling me with an ensuing wrestling match (she's a rough little girl and I LOVE IT — and I may even encourage it from time to time . . . when her mom's not around of course). Here's my point! For me — her daddy — the game is fun, but, I'm not there for the game as much as I'm there for the goal. I enter into the process with the end in mind. I set it up and I set her up in order to reach the predetermined conclusion I had before beginning. God, operating as our sneaky Father, does the same with us. He "plays" with a purpose. If He hides from us, it is so that He can be found. If He tricks us, it is so that WE can found.

> IF HE HIDES FROM US, IT IS SO THAT HE CAN BE FOUND. IF HE TRICKS US, IT IS SO THAT WE CAN FOUND.

Forgiveness turned out to be one of those divine set-ups as it set the stage for an opportunity at redemption. Once again, I found myself thrusted into, or "tricked" into the middle of a situation I was ill-equipped to handle. What did I want to do? Quit. And, I would have if I could have, but, I was way too deep into process to justify it.

At this point, I had become decent at forgiving. You might even say I was good at it, which is the very thing that made redemption so frustrating. I couldn't lean on very many of the "skills" I had built in the forgiveness phase as the competencies necessary to "play well" there seemed to be in a direct contrast to those needed to "play well" here. For example,

• WHERE FORGIVENESS "RELEASES", REDEMPTION "RESTORES"

Moving from forgiveness to redemption felt like advancing from playing a sport on the high school level to playing it on the college level. I had proven I was "good enough" to make it to the next level, but things moved at a much faster pace, seemed much bigger, and the tasks much tougher.

Forgiving my father meant that I was releasing him from serving the remainder of the years left on his sentence.

Redemption meant that I would be attempting to restore the years that were lost as a result. By comparison, forgiveness was easier than redemption for the sheer fact that I could do it from a distance. In other words, forgiveness "worked" without the need for relationship. For instance, let's say I'm driving home later today, stop at a red light, and when it turns green someone pulls out in front of me or cuts me off (it makes me angry just thinking about it). I become offended by their "trespass against me". Instead of giving them the middle finger of fellowship, I choose to "release" them from it. Do I know the person? No. Did I need a relationship with the person to forgive them? No. Forgiveness doesn't need relationship because that's not what it's about — it's about the release from the sentence. Redemption, however, demands relationship. That's the whole point of it — to restore the years that were lost previous to the release.

Wait a minute! "You're telling me that God wants me to pursue a relationship with my dad — the person who rejected me and made it abundantly clear that he DID NOT want a relationship with me?" That's exactly what I'm telling you. There's a promise that says "I will restore to you the years" (Joel 2:25). We like to quote promises, declare them in conversations, mention them as fill-ins to the awkward moments in our church small group meetings when a study question is asked and no one wants to be the first one to talk. We even like to meditate on them at night to calm our minds so that we can go to sleep. What we don't like is when we actually have to do something to see them come to pass.

Do we *have* to redeem? No. We also don't have to be considered courageous or go any deeper in the revelation of who we really are. Look! I get it. I didn't like it either. Ok, truthfully, I hated it. I loathed the consideration of pursuing a relationship with the man who walked out on me. Wasn't it enough that I forgave him? That I set him free from his charges? Did he really deserve any of it? That's when it hit me . . .

• WHERE FORGIVENESS OFFERS MERCY, REDEMPTION OFFERS GRACE

No. He didn't deserve forgiveness much less redemption. Then again, neither did I once it was all put into its proper perspective. By asking me to extend forgiveness, God was asking me to extend mercy. By asking me to work towards redemption, He was asking me to give grace. Mercy is when you don't get what you deserve. Grace is when you get what you don't deserve. I had to eventually come to grips with the fact that anything I was being challenged to do concerning my dad wasn't about him being deserving; it was about me being willing — willing to go deeper (into my pain) to find myself.

I claimed that I wanted to know who I really was — that I desperately wanted God to reveal who He made me to be. Did I still want it if it meant that my person was hidden in my greatest pain? What if it was in a confrontation where the fight looked more like forgiveness than numbness and the triumph looked more like redemption than rejection? What if it meant calling the undeserving "deserving"? Did my desperation remain or did it wane? Was I still willing to go — to do whatever it takes — or would I settle for who I had become?

Each phase (forgiveness and redemption) led me to a face-to-face encounter with my dad. Truthfully, for the first one, I could've done it without actually going to see him. However, something in me said I had to look him in the eyes. He had to see I meant business. Although the meetings were seven or eight years apart from one another, the same feelings accompanied each one — my heart racing a million miles per hour, my brain talking me into it and out of it at least a thousand times in the short 30 minute drive to his house, and my entire body shaking with nervousness as I stepped out of the car. So much so that I questioned whether or not I might pass out, either in mid-stride or mid-conversation.

In spite of my terribly suspect emotional and physical state, I somehow found the fortitude needed to bring myself to stand eye-to-eye with him. Obviously, the roller coaster of emotions that came with each event are enough to make them both unforgettable experiences, still, it is the second confrontation that stands out most to me.

The first meeting was about giving something *to* him while the second was about getting something *from* him. In a conversation with my Pastor, Stan Lester, who also happens to be one of my closest friends, he asked me, "I know you've forgiven your dad. Have you ever asked for his blessing?" Although perplexed by his question, I wanted to maintain my spiritual status, so, I pretended to know what the heck that meant and responded with a simple "no". He said, "I think you need to go ask for his blessing". I left that conversation not knowing what a "father's blessing" was, but I did know that it wasn't my Pastor making the "suggestion". It was *Jehovah Sneaky* in disguise. I didn't argue this time whether or not I was going to go — that was a given. I did argue, however, why I needed to go. I didn't desire his blessing. In actuality, I didn't want anything from the man because I didn't feel that he had anything to offer (as proven by his previous example). Boy, was I wrong.

I went to my dad a few months later. Unable to explain why I was asking what I was asking for, I said, "Pops, can I have your blessing?" Without hesitation, he said, "son, you've always had my blessing". I felt something move inside me. It was subtle, yet, sudden. You'd think there would be a flood of tears or a long embrace (kind of like what you picture in the Bible when you read about the prodigal son coming back home and his father running out to meet him). That wasn't it. There was more of a calm unlocking within me. When I first began to tell this story, I used to say, "he set something free in me". After meditating on that event over the years, it's become clear what that "something" was. It was me. He set me free in me. What also became much clearer is what a fathers blessing is: the legitimate identity of their children. When we left, I noticed a quiet self-confidence that I never had before. The tormenting, blaming, condemning voices in my head were silenced. It was a new day, I was a new person, and it was time to pursue a new relationship with my father.

I shudder to think where I'd be today if God hadn't offered mercy and grace to me ultimately giving me the ability to offer it to my dad. Things aren't perfect by any stretch of the imagination. I am not perfect, but I am progressing and that's all my Heavenly Father wants. He is not a Father that expects perfection from His children. He is one that expects progression. And sometimes, to help with that, He will hide the things we most want in the one that didn't want us, give us the requirements of finding them, and just when we thought we had done all we needed to do, He says "there's more".

STEP #3: HONOR — *RESPECT THE POSITION*

Luke 19 speaks of a meeting between a man named Zacchaeus, who is called *a chief tax collector and rich man*, and Jesus. Zacchaeus was "known" among the people. He was what most would consider a "popular" man (albeit for the wrong reasons). A point well validated by the community's response when Jesus called for him to come down from the tree because He was coming to stay at his house:

> *When they saw it, they all began* to grumble, saying, "He has gone to be the guest of a man who is a si*nner"* (Luke 19:7).

The public's reasoning for despising the man doesn't go without justification. As the chief tax collector, he would've been responsible for collecting money for the payment of taxes and his "riches" were the likely result of dishonest gain that came in the form of overtaxing (stealing from) the citizens (the likely majority of the crowd that day). But, something very strange happened. As Zacchaeus made his way down from the tree to take Jesus to his house he "*stopped and said to the Lord, 'Behold, Lord, half of my possessions I will give to the poor, and if I have defrauded anyone of anything, I will give back (RESTORE) four times as much'. And Jesus said to him, "Today salvation has come to this house, because he, too, is a son of Abraham. "For the Son of Man has come to seek and to save that which was lost. (Luke 19:1-10 NASB — parenthesis/ capitalization is mine added)*"

There are two things I want to bring your attention to: Zacchaeus' gifts ('half' and 'four times as much') and Jesus' goal ('to seek and save that which was lost'). Had Zacchaeus stopped "half" way, the story would've had a much different ending. Perhaps, very much like the ending of the rich young ruler whom Jesus came in contact with shortly before his encounter with Zacchaeus.

> *After asking what He must do to inherit eternal life, Jesus laid out a list of commandments for the young man to follow. The ruler responded, "all these I have kept since I was a boy". "One thing you lack", Jesus said, "Go sell everything you have and give to the poor, and you will have treasure in heaven. Then come, follow me." At this the man's face fell. He went away sad, because he had great wealth* (Luke 18:18-30).

Everything. This is the requirement. It wasn't until after Zacchaeus said, "I will repay (restore) "four times as much" did Jesus respond with 'Today Salvation has come to this house, because, **he too is a son** of Abraham'. There you have it. Jesus, **the Son** of man, who said his purpose in coming was "to seek and save that which was lost" reveals what He was really after in the rich young ruler, in Zacchaeus, and in me and you. It's not our possessions that He is after as the possessions were never lost in either story. Zacchaeus knew exactly where his riches were and the rich young ruler knew exactly where his "stuff" was too. Jesus was after their identity as sons. And, He is crystal-clear on how it's revealed: by not stopping half way, by giving everything and more.

After studying these two stories, it was as if God was saying, "You're almost there". This was unbelievably disheartening as I had given, or, perhaps I should say "I had forgiven" all I thought I could. Truthfully, it almost felt like a slap in the face. A total disregard for what I had already "accomplished" and the temptation was certainly there for my "face to fall" and to "walk away sad" like the rich young ruler. Then, I realized I had pressed beyond "half" into "everything" and was now being asked if I would be willing to give "four times as much". In the context of reclaiming and living out our identity as sons, "four times as much" doesn't just forgive and redeem. It also honors.

God was asking me to go beyond giving my dad a "discharge". He was summoning me to offer him an "honorable discharge". In the military, an honorable discharge is given to *service members who meet or exceed the required standards of duty performance and personal conduct, and who complete their tours of duty.*

Even being willing to do so, I was beyond perplexed at how I could give him an honorable discharge. He met very few, if any, positive paternal performance standards and fell embarrassingly short of any admirable paternal conduct scale. Then, it dawned on me. This phase wasn't to be a repeat of the first. The emphasis was not to be placed on the discharge, rather, it was to be placed on the honor.

• HONOR REJECTS THE SHAME AND RESPECTS THE NAME

In the book of Matthew, Jesus says, "*He who receives a prophet in the name of a prophet shall receive a prophet's reward; and he who receives a righteous man in the name of a righteous man shall receive a righteous man's reward (Matthew 10:41).'* From this, I've often wondered if it would work the same way with other "names", positions, or titles. Such as, if I received a teacher in the name of a teacher would I receive a teacher's reward? Or, if I received a leader in the name of a leader would I receive a leader's reward? Or, how about if I received my father in the name of a father would I receive a father's reward? I've chosen to believe the answer is "yes" and it all starts with receiving (honoring) them as such.

The reward of any "name" is directly linked to the level of respect we give to it. If I wanted a "father's reward" (identity), then, I had to "receive" my own father in the name of a father. I had to find a way to reject the unrespectable actions of his past and respect the position of authority he had been given. Like it or not, fair or not, worthy or not, God saw fit to make him my dad — to give him that "name" in my life and nothing was ever going to change that. There's not enough hate, anger, bitterness, or pain that can separate me from him or him from me. Paul wrote the following letter to the Romans:

> **Let everyone be subject to the governing authorities,** *for there is no authority except that which God has established. The authorities that exist have been established by God. Consequently, whoever rebels against the authority is rebelling against what God has instituted, and those who do so will bring judgment on themselves*
>
> *Therefore, it is necessary to submit to the authorities, not only because of possible punishment but also as a matter of conscience.*
>
> *This is also why you pay taxes, for the authorities are God's servants, who give their full time to governing. Give to everyone what you owe them: If you owe taxes, pay taxes; if revenue, then revenue;* **if respect, then respect; if honor, then honor** (Romans 13:1,2; 5,6).

The core of his letter was directed toward the political governing authorities of their day, but it also serves us to include our parents (good or bad) in that list as well. Just as we should give to Ceasar what is Ceasar's (taxes), we should also give to our parents what is our parents: Honor.

In accordance with a life that lives without rebellion toward God, working to maintain our identity as sons/daughters and desiring to unlock a father's reward, we must honor the God placed maternal and paternal "governing authorities" in our lives. Doing so through the submission of our opinions about who they have previously been and the admission of who they were made to be originally.

• HONOR CELEBRATES WHO A PERSON IS WITHOUT STUMBLING OVER WHO THEY ARE NOT: (Quote by Bill Johnson, Pastor of Bethel Church in Redding, California).

Slowly, but surely, the once impenetrable self-protective fortress I had built in my mind and emotions that believed "my dad had nothing to offer me" began to crack under the pressure of a new and more powerful perspective. Finally, the tables were turning and I found myself beginning to think more like a son and less like a bastard.

There's a side-lesson to all of this. Consider it a warning of sorts. As a bastard, life will be much easier for us as we will not be held accountable to the requirements of sons. Conversely, it is also true that we will not be eligible to receive a father's reward because bastards don't have fathers. On the flip side, life as a son means stepping into a more challenging set of standards with a higher degree of accountability attached. Life here seems harder, more stringent, more stressful, and it is. Such is the cost of qualification for receiving the reward therein.

Living from acceptance (living as a son) demanded a shift in the way I viewed my dad. Taking on a new identity, becoming an entirely new person, meant taking on a new set of "eyes" to go with it. It was no longer acceptable to look at him the way I had known him. I had to learn to see him the way God had known him. The only way to do this was to remove the lens of sin and put on the lens of honor.

Sin literally means "to miss the mark". Wouldn't that indicate there has to be a mark to hit in the first place? Sure it would. What is that "mark" then? It is a predesignated target created for each of us "before the world began" (see Ephesian 1:4,5; Ephesians 2:10; John 17:5; Jeremiah 1:5). It all started to make sense. My dad was living outside of his divine design. His actions were not an accurate portrayal of who he was originally made to be. They may have been the expression of who He was choosing to be in that moment, but they were not the truest display of his purest essence. He was simply "missing the mark".

If I appear to be protecting him it's because I am. This is what honor does. It celebrates who a person is (their divine design, their God-given image) without stumbling over who they are not or have not been. The change I wish to see in him starts with me seeing him changed. After all, that's how I changed. Someone chose to ignore my sin, to see and call out the good, and they did it consistently until it began to surface. They did it in spite of my struggles, in spite of the moments I would "backslide", and in spite of my actions. They saw something better in me, kept calling it out, until I could I see it in myself. They honored the God in me instead of acknowledging the sin in me and that has made all the difference.

• HONOR ASSUMES RESPONSIBILITY FOR THE UNASSUMED RESPONSIBILITY OF ANOTHER

One of my all-time favorite movies is a film called, "*The Hunger Games*". The setting is placed in the nation of Panem, formed from a post-apocalyptic North America. Panem is a country made up of an extremely wealthy Capitol region surrounded by 12 poorer districts. In its earlier history, a rebellion led by a 13th district against the Capitol resulted in its consequential destruction and the creation of an annual televised event known as "the Hunger Games". In punishment, the Capitol offers the yearly reminder of their authority and power by commanding each district to offer one boy and one girl between the ages of 12 and 18 to participate in the games. The "tributes" are chosen as a lottery event during the annual "Reaping" and are forced to fight each other to the death, leaving only one survivor to take claim as the winner.

At the 74th Hunger Games Reaping, a young girl, Primrose, is chosen as a tribute. Refusing to let her younger sister be taken to a probable death, Katniss Everdeen, played by Jennifer Lawrence, volunteers herself to go in her place, becoming District 12's female tribute.

There's no higher degree of honor than to give one's own life for another. In one of His teachings to the disciples, Jesus commanded them to *"Love one another as I have loved you.* Then, continued with, *"No one has greater love than this, that someone would lay down his life for his friends (John 15:12,13 HCSB)"*. Katniss' sacrifice gives us a perfect picture of "no greater love" and shows what I believe God had in mind when it came to honoring my dad. I was to volunteer myself in his place, picking up the unpaid balance of his tab, and set our future blood-lines free in doing so. I began to have a vision for and belief in the possibility of the coming generations inheriting life without a deficit (or, in this case "a curse") and this was the path to ensure that vision would become reality. By releasing previous generations from their debt, I would also be releasing future generations from it as well.

One of the most popular figures in the Bible is a man by the name of Abraham. To those of us who have spent a considerable amount of time in church settings, he is known as "the father of faith"– a title attributed to him for the trust he displayed in the promises of God throughout his life. While we are no stranger to this man or the bizarre stories that marked his existence, we may not be as familiar with how it all began for him.

He was the son of a man named Terah and the short encounter we have with him tells us, "*Terah took his son Abram, his grandson Lot son of Haran, and his daughter-in-law Sarai, the wife of his son Abram, and together* **they set out from Ur of the Chaldeans to go to Canaan. But when they came to Harran, _they settled_ there**".

Obviously, Harran was not in Canaan. In other words, Terah didn't reach his intended destination and all that was "with" him (his family) fell under the consequence of his decision. Because he settled, they had to settle as well. The short story of Terah ends with, "*Terah lived 205 years, and he died in Harran*". I'm not sure if there's a sadder or scarier statement in all the Bible as it proves it's possible to die just short of where you were intended to be. However, all was not lost,

> The Lord said to Abram, "Go out from your land, your relatives, and your father's house to a land I will show you." (Genesis 11:32;12:1). So Abram went, as the Lord had told him . . . He took his wife Sarai, his nephew Lot, all the possession they had accumulated, and the people he had acquired in Harran, and ***they set out*** for the land of Canaan (Genesis 12:1,4,5 HCSB). As Abram journeyed through the various places, on his way to Canaan, "the Lord appeared to Abram and said, 'I will give this land to your offspring (Genesis 12:7 HCSB)'".

Abram took Terah's place — assuming responsibility for the unassumed responsibility of his father — and his offspring would be the direct effect. Where Terah "settled", Abram "set out" and it created a very different outcome for the future of those who would come after them.

The phase of "honor" was much bigger than me and my dad. It required me to see that I was the generation called to stop the curse. And, it would only come through honoring my father — by assuming responsibility for his debt, paying it in full and beyond, ultimately, giving "our" future 'offspring' a different "land" to live in. Where he was weak, I would be strong. Where he was deficient, I would be sufficient. Where he failed, I would succeed. Where he cursed, I would bless. Where he "settled", I would "set out".

Honor allows me to be and to bring the change my blood-line deserves. I live with a deepening conviction and passionate pursuit that I owe my future generations a life of sacrifice through faith. I owe them a life that proves, "Anything is possible". I owe them the example that I didn't have: a story worth telling and a legacy that serves as a reference point made of their own flesh and blood proving to them that there is victory in their veins as well as an unshakable determination in their DNA inspiring them to make the firm resolve that they won't stop until they see it in their own lives.

The pen of honor has been placed in my hand and in yours to rewrite history — the future history of our children, grandchildren, great children, great-great children, to a thousand generations (see Exodus 20:6). We must refuse to allow those coming after us to repeat the narrative of curse that we've experienced. Instead, we must commit to helping them rewrite the narrative of blessing for themselves and their future because honor has been given where it may not have been deserved, but, was due.

In conclusion, Paul wrote in Ephesians 6:2,3:

Honor your father and mother, which is the first commandment with a promise, that it may go well with you and that you may have long life in the land.

"Long life in the land" is the result of generational honor. And, it is a promise that God desperately wants us to have.

It can't happen, however, if we choose to "settle" rather than "set out". Settling in forgiveness will only set the past free. Settling in redemption will only set the present free. Setting out into honor will set the future free. The future is literally in your hands. What will you do with it?

I LOOK LIKE MY DADDY

Fighting to reclaim our identities as "sons/daughters" doesn't just make us soldiers fighting a good fight of faith, it also makes us stewards of a new way of living. We now carry a responsibility to align our values with the values of our heavenly Father — those being forgiveness, redemption, and honor. It is no longer about us expressing our anger; it's about us expressing His image. It's about us looking just like our Daddy.

REFLECTION QUESTIONS:

#1. Is there anyone that you need to "release" from the prison of *your* un-forgiveness? How about restore a relationship with? Honor? Who is it? What did they do to you that's caused you to keep them in them "locked up"?

#2. What are some of the excuses you've used up to this point to avoid forgiveness, redemption, or honor? What are some "excuses" that you're going to use moving forward to stop avoiding it?

#3. Has it been challenging for you to connect to God as Father? Why or why not? It's important to have both perspectives because those who answer, "No", will be helping those who answer, "Yes" see Him and connect with Him as they do — as a Father.

MEDITATION/APPLICATION:

"Four times as much". Just when you think you have nothing left to give, God touches that part of your life and you realize you have *"four times"* the capacity you thought you did. You may not think that you 'have it in you' to reach beyond where you are now, whether that be the most basic level of forgiveness into redemption, or whether that be in any other area of your life you desperately want victory in, but you do. However, you won't realize it without taking the first courageous step. So, I ask you, what step do you need to take to tap into the greater capacity within you — the *"four times as much"*?

PART II

VALUE
WHAT AM I WORTH?

*"When you learn how much you're worth,
you'll stop giving people discounts"*

—ANONYMOUS

10

THE GOD OF ABRAHAM . . . MASLOW

Value is determined by "whose" you are.

(THE NAME OF JESUS)

Taking on our identities as "sons/daughters" marks the end of one phase in the *Great Commission* and the beginning of another. It serves as the bridge between being "baptized in the name of the Father" to being "baptized in the name of the Son". Where an immersion (baptism) in the Father's authority (name) unveils our identity to us, an immersion in the Son's authority unveils the inheritance within us. The first is initiated by the question of *Who Am I*; the second is initiated by the question of *What Am I Worth*.

THE INGLORIOUS DAYS

Not many things have robbed humanity's potential like that of self-worth. Generally, there are two categories that mankind tends to fall into: *no self-worth* and *low self-worth*. The first is usually the result of ignorance while the second is the result of experience. Neither are good, however, it's difficult to arrive at a conclusion of which is worst — for a person not to know they have value or to consider the value they have as meaningless. Some may consider a meditation over such a comparison to be futile, nevertheless, it's still a wise starting place for providing a solution, or, better stated, an answer to a much deeper beckoning within the core of humanity at large which calls out *WHAT AM I WORTH?*

I know what it is to be surprised by a dormant value — one you've always possessed and didn't know you had. Likewise, I also know what it's like to live with a poor assessment of the value that you do know you have. Both are equally as painful, but for different reasons.

The first (no worth) is an acute, sharp pain that comes at a moment of discovery — a prophetic word spoken over your life, a scripture divinely highlighted to you, a coach who tells you, "you've got the goods", a weight you lift that you never dreamt in a million years you could, a "move" you make on the ball field that you haven't made before. These can feel like the best of times and the worst of times. On one hand, you're thrilled to show an ability to do what you've never done before. On the other hand, you wonder why it took so long to show up. To make matters worse, you contemplate when you go back out next time why it feels like you couldn't do it again even if your life depended on it. The weight which felt like a feather yesterday feels like a mountain today. You begin questioning if the "word" you got last week about "preaching to the nations" is false because this week you tried preaching to a small youth group and it was horrible. "The goods" your coach was quick call out and brag on in your first practice session together looked more like "the bads" in your first competition or game together. You find yourself beyond frustrated, perplexed by the inability to replicate it, and speculating *"was it all just a fluke, or an accident, or some kind of transitory reward or punishment from God for a good or bad deed you did that particular day?"*

No self-worth will turn into low self-worth unless there's someone there to tell you that the undiscovered worth must be worked. That's why I'm here — to tell you just that. Your untapped potential also means it is undeveloped potential. Much like the muscle that lifted the once seemingly impossible weight, the potential to do so was always there. It was subject, however, to a required process of development to bring it out. Do you realize that it's the same person in the same body with the same muscle? The only thing that has changed is years of exercise. *"Most people overestimate what they can do in a year and underestimate what they can do in ten years (quote by Bill Gates)"*. Don't let your personal revelation lead to personal degradation based on inconsistencies of beginning performances or incongruences between who you are right now and who you will be later. As the old adage goes, "Rome wasn't built in a day" and neither will we be. The art of *becoming* begins with realizing the path from ignorance to competence is experience. There's simply no other way.

The second pain of worth is low self-worth. It's a chronic, dull pain that haunts you on a daily basis, never leaving your awareness. Every move you make is affected by it. Move to the right and you feel it. Move to the left and you feel it again. Stand up, sit down, walk forwards or backwards and it's there — a constant nagging reminder, not necessarily of how bad it hurts, but, of why it hurts.

> THE ART OF *BECOMING* BEGINS WITH REALIZING THE PATH FROM IGNORANCE TO COMPETENCE IS EXPERIENCE.

There are so many negative effects that came from my father leaving. What stands out above all else, though, is the impact it had on my self-perception and, consequently, self-confidence.

There was a time when I despised mirrors because I didn't like the reflection of what looked back at me when I looked in them. In fact, I hated it. Down to the smallest, most insignificant things that no one really cares about — the size of my feet, the shape of my hands, the color of my hair and skin, the length or my arms and legs — I would find something wrong with it. I truly didn't like anything about me. I would say and, worse yet, believe things like, "*I wear a size 11 shoe and most really athletic people wear a 10 ½ so that means I'm not meant to be one of the 'superstars'. I have red hair and light skin so there's no use in asking "that" girl on a date because she's probably into dark hair and dark skin guys. I can't be friends with "that" person because he or she is rich and I'm not, so, they probably won't like me getting their furniture dirty when I sit on it (that one is hilarious and still baffles me to this day. What the heck? Did I really believe that poverty would really result in physical filth?)*".

The one area that I recall it showing up in the most growing up was sports. There's no way I would've said back then what I'm getting ready to say now, but, I was good athlete. Something to be proud of right? Wrong. I was a *good* athlete that never became *great* although I possessed everything needed to be. No, this is not an older version of me "reliving the glory days" because, quite honestly, they weren't all that glorious and thinking back on them certainly isn't either. I tend to think back with a ton of regret and tortured by "what if". My poor self-perception resulted in an extreme lack of confidence and caused me to leave so much on the table and it hurts. It hurts on a level that's hard to put into words. I feel as if I robbed, not only myself, but also my teammates of a better experience and better opportunities. What if I would've saw myself as a playmaker in football instead of a role player? How many more passes would I have intercepted or caught for touchdowns? How many more tackles would I have made? In baseball, what if my approach to the plate as a hitter was centered more on getting a hit rather than striking out? What if I were able to see in me what many of my coaches saw in me and tried to encourage? In addition to seeing it, what if I had the confidence to risk being it? Things may or may not have been different and that's really not the issue at this point. The issue is I'll never know because I didn't have the confidence needed to take the risks. Even so, all is not lost. While I can't claim to have the outcomes I desperately wanted in my childhood and teenage years, I do have experience — an invaluable set of skills fashioned from having undergone that now allows me to overcome.

We've all heard the familiar mantra of the masses declare how they "wish they could go back and do it all over again knowing what they know now." I've never made that wish. One, it's impossible. Two, I don't want there to be chance of repeating the same process — of enduring the same pains. Three, a "redo" would change my experiences and, therefore, my impact. Paul interceding on behalf of the Ephesians said, "*I pray that the eyes of your heart may be enlightened in order that you may know . . . (Ephesians 1:18 NIV)*". To be enlightened is "to give understanding to or to imbue with saving knowledge". To "know" is "to experience first-hand". Enlightenment comes from experience. Einstein agreed saying, "All source of knowledge is experience". This is the reason I don't want a do over. My experiences are what makes me unique. They don't just make me who I am, they give me my value by making me valuable to others. A redo means I would have to give up my education and others liberation. By learning how to set myself free, I was, unknowingly, learning how to set others free as well.

Famous Russian author, Leo Tolstoy, said, *"The only purpose of education is freedom; the only method is experience"*. The silver lining in all the years I spent in self-deprecation is it allowed me to gain an experiential education in worth determination. While there's no way I'd volunteer myself for a "second try", it's also true that I wouldn't trade the "first try" either. Because of it, I know what causes value to fall and I know what causes it rise. And, it's what I know that's give me, not only my freedom, but also my commission because, *"Freedom is not worth fighting for if it means no more than license for everyone to get as much as he can for himself (Dorothy Canfield Fisher)".* **In this kingdom, the kingdom of Almighty God, there's no such thing as hoarded victories**. Everything gained must be shared (see Matthew 10:8). In alignment with the ways of the kingdom and in the words of the apostle Peter, "What I have, I give to you" (see Acts 3:6).

IN THE NAME

Like the question of identity (Who Am I), the question of value (What Am I Worth) is instinctive. It craves an answer and it will satisfy its craving by any means necessary. It shows no preference towards the answer being inferior or superior, good or bad, empowering or disempowering, so long as its thirst gets quenched. This is why it's so vital for us to take hold of the reins of our search — so that we can redirect our intuitive pursuits to being more intentional than accidental. Hence, the reason we were commissioned, first, toward the discovery of our identities.

Knowing "who you are" is the perfect buffer for and transitional piece to knowing "what you are worth" since knowing "who you are" begins with knowing "whose you are". Jesus had what seemed like an irresistible habit. He was constantly telling people who His daddy was. Was He doing it braggingly? I don't think so. He was doing it as a reminder to Himself and to those around Him of what He carried — of His value. As a Son, He knew He possessed an unlimited inheritance within Him — an endless supply of "blank checks" to meet the endless demands of humanity's need. Contrary to popular belief, the value of His inheritance wasn't in what the check was "for"; it was on the "signature line". You see, when it comes to writing checks, every line item can be filled out, funds can be readily available for withdrawal, still, without the signature, there will be no transaction. The name is what gives the authorization. It is where the true power of the transaction lies. Why do you think *the Great Commission* is centered on a baptism in three names? Because He meant for our immersion to become our authorization — our permission to move forward **IN HIS NAME.**

There's a popular story in the book of Acts where Peter and John were on their way to the temple for a time of prayer. While going, they came across a lame man who was carried to the gate (the entrance) of the temple every day in order to beg from those going in. One day, as Peter and John approached gate, the lame man asked them for money. Then, as scripture records:

> *Peter said, "Look at us!" So the man gave them his attention, expecting to get something from them. Then Peter said, "Silver or gold I do not have, but what I do have I give you. **In the name of Jesus Christ** of Nazareth, walk." Taking him by the right hand, he helped him up, and instantly the man's feet and ankles became strong. He jumped to his feet and began to walk. Then he went with them into the temple courts, walking and jumping, and praising God. When all the people saw him walking and praising God, they recognized him as the same man who used to sit begging at the temple gate called Beautiful, and they were filled with wonder and amazement at what had happened to him (Acts 3:4-10 NIV).*

Like those in the temple, we tend to become filled with wonder and amazement at what happens to people and miss the reason the transaction was able to occur.

> *While the man held on to Peter and John, all the people were astonished and came running to them in the place called Solomon's Colonnade. When Peter saw this, he said to*

*them: "Fellow Israelites, why does this surprise you? Why do you stare at us as if by our own power or godliness we had made this man walk? The God of Abraham, Isaac and Jacob, the God of our fathers, has glorified his servant Jesus . . . **<u>By faith in the name of Jesus</u>, this man whom you see and know was made strong. <u>It is Jesus' name and the faith that comes through him</u> that has completely healed him, as you can all see.** (Acts 3:11-13,16 NIV; emphasis mine)*

Peter and John did not give the man healing; they gave him "the name of Jesus Christ". They gave him "what they had" and it's what you and I have as well. It's the inheritance given to us as both His progeny and as His product — the inheritance of "His name". As His progeny, His name brings value by telling us we are accepted. As His product, His name brings value by telling us we are approved.

THE PROGENY OF GOD

Progeny is just another word for "child or offspring". When it comes to the "name of Jesus" in Christianity, it's certainly not a new topic. However, it is often times viewed more as a weapon of warfare than a brand of birthright. We are taught to cast out demons "in His name", heal the sick "in His name", pray "in His name", and wake ourselves up from nightmares "in His name", yet, rarely, if ever, do we slow down to consider these as derivatives stemming from our adoption "in His name". Much like my daughter, Avery, received my last name when she entered into the world, we receive His name when we are born again into His. And, it is that name that gives us our identities which points us to our inheritances revealing not just the power in it, but more so the worth in us. A child is able to easily pull a measure of self-worth from the name they have because it is a direct link to their belonging, which greatly impacts their believing, creating a clearer and straighter path to their becoming.

BELONGING, BELIEVING, BECOMING

Of all the things God has given me as an inheritance, none can compare to the gift of His name. When I find myself in doubt about or confused by any of life's contradictory conundrums or feeling deficient in self-esteem, remembering that I have been given His name stabilizes me. The reason being is it points me to my acceptance. It tells me that I am a member of a family and that I belong.

No matter where you look throughout history, the world's greatest influencers agree that "belonging" is the precursor to "believing". Although they don't come out and say it openly, and it may even be unbeknownst to them they are doing it, they have still made it abundantly clear that belief (particularly self-belief) is the byproduct of meaningful associations and connections.

Abraham Maslow, a world renowned psychologist, was one such influencer best known for creating *Maslow's Hierarchy of Needs": a motivational theory in psychology comprising a five tier model of human needs, often depicted as hierarchical levels within a pyramid.* In short, Maslow's impetus for developing the needs theory and subsequent model was a desire to understand what motivates people. He believed that mankind possessed a much deeper set of motivations that were not related to "rewards" as proposed by B.F. Skinner in his *"Operant Conditioning"* theory, or "unconscious desires", as proposed by Sigmund Freud in his *"Id, Ego, Superego"* theory. His aim was not necessarily to prove them wrong as there is an element of truth in all theories that are helpful for gaining knowledge. His goal was to prove man's depth. He did that by presenting the following hierarchy:

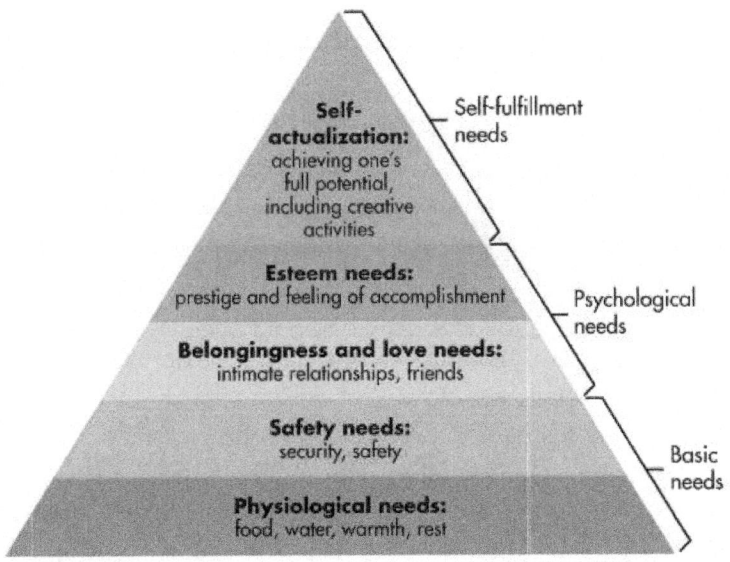

As you can tell, his rationale was built on the idea that people are predominantly motivated by certain "needs" and that some take precedence over others. Starting at the bottom, he proposes that our most basic need is physical survival and suggests that this will be the first thing motivating our behaviors. The dominating thought that should be taken from his premise for the point we are wanting to make is that each level of need greatly impacts the next.

Notice the highest need: *Self-Actualization*. This is the stage where people reach "convergence", a term used by Dr. J. Robert Clinton in his book *The Making of a Leader: Recognizing the Lessons and Stages of Leadership Development*, to describe a person who has stepped into a role or assignment, or in Maslow's theory, has reached a place "self-fulfillment", where that person is doing what they the love to do the most and what they are gifted to do the best. More simply stated, they are achieving their full potential on all levels and in all areas of life — physiological, emotional, relational, and psychological.

I think most would agree with Maslow that an "actualized" life is the ultimate aim of our existence. An unfortunate reality we face, as proven by Dr. Clinton in a 30-year group case study at Fuller Theological Seminary, is that only 20% ever reach it. Using the hierarchy, we can draw some strong conclusions as to why that is and make a strong case for our originating impression: **belonging is the precursor to believing**.

The difference between the 20% who make it into the promised land of "self-actualization" and the 80% who stop short is that the 80% who end up "wandering in the wilderness" do so because of a lack of "belonging" and/or "esteem". For the most part, I've found that people will find a way to meet their most basic needs of survival and security, even if it means digging in a trash can for food, begging on the street corner for money to buy something to drink, or using a cardboard box for a home. In the worst of worst situations, death is a heavily motivating factor. However, when it comes to their psychological needs, they end up lost because death is not the driver of esteem (belief), belonging is. Where there is no sense of belonging, there will be no sense of value, and where there is no sense of self-value (esteem), there will be no self-actualization, or what Jesus referred to as "abundant life".

> *I came that they may have life, and have it abundantly*. *I am the good shepherd; the good shepherd lays down His life for the sheep. "He who is a hired hand, and not a shepherd, who is not the owner of the sheep, sees the wolf coming, and leaves the sheep and flees, and the wolf snatches them and scatters them. "He flees because he is a hired hand and is not concerned about the sheep. "I am the good shepherd, and I know My own and My own know Me, even as the Father knows Me and I know the Father; and I lay down My life for the sheep* (John 10:11-15 NASB: emphasis mine). "

The shepherd and sheep dynamic is a dynamic of belonging and trust. To the sheep, the shepherd is the source of survival as he leads them to pastures with food and water. He is the place of safety and security protecting them from dangerous predators. They belong to the shepherd, and, therefore, believe he can be trusted.

Seems that Maslow's theory of actualization wasn't too far off from God's idea of abundant living does it? Perhaps this is what provoked Solomon to write, "A *good name is to be desired more than great wealth (Proverbs 22:1)*". The wisest and richest man to have ever walked the earth realized that the greatest wealth a man can acquire is that of self-wealth — which comes from inheriting "a good name". After all, this was his experience.

God appeared to Solomon in a dream soon after he was made king offering him "one wish" for "whatever he wanted" (see I Kings 3:5). Solomon opened his request with,

> *"You have shown great lovingkindness to Your servant David my father, according as he walked before You in truth and righteousness and uprightness of heart toward You; and You have reserved for him this great lovingkindness, that You have given him a son to sit on his throne, as it is this day." Now, O LORD my God, You have made Your servant king **in place of my father David**, yet I am but a little child; I do not know how to go out or come in. "Your servant is in the midst of Your people which You have chosen, a great people who are too many to be numbered or counted. "So give Your servant an understanding heart to judge Your people to discern between good and evil. For who is able to judge this great people of Yours?"*

> **It was pleasing in the sight of the Lord that Solomon had asked this thing.** God said to him, "Because you have asked this thing and have not asked for yourself long life, nor have asked riches for yourself, nor have you asked for the life of your enemies, but have asked for yourself discernment to understand justice, behold, I have done according to your words. Behold, I have given you a wise

and discerning heart, so that there has been no one like you before you, nor shall one like you arise after you. "I have also given you what you have not asked, both riches and honor, so that there will not be any among the kings like you all your days. "If you walk in My ways, keeping My statutes and commandments, *as your father David walked, then I will prolong your days.*" (I Kings 3:6-14 NASB; emphasis mine).

I am tempted to believe that Solomon's wisdom didn't begin at the Lord's pleasure or the gifts and promises that followed. I believe these were more of an "amen" to the wisdom he was already displaying by coming to God "in his father's name". Maybe this was the real genius to Solomon. He knew that he belonged to someone, evidenced by his use of their name, and he knew how to leverage it to work in his favor. **He understood that a good name provides a person with proper identification which will directly impact their self-evaluation setting them on the path toward the pinnacle of self-actualization.**

THE GREATEST WEALTH

A name done right gives you all of that — a way to identify yourself, a way to evaluate yourself, and a way to actualize yourself. I'm encouraged by this because my daughter will not have to worry about the same things I had to worry about growing up. She will not know what it's like to live without a father or without a sense of emotional security that only comes from acceptance. She will not have to overcome the same deficits of self-esteem or worth I had to because the name she carries (Brooks) will provide her with a different answer than it did me since she has a daddy that has chosen to alter the course of our family tree by stepping up to the plate and being in her life. She'll know that she is valuable — that she belongs — because of my presence (more on this later), but in the event I'm not around or after I'm gone, she will never have to be in doubt about her significance or her security because she has my name to remind her. If I do a good enough job her name will tell her everything she needs to know about herself and about her worth. It will tell her she is loved and will give her permission to love herself. It will tell her that someone is proud of her giving her permission to be proud of herself. It will tell her that someone believes in her giving her permission to believe in herself. It will tell her that she belongs giving her permission to become. "Brooks" will not be a legacy I leave *for* her; it will be a legacy that I leave *in* her, thereby, providing her with the greatest wealth any of us can receive: the wealth of a "good name".

REFLECTION QUESTIONS:

#1(a). Have there been "moments" in your life where you surprised yourself — where a gift or talent emerged that you didn't know you had? Did you consider it to be accident, a lucky "shot", or a coincidence — or have you considered that maybe, just, maybe it's always been there but your lack of self-confidence and esteem has kept it subdued? Do you recall any specific times where that happened?

#1(b). What can you do to develop that gift even more?

#2. Have you ever looked in a mirror and hated what was looking back at you? What criteria were you using to judge that person by? What criteria can you use moving forward to give the man or woman in the mirror a "fair trial"?

#3. Belonging precedes believing. Have you ever been in a place where you sensed you didn't belong? What was the immediate emotional effect? Now, compare that to a place where you felt you did belong? How did that impact you emotionally? What can you do moving forward to create places and spaces of belonging at all times?

#4. Do you realize that you literally belong to God and that He gave you His name? What does that do for your sense of self-worth? Do you still feel worthless or insignificant?

MEDITATION/APPLICATION:

Solomon proved the power of coming to God "in his father's name". Keep in mind that he did it under an inferior covenant. We live in a more superior covenant — the covenant of Jesus — which is described in the book of Hebrews as *"a better covenant built on better promises"* (Hebrews 8:6). Therefore, if Solomon found value in himself through his daddy's name, how much more should we? Shouldn't this cause us to approach "his throne of grace boldly" knowing that we are coming to a King who is also our daddy? The next time you pray, try to pray, not as a slave to a master, but as a son/daughter of Father. Record what happens.

11

VAN GOGH, APPLE, AND A DEAD SQUIRREL

"Value is determined by the guarantee backing you"

(THE WORD OF GOD)

D a Vinci had *the Mona Lisa*, Vincent Van Gogh had *the Starry night*, Rembrandt had *the Night Watch*, and Picasso had *Guernica*. Like these great artists, God also has many famous works that He's known for — *The Blind Seeing* (see John 9:1-12), *The Legions Leaving* (see Mark 5:1-20), *The Dead Man Rising* (see John 11:38-44), and *The Fermented Water* (see John 2:1-11). As beautiful as each of these are, none compare to His greatest masterpiece: *The Creation of Mankind* (see Genesis 1:26-28).

UNFINISHED BUSINESS

The arts are a highly admired arena due the fact that it's a premeditated arena, meaning, very little happens by accident or without cause. In other words, artists begin with the end in mind. They have an idea of what they wish to accomplish — what they want the final display to be before they ever touch the canvas. In the words of Michelangelo, they, first, *"see the angel in the marble and carve until they set him free"*. Without a doubt, the process toward the finished work will demand them to remain somewhat flexible, but, the proceeding adjustments will never violate the predetermined aim.

Another famous quote from Michelangelo says, *"The marble not yet carved can hold the form of every thought the greatest artist has"*. There are multiple ways to interpret this, however, I see it as Michelangelo revealing the "greatest artists" most valuable secret in creating timeless masterpieces as well as disclosing their most exceptional skill: the ability to bring every thought into one — every potential plan (sculpture, drawing, painting) into one definite purpose and, then, for the sake of its completion, submit the one definite purpose back to the many different plans. That's where the real art lies. In the dance between the purpose and the plan — of knowing the exact destination, yet, leaving room for alternate directions. And, nobody does it better than the Great Creator Himself.

Ephesians 2:10 reads, *"For we are God's workmanship (another translation says 'masterpiece'), created in Christ Jesus for good works, which God prepared beforehand so that we should walk in them."* This idea of us being referred to as "His workmanship/masterpiece" cannot be fully grasped without being placed into the "work-in-progress" context. "Workmanship", in its original linguistic format, the Greek, is the word "poiema". This is where we get our English words "poem" and "poetry". Re-written, the opening statement in Ephesians could read, "For we are God's poem". Admittedly, I am not an avid reader of poetry, however, I do have a deep appreciation for the artistic flavor it contains — for its complexity, its depth, and, most of all its imperfection. Paintings and poetry seem to have this in common. Imperfection is accepted and even appreciated, considered, in some cases, to be the main attraction by many of the industry's enthusiasts — the purposeful expression of their favorite artist's or author's intention. Maybe Paul had his favorite Artist in mind when he later wrote to the leaders in Philippi, *"I am sure of this, that He who started a good work in you will carry it on to completion until the day of Christ Jesus (Philippians 1:6)"*. Often times, I wonder if our incompleteness and imperfections should be more of what we use to determine our worth than their counterparts. According to Paul, it's the unfinished "good works" that show us we are His masterpiece.

CALLED, JUSTIFIED, GLORIFIED

God chose us before the world began to be the canvases by which He could display his "good works" on and through. Though it receives little to no consideration of relevance, the canvas is just as much a part of the overall work as the painting itself. In fact, we could make a strong case to the canvas being the most valuable piece of all. Without it, there's nothing to excite the artist's imagination, nothing to hold the form of their thought, nothing to showcase their talents on, or put their tools to, and nothing to receive their final stamp of approval: **their name**.

On most completed works, traditionally at the bottom right hand corner, you will find the artist's signature. It is their finishing touch signifying not only the work's completion, but also the artist's approval of it.

WHERE THE CREATORS ON EARTH WAIT UNTIL THE END TO GIVE THEIR WORKS THEIR SIGNATURE, THE CREATOR OF HEAVEN LEADS WITH IT

As His "masterpieces", we carry the same confirmation of approval, His name, although, it is applied with one slight difference. Where the creators on earth wait until the end to give their works their signature, the Creator of heaven leads with it (see John 1:1-3; Colossians 1:15-17). Selah — pause, meditate on, and lean into the implications of that statement. God puts His signature on the project before it is complete.

To understand why this matters, you must understand what a name means to the work it has been placed on.

> *For those God foreknew he also predestined to be conformed to the image of His Son that He might be the firstborn among many brothers and sisters. And those He predestined, He also **called (gave his name to)**; those He **called (gave His name to)**, He also **justified (gave His approval to)**; those He **justified (approved)**, He also **glorified (valued; gave value to)*** (Romans 8:29,30; Emphasis and Parenthesis mine).

All artistic surfaces, be they paper, rock, or walls (if you're raising a three and half year old), have been predestined to carry an image, however, not every surface is guaranteed to carry the name. Why? As you can see from Paul's statement to the Romans, a name "justifies" and "glorifies" the artist's work. It is an open display of their approval and what ultimately brings the work its highest value. This is the very reason most artists refuse to give any "piece" their name until it's finished. They're judging whether or not the work is worthy of their approval because their approval is . . .

1. AN EXPRESSION OF THEIR PLEASURE *"IN"* THE WORK
2. A DECLARATION OF THEIR COMMITMENT *"TO"* THE WORK
3. AN ASSUMPTION OF THEIR RESPONSIBILITY *"FOR"* THE WORK

AN EXPRESSION OF PLEASURE IN THE WORK

> *You are worthy, our Lord and Our God, to receive the glory and the honor and the power, because you have created all things, and by your pleasure they exist and were created* (Romans 4:11).

God doesn't just love us, He actually likes us. That phrase is one of the most impactful things anyone has ever said to me. As a newly begotten son, all I wanted to do was make my Father proud. As a matter of fact, I recall the majority of my desires, especially in the beginning, being centered on Him opening the heavens to make the same unashamed announcement to the world about me that He did with Jesus: *This is My Beloved Son, in whom I am well-pleased* (Matthew 3:16,17).

Everything flows from His love. I get that. It's not a topic that's up for debate. All I can tell you is that at one point in my life (and sometimes now), His "liking" is what I wanted more. We hear it all the time – *"my parents tell me they love me, or I'm beautiful, or I'm smart because they have to — they are my parents"*. Right or wrong, that's exactly how I feel concerning His "love" — that it's more of a parental obligation than a pleasured aspiration or that it's more like something He *has* to do than He really wants to do. And, it feels like something He can do from a distance — like from heaven. In my mind (as twisted as it may be), for Him to "like" me, for Him to express His pleasure 'in' me, He'd have to get close — close enough for me and others standing by to hear Him say it. He'd have to "break open the heavens and come down" (see Isaiah 64:1).

Recently, I decided to go to the bookstore and search for a new book to read. Reading books are not abnormal for me. What is, however, is the "searching". I'm not sure if it makes me impatient or makes me a man, but 'shopping' is just not my thing, so, you can imagine what a trip to any store looks like — get in and get out as fast as humanly possible. For that to happen, I have to follow a few simple rules:

RULE #1: ALWAYS know what you're looking for before you enter the store — size, color, price, etc.
RULE #2: RARELY try anything on while inside. If it doesn't fit when you get home you can send it back

through mail and order your size online and have it shipped to your house. (P.S.: the only exception is when your wife wants you to be her "how-I-wish-you-dressed" model for the day).

RULE #3: NEVER go shopping with my mother-in-law (she shops like men hunt — go all day and come back with nothing but a story of how you "almost got one").

On this particular trip to the bookstore, I broke a few of my rules. It's probably not something I will do for another 34 years, although I have to admit I'm glad I did. After about five minutes of aimless wondering, picking up various books with somewhat intriguing titles and flipping through a few of the pages, my impatience began to set in and I did what most everyone does when they've been outside of their comfort zone for an extended period of time. I defaulted to my old, comfortable habits by giving myself an "aim". I remembered a friend earlier that week mentioning Deepak Chopra and how he was a big fan of his writing. Walking over to the section I thought he might be in, I grabbed the first book of Chopra's I came to called *"The Book of Secrets"*. Opening it to the table of contents, my eyes were drawn to the title heading of Chapter 4: **What you seek, you already are.** Although I've yet to read the book, I bought it because of the impact of that chapter's title.

Suddenly, it hit me like a ton of bricks. The approval I so desperately strived for and the "way" I wanted Him to show it had already happened. I had a hard time recognizing it because it didn't look or sound like I thought it would. It looked and sounded like ME. Pleasure was not something to be revealed through a form without (a dove from heaven, a burning bush in the desert, or an angel in my room). It would only be revealed through a voice and value within. To hear Him, I would have to hear myself. To receive His "liking", I would have to "like" myself because everything I sought, I already was.

And those He predestined, He also He called. Those He called, He also justified (approved). He gave me His approval "before" He gave me my arrival. In fact, my arrival is the result of His approval as no great artist will ever approve a work for public display until He is, first, pleased with it.

A DECLARATION OF COMMITMENT TO THE WORK

> But the LORD abides forever; He has established His throne for judgment, And He will judge the world in righteousness; He will execute judgment for the peoples with equity (Psalm 9:7,8).

Unfortunately, words like "justification" are not usually associated with approval. More often than not, they lend themselves more toward images of an angry judge (this is usually where we insert God) ready to inflict the harshest sentence possible to some worthless criminal (this is usually where we insert ourselves). This is NOT what God had in mind when He moved Paul to write those words to the Romans. If you'll notice the core of the inspiration is focused on "the image of His Son" revealing that His resulting decree of "innocence" concerning us was more the result of admiration than adjudication. In other words, our judiciary image, where we place God in the seat of presiding authority over our lives is correct; the way we envision ourselves in that image and the way we envision Him coming to a ruling is not. We are not criminals on trial awaiting the conviction of some elected governmental official. We are children under the willful covenant of an everlasting loving Father. Understanding the message any other way is to misunderstand it all-the-way.

Scripture records over 900 titles for God. And, one of them happens to be "Judge". In fact, 76x from Genesis to Revelation, He is referred to as such. That's a point, position, and power that can't be challenged. What can be and must be, however, is the misconception we have of Him in that role. It may appear to be a harmless blunder, nevertheless, our customary referencing of Him as "Judge" lacks an extremely vital piece that doesn't just tell *who* God is; it tells 'how' He is. It tells us about His nature (which is the sole purpose of so many names). He is not just a judge, He is a "just" judge (Psalm 7:11), meaning, that He makes everything right in its time. Contrary to our usual assumptions, "right", or "righteousness", is the aim of His rulings, not "wrong". Does He notice the wrong? Of course He does. However, He sees it and judges it from a Father's perspective — a perspective driven by innocence (approval) and blinded by love.

Any and Every name, position, or title He possesses (Creator, Provider, Healer, Teacher, Judge, etc.) has been made subject to His paternal perspective. Said another way, God the Creator, God the Provider, God the Healer, God the Teacher, and God the Judge lives under the influence of God the Father. The moment we remove or reverse this order is the moment we position ourselves for a misinterpretation of who He is and a misevaluation of who we are. Case in point. If we extract God the Father from God the Creator, we may be called His development but we won't be called His descendants. If we remove God the Father from God the Provider, we may be fed, but we won't be filled. If we eliminate God the Father from God the Healer, we will feel well but we won't feel wanted. If we separate God the Father from God the Teacher, we may receive instruction but we won't receive an inheritance. Finally, if we exclude God the Father from God the Judge, we may have His conclusion, but we won't have His commitment.

Herein lies the beauty of a Judge and Father existing in the same person. A unique dynamic is created whereby the power to conclude meets with the promise of commitment, where justice is less about abiding by law and more about abiding in love, where verdicts are pledges of His allegiance *to* us rather than pronouncements of acquittal or accusation *against* us. Fatherly-justice, as beautifully expressed by Bill Johnson, *"is fiercely aimed at removing anything that interferes with love"*. With this, I pose the same admonition to you that the author of the book of Hebrews posed to His audience:

And have you forgotten the encouraging words God spoke to you as his children? He said,

> *"My child, don't make light of the LORD's discipline*
> *and don't give up when he corrects you.*
> *For the LORD disciplines those he loves,*
> *and he punishes each one he accepts as his child."*

As you endure this divine discipline, remember that God is treating you as his own children. Who ever heard of a child who is never disciplined by its father? If God doesn't discipline you as he does all of his children, it means that you are illegitimate and are not really his children at all. Since we respected our earthly fathers who disciplined us, shouldn't we submit even more to the discipline of the Father of our spirits, and live forever?

For our earthly fathers disciplined us for a few years, doing the best they knew how. But God's discipline is always good for us, so that we might share in his holiness. No discipline is enjoyable while it is happening—it's painful! But afterward there will be a peaceful harvest of right living for those who are trained in this way Hebrews 12:5-11 NIV).

AN ASSUMPTION OF RESPONSIBILITY FOR THE WORK

I will surely tell of the decree of the LORD: He said to Me, "You are My Son, Today I have begotten You" (Psalm 2:7).

Apple has been called "the most successful company in history". What an accolade. Just when I think I've made my dreams big enough, a statement like this comes out and forces me into a massive revision of my goals. Like most business owners, Apple is definitely a company I look up to, though not for the reasons you may think. Many people look at them and see the money. Don't get me wrong — a conservative, "drastically undervalued" (quoted Carl Icahn) stock price of $728.35 billion is nothing to balk at and I'd take it in a heartbeat, however, my greater interest is in how they've continued to climb year in and year out until somebody or "somebodies" of credible clout decided it was time to put the champion's belt around their waist. Honestly, you'd think at some point they'd run out of creativity or become a bit lax in their passion since there really is no legitimate contender for taking the title from them anytime soon, yet, this isn't the case. They just keep getting better driving the gap between them and their competitors farther and farther apart. So much so, that even the most destructive and immature of all teenagers wouldn't dare think of putting a décor of stickers (usually of other companies logos) anywhere near the logo on the back of their Mac computers for fear they may cover it up because, to them, there are none worthy enough of co-existing in the same space.

What is it about this company? How have they created such a great divide? How have they branded themselves, their products, and their culture in such a way that their users represent them with a pride that rivals that of their favorite sports teams? Where does the unending amount of creative juices and the eerily accurate assessments of what the market wants and needs come from (even when the market hasn't openly said they wanted it or needed it yet)? What makes Apple . . . Apple?

That's the million dollar question, or, in Apple's case, the near trillion dollar question isn't it? There's certainly no lack of references and coinciding research to prove just how great of an interest this entity is to society as they have found a way to not only cross cultural and professional lines, but have also figured out how to impact them with immediate and sustainable value when they get there. An incredibly great feat indeed — one that many considered 'impossible'. Nevertheless, as impressive as their accomplishments have been and continue to be I can't help but think of the pressure they must live under. The more hands their products go into, the more value they add to their users, the more they enhance and advance the capacity of their technology, the more they raise the expectations of consumers for the "next" product. Think about it! This is a point well proven every year when Apple releases the newest version of the iPhone. In a weekend, they have reported as many as 10,000,000 new phones being sold. That's astounding, to say the least, but, let's also remember that it's also 10,000,000 people with extremely high expectations who will undoubtedly compare and critique alongside of last year's already remarkable version. This is the very reason they will never give their logo to (put their name on) anything that has not endured a rigorous, thorough process of research, development, and testing. The logo is a sign of their personal approval to the world. It's their full assumption of responsibility *for* the product(s) — for their originality and their functionality.

Since its inception, Apple has given much to the world: Mac Computers, iPhones, iPads, iPods, iTunes, the App Store, and more. They have literally been the founding fathers of convenience — of taking the complex and making it simple . . . of taking the slow and making it fast. Pioneering such an advancement brings with it great rewards, such as being called, "the most successful company in world history", as well as great risks, such as meeting the ever-growing demand of consumers for more of the same except better, faster, and simpler. All the while their reputation hanging in the balance. Jesus was right in saying, *"From everyone who has been given much, much will be required; and from him who has been entrusted with much, even more will be demanded (Luke 12:48 BSB)"*. There's nobody more qualified to make such a statement because there is nobody who has been "entrusted" with as much. Apple and Jesus both know what it is to bring change to the entire world. They each know just how great the demands can be for doing so. And, they each assume full responsibility *for* their works by backing them with their own personal promises better known to consumers as "warranties"

Warranties are guarantees from the manufacturer to the consumer that the products, goods, or services will operate according to the proper standards set forth by the manufacturer's original design. In the event the event that they don't, the warranty covers them with the legally binding assurance of replacing or repairing the product. While the warranties on earth and those in heaven are similar in many respects, they are also different in many others. And, it's these distinctions that disclose even more of the value we have as His product. For example,

#1. EARTHLY WARRANTIES OFFER LIMITED GUARANTEES; HEAVENLY WARRANTIES OFFER LIFETIME GUARANTEES:

On my way to work this morning, I saw a crow on the side of the road "feasting" on a dead squirrel. As grotesque as it was, I was immediately reminded of the command that Jesus gave us:

> *"Therefore I tell you, do not worry about your life, what you will eat; or about your body, what you will wear. For life is more than food, and the body more than clothes. Consider the ravens: They do not sow or reap, they have no storeroom or barn; yet God feeds them. And how much more valuable you are than birds! Who of you by worrying can add a single hour to your life? Since you cannot do this very little thing, why do you worry about rest? (Luke 12:22-26 NIV; emphasis mine).*

Do not worry about your life? How is that possible? I know He would've never spoken it if it wasn't, but some things are easier said than done aren't they? Externally, if you were to meet me you wouldn't consider me a "worrier". The truth is, however, I catch myself worrying about everything (and it seems to have been magnified exponentially since having a child). While I'm in the mood to "bare all", I'll also admit to being an irrational worrier — you know the worry that results from the latest off-the-wall mental soap opera you've playing in your head that has no basis in reality whatsoever. Just this morning, on the way down the driveway, before admiring the crow and his breakfast, I was worrying whether or not I was worshipping God correctly, whether or not He was paying attention to me, whether or not my heart was really in in, and whether or not I was being one of those who "praises Him with their lips, but, their heart is far from Him" (see Matthew 15:8; Isaiah 29:13). I'm convinced He was trying to encourage me with the bird and squirrel encounter, still, I found myself speculating, "Was the squirrel born to be the God's provision for the bird?" Which one was I? I know it all sounds overly analytical and ludicrous. The point is I worry way too much — about things I shouldn't and I've been commanded 'not to'. And, He clearly reveals the antidote, if you will, by asking *"how much more '**valuable**' are you than the birds?"*

Not some of the time and not most of the time, but every single time I feel trapped in an anxious state it can be directly linked to a lowered, lesser, or lost evaluation of myself. I stop valuing me the way He values me and start allowing thoughts to slip into my head about me that's not in His. I somehow forget that I am His product and He gave me His name which carries His approval which points to my worth and to the '**life**time warranty' backing it — the promise that my life is in His hands (see Matthew

> WE HAVE A LITERAL WARRANTY COVERING OUR WORRY.

6:25-34; Luke 12: 22-34). We have a literal warranty covering our worry.

So, the next time you feel worried, simply let it be a reminder of the warranty covering your worth. If it helps you can always think of a bird eating the dead flesh of a squirrel ;).

#2. EARTHLY AND HEAVENLY WARRANTIES ARE MADE VOID BY UNAUTHORIZED DEALERS:

When companies such as Apple sale their products, they put them in a box before placing them into the hands of their new owner. Once the owner has a chance to open it, the first thing they see will not be the iPad or the iPhone. Rather, they will find, packaged neatly on top of the product an "owner's manual" that will read something like, *"Before operating this product, please read 'me' completely"* (which very few of us ever do).

The word Manu- is a prefix meaning "of the hands". In other words, the instructions set forth in the manual are the exact directions from "the hands" that made it showing the way it was built to function. As you read through the book, you will discover the bulk of the pages are dedicated to revealing to the new owner a list of "laws" (the do not's) and "promises" (the do's). Coming to the final pages, you will notice the "warranty" that provides a multi-faceted guarantee. First, it guarantees "product performance" contingent on proper care stating that the product will perform exactly as promised IF it is handled "by the book". Then, it guarantees "personal protection" for defects warning, "IF an issue arises with the product 'do not' attempt to fix it yourself and 'submit only to an authorized dealer".

Like Apple, God sends His "products" into the world with an "owner's manual" (the Word of God) which contains the "laws" and "promises" of how the manufacturer created His products to function. Neglecting to read it will make us ignorant of who He has made us to be and how He has made us to be, thus, increasing the risk of malfunction. Once the inevitable "defect" appears, we won't know "where to go" — where to send ourselves (the 'product') — because we won't have any idea "whose" we are. We won't know anything about the One who built us. The danger amplifies the longer we stay in our state of ignorance by refusing to "read the manual". As with any abnormality, we will know something is "off" but, we will be forced into making "educated guesses" on the solutions since we have chosen to bypass the "educated directives" we've been given resulting in greater confusion. The more confused we become, the more inaccurate our self-evaluation will be ultimately making us more susceptible to placing ourselves in the hands of unauthorized dealers and voiding the warranties over us.

There are a lot of "dealers"– Buddah, Mohammed, Confucius, Satanism, Atheism, and the like — however, they are not authorized and the warranty is made void in their hands because they don't carry the *author*ized story of the originating manufacturer. They don't know His mind and they haven't received the official seal of approval — His name.

The book of Acts tells the story of a Jewish high priest named Sceva who had seven sons. They watched as "*God was performing extraordinary miracles by Paul's hands, so that even facecloths or work aprons that had touched his skin were brought to the sick, and the diseases left them, and the evil spirits came out of them*". In effort to display greater power as "exorcists", they (the seven sons) "*attempted to pronounce the name of the Lord Jesus over those who had evil spirits, saying, "I command you by the Jesus that Paul preaches!"*

Then, something strange happens:

The evil spirit answered them, "I know Jesus, and I recognize Paul—but who are you?" Then the man who had the evil spirit leaped on them, overpowered them all, and prevailed against them, so that they ran out of that house naked and wounded Acts 19:1-17).

These "sons" observed Paul closely, watching his every move, listening to his every word and duplicated it, yet, they still weren't able to get the same results. In fact, they didn't just fail; they suffered an embarrassing and painful defeat. What happened? The evil spirit reveals it — *I know Jesus, and I recognize Paul — but who are you?* They were unauthorized dealers attempting to operate *with* the name of Jesus but not *in* the name of Jesus and were, therefore, void of the warranty that comes with it — the promise of power (see Acts 1:8) and protection (see II Thessalonians 3:3). Paul, on the other hand, was authorized and the guarantees of the warranty proved it.

We all bypass the manual from time to time and end up buying into the advice, and worse yet, the acceptance of other unauthorized dealers. We read their books, listen to their tapes, memorized their quotes, and find comfort in the crafty, flesh-appealing compromises of their "warranties". Soon, as fate would have it, we learn an embarrassingly painful lesson: *you can't serve two masters (can't live under two warranties). Either you will hate the one and love the other or you will be devoted to one and despise the other (see Matthew 6:24; parenthesis is mine added).*

The deception in reading other unauthorized manuals is they give the appearance of being authentic. They contain laws, promises, and instructions just like all the others, however, their warranties are limited. In the previous section, we said that God's warranty comes with a "lifetime guarantee". It's true and He will never remove it from you, however, it is possible to remove yourself from it. Hence, the parable of the prodigal Son (see Luke 15:11-32). There's good news though. The Originator of our lives — the Father — is always anticipating our return, looking out over the horizon, awaiting the day where He sees us in the distance so that He can run to us and receive us back into His home placing us back under His warranty. All we have to do is get within sight and He'll do the rest.

#3. EARTHLY WARRANTIES OPERATE BY CONTRACT; HEAVENLY WARRANTIES OPERATE BY COVENANT

There's a level of comfort that comes with warranties. They ensure us that our "stuff" is "covered" in the unfortunate event of a defect showing up. The most successful companies understand the amount of value we place on our "peace of mind" and the effect it will have on the value we place on them in return. So, they'll work to not only fulfill the promises of "repair-and-replace" made within their guarantees, but will often times go the extra-mile by taking the expense of mailing, packaging, and fixing the broken product on themselves.

The "extra mile" is good business practice, an honorable gesture of service, and gives us the feeling that we're not in this alone. It makes us feel like someone has our backs and is fighting for us. The reality is, however, "our backs" are not their primary concern . . . theirs is.

When companies create warranties or take on extra expenses it not because they "like" us. The truth is they don't even know us. They create warranties and "shoulder" the expenses because they want you to "like" them. Undoubtedly, if and when we read the manuals, it will appear as if the chief stimulus backing the "protection clauses" within are done for our sake. This is simply not the case. They are actually doing it, first and foremost, above all else, for their **name's sake**.

In the Bible, "reputation" and "name's sake" are the same word. You see, if a product doesn't succeed. If it doesn't perform to the standards they promised it would, their reputation, or their name, is in trouble. This is why they will move heaven and earth to exceed your expectations — because their name is on the line.

Everything a company does through warranty is to protect the reputation of the manufacturer. From this perspective, the warranties of *Heaven, Inc.* are no different. Receiving the "Name" of this entity means you have built by a Manufacturer who carries the *"Name that is above all names"* (see Philippians 2:9) and a *"Word that will not return void"* (see Isaiah 55:11). With that kind of reputation to uphold, you better believe it will be more than protected because fulfilling the promises associated with this Name is to fulfill a covenantal obligation, not a contractual one.

Warranties are in *word-form* what they were in *work-form* — they are the words of the work. If products could talk the warranty is what they would tell us. They would take us back to the process of their creation introducing us to their make-up and their maker and disclosing to us the intricacies of the invention in addition to the intentions of the inventor. We are a different kind of product because our Manufacturer created us through covenant instead of contract. We have been built through and backed by the unconditional influence of Love instead of the conditional influence of terms. Love is the "logo" of our Manufacturer. It is His name (see (I John 4:8). In this name we were created. In this Name we have been sent. In this Name the warranty was written, and in this Name He will protect. Products created in Heaven and sent in Love were not designed or delivered with disease, sickness, poverty, or pain — these are "defects". In the event that any of these should occur, remember the instructions and the oath of the manual: GO TO THE MANUFACTURER!

WORD OF WORTH

An article written by Daniel Grant entitled, "What's the value of a signature on an Art Print?" stated:

VAN GOGH, APPLE, AND A DEAD SQUIRREL

"An artist's name on a print can increase the price by two or more times'. Many artists and dealers contend that by signing a print the artist approves and endorses it, and, implicitly, claims it as his or her own work."

The name lays "claim" to the work. Within that claim of possession is also the claim of protection that doesn't just tell the world who the work belongs to; it also tells the world who it is backed by — 'whose 'word' is covering the warranty.

How much value does Apple's logo bring to their products? What about Nike — what is the exponential value the "Swoosh" bring to their shoes? How about Under Armour? Walt Disney? BILLIONS. That's right. BILLIONS with a "B". Simplifying and scaling this idea of "brand value", let's bring it down to a much smaller, personal level. Right now, let's say you remove the "Apple" from your iPhone/Computer, or the Nike "Swoosh" from your favorite pair of shoes. Isn't it true that even though you would have the exact same computer and the same exact pair of shoes, the value attached to it would decrease, for you and for those around you, apart the presence of the logo? What this reveals is that a consumer's loyalty is not as much about the uniqueness of the product as it is to the logo and what it represents.

If "brand marketing" could be summed up into one word it would be "loyalty". Notice I didn't say 'consumer loyalty' because that would only be a part of the equation — the final part. This does not mean it's unimportant as legendary branding experts, such as those we've listed above, and less-than-legendary experts are ultimately seeking the same outcome with their marketing campaigns: long-term, residual, consumer loyalty. The main distinction between the two is that the less-than-legendary focus on "getting" while the legends focus on "giving". Apple, Nike, Under Armour, and Walt Disney have all figured out that the predominant pathway to creating consumer loyalty is through company loyalty. One of the main ways, if not the main way, they do this is through the promise and protection of their "word" — by fulfilling their 100% money back satisfaction guarantees and/or their 100% repair-and-replace warranties. As great as these companies are at doing this, they are still a mere reflection of the Company that created us all.

REFLECTION QUESTIONS

#1. You are God's work (His greatest masterpiece) and because of that, His word is backing you. Have you approached God, either for yourself or on someone else's behalf, with this in mind? How would this change your approach if you did?

#2. *He who began a good work in you is faithful to bring it to completion.* Are there any "good work in you" that you feel are incomplete? If so, what are they specifically? Have you talked to the "Manufacturer" about it?

#3. God is pleased with you, committed to you, and responsible for you or else you wouldn't be here. What does this truth do for your self-worth? Are you starting to see that you are not worthless? Are you ready to come to God and go to the world as such?

MEDITATION/APPLICATION

THE PROOF IS THE PUDDING

Just this past weekend, while on a short get-away with my family, I was reminded of the 'loyalty' that Heaven has to its name and to its Creation. Every year, my family, along with my in-laws will take a mini-vacation together. When we go, the schedule stays extremely consistent. We use one of the days to go to the amusement park and the other day we will go shopping at a nearby outlet mall to capitalize on all the 'deals'. On the final day, while we were shopping, my daughter (three and half years old) decides that she wants to sit down in the middle of one of the extremely busy stores. I walked over to her to pick her up and proceed to grab her hand/wrist to help her up. As I'm doing this she thinks we're playing a game and collapses back to the floor so that I can 'drag' her around the store. When she does, she twists just a little and her elbow slightly dislocates. It was a minor dislocation — so minor that we really didn't know why she was screaming bloody murder. We knew something was wrong because that level of crying is totally out of character for her, but she stopped crying fairly quickly and was immediately back to wanting to ride the "quarter" rides located at variously places around the mall. Thinking everything was normal we noticed her holding her elbow while she walked, although, still not crying. Then, her mom took her to restroom. After finishing, she attempted to wash her hands by rubbing them together and started screaming again. I could hear her from the men's restroom and I did what other parents do, especially the guilt ridden ones who realize they've accidentally hurt their child. I prayed. I was working on this very chapter right before leaving and suddenly it came to mind and I prayed, *"Father, my daughter is hurting and we don't know what to do. Just this week, You've taught me that 'pain is defect' and Your warranty says 'in the event of a defect' that I should 'go to the manufacturer. So, I come to You, You are the Manufacturer and you know how to fix her. Please help."* The prayer was really that simple (although much more passionate than I'm able to convey here). About ten minutes later, we went into the Disney store to buy her a princess dress and her mom grabbed her arm and said, "Avery, let me look at it". Reluctantly, she let her look and my wife gently rotated her elbow inward to look at the back of it and she felt it pop. Avery cried for about 30 seconds, then, started using it immediately with full strength restored as if nothing ever happened. Later, we found out that it's common for a child under the age of 5 to get what's called "Nursemaid's elbow" — occurs when children are pulled up to hard by their hand/wrist. Although common to some, it was uncommon to me and her mom. You know who it wasn't uncommon too? The Manufacturer of her life. He put His name on her and gave His word to her — neither of which was He going neglect. All that was needed was for someone to bring Him in remembrance of *who* He is (the Word — the Logos — also, where we get our English term 'logo' — see John 1:1-3) and of *what* He said (see Isaiah 43:25,26). It is a bold reminder that He told us to give Him — a reminder that His reputation (name's sake) is on the line.

12

THE PRICE OF LIFE

Value is not determined by the price that's set; value is determined by the price someone is willing to pay

Recently, I had a conversation with a friend and told him that my wife and I had just sold the first and only home that we lived in a few months ago and have been searching for a new one ever since. As you can imagine, we're excited about our "upgrade", although, the search has proven to be more challenging than we anticipated. While I wouldn't say that the "homes for sale" in our area are scarce; I also wouldn't say they are plentiful either. Combine the lack of availability with an inability to find a close match with the specific details of what we want in and around our next home and you have a recipe for delay.

Our first home purchase moved much quicker because we didn't have to deal with as many details back then as we do now. Mostly due to the fact that there wasn't enough money in our preapproval to be picky. We also didn't have to take area schools into consideration since we weren't parents yet. And, we didn't own a loan mower to cut any size lot of grass much less the two or more acres we want now. We were your typical first-time, fresh-out-of-college, still-in-the-honeymoon-phase, newly-wed home buyers: rich in love and poor in pockets.

Sharing all this with my friend, I eventually arrived at my biggest complaint. *"The homes we like and would consider purchasing are way over-priced. They exceed homes similar to them by as much as $40-$50 per square foot . . . IN THE SAME NEIGHBORHOOD. Nobody is going to give them that much for it"*. To which my friend laughed and interjected after patiently enduring my rant, *"You might be surprised"*. He went on to explain that he and his family just went through a similar transition a couple of years ago when a job change required him to move from South Carolina to Georgia. He shared that he also had many of the same complaints as me and in the process of selling his old home and purchasing his new one he learned, in his own words, that *"value is not determined by the price someone sets; value is determined by the price someone is willing to pay"*.

My friend kept talking in an attempt to offer me further advice, although, I can't tell you much of what he said past that previous statement. I had heard others say it before, but this time it carried something with it — something unique, something of spiritual significance, and something in the shape of a much needed reminder of the price that was paid for as well as a new found revelation of my value because of it.

THE HIGH PRIEST AND THE HOME BUYER

The Book of Hebrews reminds us that we have a *"High Priest who sympathizes with us — who is not out of touch with our reality because He has experienced it all* (see Hebrews 4:15 NASB and MESSAGE). In other words, if we've been through it, He's been through it. Anything and everything we encounter in this life He encountered in His. Even the simple and seemingly meaningless process of buying a home, He is able to relate to it because He, too, has been a "Home Buyer". In fact, this was a huge reason that He chose to leave the comfort of His former home in Heaven — to search for and acquire future homes on Earth. These homes would not be made of the usual material such as wood, brick, concrete, or steel. As a result, their values would not be set at usual prices or satisfied through the common monetary exchange. No, His real estate of interest would be those made of flesh and blood, joint and marrow, heart and soul. Their asking prices would be "life"– His life — and their only acceptable form of payment would be the *willing sacrifice* of "innocent blood" — His own.

We are those homes — those that he took up residence *"among"* (see John 1:14 HCSB) so that He could eventually take up residence *"within"* (see I Corinthians 3:16, Hebrews 3:6, II Corinthians 6:16). We are those who, by natural standards, would've been considered a terrible investment because we carried an excessive estimate — a price tag that was not only unreasonable, but was also unnegotiable. We were homes whose worth reflected more of those that should've been condemned rather than those that should've been redeemed. For many of us, our "foundations" (identities) were destroyed before they even had a chance to be finished. The "coverings" (parents) meant to protect us from the "elements" (thoughts, words, teachings, attitudes) of "external environments" (so-called friends, negative teachers, bad pastors or coaches, etc.) were blown away (ran away from) by the first storm (adverse, challenging circumstances) they ever faced after being attached to us. Inside, the "lights" (dreams, visions, desires, and imaginations) had grown dim and died. And, the exposed "rooms" (heart, mind, soul, and spirit) had become a resting place for "snakes" (demonic influence). Nevertheless, He came. He came not because of what was 'in' us; He came because of what was 'in' Him.

JESUS PAID IT ALL

Coursing through His veins was the payment for every property that would come into His possession. This payment, although different in form, remains similar in outcome to those being made under natural transactions in that it is the agreed upon exchange for everything — for the whole house, not just parts of it. The same is true for me and my wife. When we eventually find the home we want to move into, the moment we put our signatures on the final documents agreeing to the price we negotiated we will assume ownership of the entire property. The closing of any home, natural or spiritual, will never be reached without an "all-or-nothing" purchase.

While it's true that we won't close on any home *in part*, it's also true that we won't close on any home without its parts. It is the parts that make the whole, that make the house a home, that make it livable, and that make it valuable. Typically when Jesus' sacrifice is mentioned, it is from the perspective of the "closing table"– the Cross — because it is here that He took His final breath. It is here that the last drop of living blood had fallen from His body signifying that the purchase was complete. Yet, there's more. There's more to a purchase than just the close and there's more to the price He paid than just His last hours on the Cross. There's the details — the stages of events leading up to those last moments that we can't continue to leave out because it's in these stages that the entire exchange is revealed. It's here that we move from knowing He made a purchase to knowing exactly what He purchased. It's here that His true glory is revealed and our true value is realized.

In all, Jesus' blood was shed seven different times leading to and through the Cross. Each time disclosed another "stage" in the purchasing process and another "part" of the property He would be possessing in return. Those seven "stages" and their coinciding "parts" were (in order):

1. OUR EMOTIONS — The 1ˢᵗ shedding of His blood
2. OUR IMAGE — The 2ⁿᵈ shedding of His blood
3. OUR MIND — The 3ʳᵈ shedding of His blood
4. OUR BODY — The 4ᵗʰ shedding of His blood
5. OUR WORK — The 5ᵗʰ shedding of His blood
6. OUR WALK — The 6ᵗʰ shedding of His blood
7. OUR FAMILY — The 7ᵗʰ shedding of His blood

OUR EMOTIONS — *THE 1ˢᵀ SHEDDING OF BLOOD* — Luke 22:39-43

The first drop of blood to fall from Jesus' body was unique from the others because it was the only time that it didn't come from hands of another person. Instead, it would be the result of a self-inflicted shedding, where *"His sweat became like drops of blood falling to the ground"* caused by the *"agony"* He felt in His soul as He sensed the time had finally come to fulfill His purpose in becoming the Savior of the World.

For hundreds of years, the prophets had prophesied about this moment. John the Baptist, the last prophet in the Old Testament, had the privilege of seeing Him in the flesh and confirming *"Behold the Lamb of God who takes away the sin of the World (see John 1:29)."* Jesus Himself echoed it through many open discussions with His disciples in order to prepare them for a life without Him physically being with them. He even went as far as to boldly declare it among the religious and political leaders of His day knowing that every time He did their hate toward Him would grow all-the-more and would eventually become the impetus behind their desires to crucify Him. Now, the "the hundreds of years" had found their "day" where the talk would be ending and the walk would be beginning.

He knew what awaited Him in the hours ahead and could feel the pressure of the "culmination of times" mounting on Him. So, He did what we all do when our emotions start getting the best of us. He withdrew Himself and cried out. Caught between a willing spirit and weak flesh, He prayed, *"Father, if you are willing, take this cup from me — nevertheless, not my will, but Yours, be done". (Matthew 26:39)*

Jesus wanted to quit. That's extremely scary to admit considering He was our only hope for our salvation. Nevertheless, it's true. He came within inches of it, even to the point of asking the Father "take this cup from Me", but, something happened — something that shifted His attention from "take it from Me" to "Let Me keep it". In a matter of seconds, He went from wanting to throw-in-the-towel to declaring, *"Nevertheless".*

Although I can't prove it, I have this picture in my mind of Him kneeling to pray, wrapping both arms around His belly, anxiously rocking back and forth, with His face aiming towards the ground contemplating whether or not He really wanted to go through with this, speculating whether or not He had what it takes, and questioning whether or not it would be worth it. I believe it was at this point, in the tension of "let this cup pass from me" and "Your will be done", that the blood (which He mostly likely assumed was sweat running down His face) fell and hit the ground in front of Him triggering the reminder of what was "in" the cup (the *new covenant*: Luke 22:20) and what was "in" Him (the required "sacrifice" to fulfill the requirements of the *old covenant* :Matthew 5:18).

At the Passover dinner just a few short hours before this, He had taken communion with His disciples where He handed them a cup saying, " *This cup is the new covenant in my blood, which is being poured out for you (Luke 22:20). Do this in remembrance of Me (I Corinthians 11:25).* The sight of His own blood brought to His "remembrance" the "new covenant" within it as well as the reminder that it could not be established without it.

God's deepest desire was, is, and will forever be an unhindered, unbridled, unbroken relationship with us where we have constant, eternal access to Him and Him to us. This is what the "new covenant" was all about: Him living *with* us, and, more importantly, Him living *in* us. However, it was not possible without the forgiveness of sins which could not come apart from His sacrifice.

Now you see why the struggle was so great and so needed in the Garden. Without the "agony", there wouldn't have been blood, without the blood there wouldn't have been the reminder, without the reminder there may not have been the strength to continue, without the strength to continue there wouldn't have been a payment made, without the payment being made there wouldn't have been the forgiveness of sins, and without the forgiveness of sins there is no "new life in Christ". The irony of it all — the detail that's so easy to miss — is the impact that emotion had in creating, advancing, and sustaining the covenant. Uncontrollable desire created it, unbearable agony advanced it, and unconditional love sustains it. This is why the price He paid included it.

The first piece of property that came under Jesus' purchase, through intentional order, was our emotions. But, why would He start there? Because acquiring our emotions meant He would be acquiring our soulds and acquiring our souls meant He would be acquiring the "life" within them.

We spent a considerable amount of time on soul and emotion connection in the section on "identity", so, we won't go over the entire introductory details again. Just recall that the original Hebrew word for "soul" is defined as "the seat of emotions and passions". This is where life happened and where life still happens (see Genesis 2:7 and III John 1:2). By saving our emotions, He was saving our souls, and by saving our souls, He was saving the "life" that He breathed into them (see Genesis 2:7).

The "life" which makes each of us "living" is made of the eternal and the temporal. Jesus died for both. This may come as a surprise to some since the first, eternal life, has been the more highlighted, pursued, celebrated, desired, and exalted out of the two. To the extent that it has totally eclipsed it's counterpart in *spiritual* significance and some circles have not only made it inferior, but have even went as far as to consider it "evil". This is a huge mistake. The temporal life is the one Jesus came to redeem. It is the one where sin and its "wages" rule and reign (see Romans 6:23). And, it is the one that determines where and how we will spend eternity. Therefore, who you are NOW, where you are NOW, what you are doing NOW, and how you are living NOW matters. It obviously mattered to Him or else He wouldn't have given His life for it and it should begin to matter to us. Perhaps, even more so, at this juncture of our existence, than the eternal since it is the one we occupy.

Living as one whose life is centered on "waiting to die" so that he or she can go to heaven is selfish because it robs those living at the same time as us of "us" — of the "life" (our identity, gifts, talents, calling, and creativity) we've been placed here, in the temporary, to express. I can't help but to think what would happen if we would allow ourselves to believe that His death covered now and later.

How many more risks would we take? How many more businesses would we start, books would we write, or songs would we sing? How many more friendships would we have? How much less time would we spend *"gazing into the sky" (see Acts 1:1)* in anticipation of a "rescue-by-rapture" and instead start living as those who have been acquired in order to *"occupy until He comes" (see Luke 19:13)*?

He didn't die so that we could die; He died so that we could live. Out of His own mouth He said, *"I have come that they may have life and have it more abundantly (John 10:10)".* The "abundant life" is the "blessed life" (Genesis 12:2). It's the one that yields

> HIS DEATH COVERED NOW AND LATER.

more-than-enough. It's a life of overflow — one designed to impact and influence with the "extra" coming from it. How is any of this possible if you're dead? It's not, so, we might as well start living and in truly living *win for the Lamb the reward of His sufferings*. (song of the Moravians).

#2. THE "NEW COVENANT" WAS ABOUT LIVING FROM THE "INSIDE-OUT"

"This is the covenant I will make with the people of Israel
after that time," declares the LORD.
"I will put my law in their minds
and write it on their hearts.
I will be their God,
and they will be my people.
No longer will they teach their neighbor,
or say to one another, 'Know the LORD,'
because they will all know me,
from the least of them to the greatest,"
For I will forgive their wickedness
and will remember their sins no more."
—Jeremiah 31:33-34-

The effectiveness of the new covenant cannot be understood without the ineffectiveness of the old. While it's "blessings" and "curses" brought a measure of impact to those it was given to, the impact was short-lived. Kind of like when we were in school learning a certain subject, we would hear the information, we would see it written on the board, we would complete all the homework assignments that came with it allowing us to know it enough to pass the test, but we would never get on an intimate (emotionally connected) level with it. As a result, the test would end, and we would end up disengaging from it, forgetting about it, and moving on to the next set of "requirements" in order to "pass the next test".

Such was the cycle the children of Israel found themselves in operating under the old covenant. They knew the information, however, they knew only knew it as a "law" (rule or requirement) in order to remain "blessed" (aka: pass the test). Meaning, they never came to know the "Blesser" — which was meant to be its purpose. Although established as a means to bring them into a relationship with God, it fell short. Why? It was an outside-in covenant based on rules instead of relationship, and, therefore, one that never reached their heart and soul.

The "new covenant", however, was about living from the inside-out. In the words of Jeremiah, it was a covenant that would be placed "in their minds" (another word for "soul") and "written on their hearts" (another word for "emotions"). It did come to replace the old, just not in the way you may think. Recall the words of Jesus who said, *"Do not think that I have come to abolish the Law or the Prophets; I have not come to abolish them but to fulfill them (Matthew 5:17)."* Replacing it was not about *removing* it; it was about *repositioning* it. We could say the old covenant was more misplaced than ineffective. This is a vitally critical distinction. If He removed it, then He would also be removing its original purpose — to reconcile God to man and man to God. If He repositioned it, however, it simply meant He would be transferring or transitioning it from one place to another, such as from *stone tablets* to *heart tablets*, and the purpose would remain.

According to Jeremiah, this was the exact plan — to transfer the covenant of letter and law to a covenant of heart and soul. But, How? Jesus made it clear: *Do not think that I have come to abolish the Law or the Prophets; I have not come to abolish them but to fulfill them.* The *transferring* was in the *fulfilling* and the *fulfilling* was in the *shedding*.

So, within that first drop of blood was not only a *reminder*, but also a *fulfiller* and an *initiator*. By fulfilling the requirements of the previous, He was initiating momentum for the new. As soon as that first drop of blood hit the ground, a "ripple effect" occurred shifting the covenant from the outside-in to the inside-out. No longer would we be working *against* the current of rules and requirement. Instead, we would be working *with* the current of redemption and relationship. We would be working *from* the seat of emotion, the soul, which is directly linked to every single part of "life".

OUR IMAGE– *THE 2ⁿᵈ SHEDDING OF BLOOD* — *Isaiah 50:6*

As the ripple effect of the new (inside-out) covenant began to move its way outward, "our image" stood in its path. In the next chapter, *"Natural Born Conformers"*, we will go into much greater depth on how this all works. For now, it serves us now to know that our bent toward conformity — the desire to "fit in", to be or become like someone else — is an inherent part of our essence. It's not something we will ever be able to resist or reject as it is one of the most primitive pieces of our original design. After all, God did say, *"Let Us make man in Our Image, according to Our likeness."* The obvious challenge we face with our natural disposition is that it seeks to "fit in" to unnatural positions — those that it wasn't designed to be a fit for and those that have become the reasons we've unknowingly become enemies of our own selves by calling conformity and its subsequent influences "bad".

Conformity is not evil. In fact, it can be an extremely powerful force if we can learn how to make it work for us instead of against us. Hence, another reason for His coming. Becoming "like" Him was more than just a mere wish. It was more than just a good thought that He passively hoped would happen. He actually shed His blood and died to make it happen.

Ripping the beard from His face caused His blood to be exposed (shed) for the second time. With it, another part of the acquisition was made: our image. II Corinthians 3:18, Paul writes:

> *But we all with unveiled faces, beholding as in a mirror, the glory of the Lord, are being transformed into the same image from glory to glory, just as from the Lord, the Spirit.*

Glory. This is where I want to bring your attention to because, according to Paul's letter, this is where our "face lift" (transformation of image) occurs. "Glory" is defined as "opinion, judgement, or view". All of which directly reflect the personal perspective (the intrinsic value) of the person making the "call" (what they esteem [or not] as an individual). Simply put, it is an open display of what a person (in this case, God) really thinks about the value they give to someone or something (us). When we *"behold, as in a mirror, the **glory** of the Lord"*, we are *"beholding the **value** of the Lord"*. We are looking at someone whose value (and image) is tied, not just to a word, but to a sacrifice. And, not just any sacrifice. The sacrifice of His own life. This can't be said enough: He paid the highest possible price for us — the price of His own life — because he saw us as being "worth" it.

Though it's not recorded, it's hard to imagine the garden of Gethsemane being the only place He contemplated "letting this cup pass from" Him. Every event that brought blood from His body– the agony in the garden, the tearing of His beard from His face, the crown of thorns being placed on His head, the 39 lashes He took to His back, the nails being driven into his hands and feet — brought with it an unfathomable pain and, without a doubt, the question of "is this (are they) worth it". He was strong, yet, the choice to continue was not about His strength. Nor was it about His courage or His endurance. It was about our image. Each time He chose sacrifice over surrender another "mirror of glory" was released for us to see ourselves through and conform our images to.

OUR BODY– *THE 3ⁿᵈ SHEDDING OF BLOOD* — *Matthew 27:26*

Infectious disorders, infertility disorder, neoplasms, perinatal conditions, endocrine disorders, skin and subcutaneous disorders, musculoskeletal, connective tissue disorders, fluid and electrolyte disorders, congenital anomalies, inherited metabolic and immune disorders, nonspecific abnormal findings, hematologic disorders, other and unspecified mortality and morbidity, psychiatric disorders, injuries, substance abuse, poisonings by drugs/medicaments/biologicals, neurological disorders, ENT and eye disorders, effects of foreign body entering through orifice, cardiovascular disorders, toxic effects of substances, varicose veins/hemorrhoids/lymphatic, other disorders and unspecified effects of external causes, certain adverse effects not elsewhere classified, respiratory disorders, complications from a procedure or device, dental disorders, complications of medical care, digestive system disorders, gynecological disorders, factors influencing health status and contact with med care, breast disorders, health services (V codes), pregnancy/childbirth/puerperium, morphology of neoplasms (M Codes).

For some, this list doesn't carry much meaning. In fact, I'd be willing to bet that 80+% of those who started reading it didn't finish it. Others may even consider it "boring", much like reading through the genealogy of names in different parts of the bible that none of us in the Western part of the world can pronounce correctly, much less find interesting. Perhaps you're in the medical field or a field similar to it and it caused you to break out into a cold sweat (like it did me) from the flashbacks you had of your "Medical Terminology" class in college. Or, maybe you're one of those who didn't study or become a medical professional, but found yourself or a loved one in the care of those who did because of the effect of one or more of the conditions listed. For the ones who considered it "meaningless", AFTER you finish reading this section, I'd like to suggest you go back and read it again, except slower this time as it will take an a whole new meaning to you. To the "uninterested", there's only one name you'll need to know how to pronounce when you're finished here: JESUS. To my medical professionals, you are stewards of "life" not "death", of "wholeness", not "disorder". This is the new "aim" I want this section to give you. To those being directly or indirectly affected and "infected", my hope is that the following message will somehow cause your pain to be a reminder of His provision and your sickness of His sacrifice — it is there that you'll find what you want most: your healing.

These are bold claims, to say the least. What make me so confident? The list we keep referring to was released by the World Health Organization in 2010 representing a revision in the ICD (International Classification of Diseases) coding systems used to categorize disease and illness that expanded it from 17 — 39 major categories. *Big deal, Chevis, what's your point?* My point is *"He was wounded for our transgressions, He was bruised for our iniquities: the chastisement of our peace was upon Him; and **with His stripes we were healed (Isaiah 53:5)."***

The third shedding of Jesus' blood came when Pilate sentenced Jesus to be flogged. How many "lashed" were customary in those days? **39**. 39 lashes, 39 categories of diseases and illnesses. Coincidence? I'll let you decide for yourself. All I know is 750 years previously, Isaiah, under the influence of God, said that His stripes would be for our healing. Little did Pilate know the sentence that he gave Jesus was not a sentence of flogging, it was a sentence of healing — healing for Pilate, healing for His accusers, healing for those who actually whipped Him, healing for us, healing for our children, and healing for the world.

OUR MIND — *THE 4ᵗʰ SHEDDING OF BLOOD* — *Matthew 27:29*

Minutes after the near-death flogging had ended,

> *"The governor's soldiers took Jesus into the Praetorium and gathered the whole company of soldiers around him. They stripped him and put a scarlet robe on him, and **then twisted together a crown of thorns and set it on his head**. They put a staff in his right hand. Then they knelt in front of him and mocked him. "Hail, king of the Jews!" they said. They spit on him, and took the staff and struck him on the head again and again."*

When the story of His sacrifice is told, we tend put a great deal of emphasis on the pain and abuse He endured. It's done in an attempt to show others (particularly those who have yet to hear His message and in turn have yet to give their lives to Him) and, often times, remind ourselves how much He cared. Unfortunately and unintentionally, by overemphasizing the price, we underemphasize the purchase. The *crown of thorns* moment is a perfect example of what I mean. We embrace the pain (price) of the thorns and miss the purpose (purchase) of the crown.

The story of His sacrifice, as traditionally told at least, has always bored me. I've sat through messages and movies, such as *The Passion of the Christ*, where everyone around me was crying and I wasn't. I just sat there as if there's not an emotional bone in my body, which I know is not true considering my wife bought me the movie *'The Notebook'* one year for my birthday because I 'teared up' a little while watching it (ok, I cried my eyes out at the end). Secretly, it bothered me. "*Why am I not 'moved' at all by this? Why do I feel so disconnected from it? Had I heard it so much that I had become 'too' familiar with it that it had lost its impact? Did it really not mean that much to me? What is wrong with me?*" When I finally decided to stop beating myself up, I realized the "disconnect" was the result of embracing the price without the purchase. I knew a payment had been made. I just never gave much thought to what was being received in return. I never placed myself in His story. Don't get me wrong. I knew that He did it all *for* me (*for* the forgiveness of my sins, *for* my salvation, *for* me to go to heaven), however, it never crossed my mind that He was also doing it '*as*' me. He took what I deserved so that I can get what He deserved.

The *crown of thorns* being placed on His head caused His blood to be shed for the fourth time. Within this shedding was pain. The pain pointed to a greater purpose: the exchange. We deserved to be crushed instead He took our place and gave us a crown. The crown represents royalty. The thorns being place on His head represents the mind. With the blood that came from the crown of thorns, He was paying the price for us to have a mindset of royalty.

In the years preceding the "bloodshed", Jesus made His message and mission very clear: *"Repent for the kingdom of Heaven is at hand"* (Matthew 3:2;4:17). He was here to establish, or I should say re-establish, a kingdom — the kingdom of heaven on earth. Every teaching, every parable, every healing, every deliverance, every miracle was dedicated to this pursuit: putting the kingdom within reach to everyone. As it would turn out, the challenge would not be getting the kingdom into their hands, it would be getting it into their heads and hearts. And, without getting it into their heads and hearts, He wouldn't be able to get it beyond His own life. This is why He led with "repent" (to change one's mind). He understood the kingdom mandate would be short-lived without a kingdom mindset. So, as a solution to the problem, He grabbed a group of 12 *learners* (disciples) that He wouldn't just pour Himself out for, but that He would also pour Himself into.

Oddly, just as they were His greatest challenge, He was theirs. Not only was His message different from what they had ever heard, He Himself was extremely different from anything they had ever seen. What set Him apart was not just the mission. It was the mentality it came with. He thought like a King, walked like a King, and talked like a King WITHOUT actually being a King (in the literal or natural sense). You know, without having a physical crown or castle to prove it. And, His unwavering expectation was that they would eventually do the same. They would think of themselves the way He thought of Himself. Even to the extent that they could look a governor in the eyes (who was appointed by their actual king and who held the power of life or death over them) and have the courage, the conviction, and the commitment to say, *"You say rightly that I am a king. For this cause I was born and for this cause I have into the world"* (see John 18:37 NKJV).

__OUR WORK__ — *THE 5ᵗʰ SHEDDING OF BLOOD* — *John 19:23*

For most, the crucifixion of Jesus is where the story of bloodshed begins. However, as we can see, it falls into a series of "sheddings" (fifth overall) that we've been exploring up to this point. And, it provides insight into, yet, another part of our existence that He came to redeem: **our work.**

Lance Wallnau once said, *"Work wasn't the result of man's fall; Frustrated work was the result"*. Perhaps, Lance's statement caught you off-guard like it did me. I can't pinpoint where I picked up the notion that "work" was the resulting consequence of Adam and Eve's disobedience, nevertheless, it was the ideology I carried with me for a very long time. Maybe it's because we live in a society where the greater percentage of those with jobs absolutely despise what they do on a daily basis and are not ashamed to voice their discontentedness with whomever will listen (or not). They make their careers sound like some type of curse on their lives. Since Dr. Wallnau's statement, I've taken a deeper look into what exactly he meant by what

He said and what I've found has led me to a vastly different perspective — one that's not driven by or derived through complaint, instead, is driven by and derived through the cross.

Work existed before the fall. Genesis 3:15 says, "*The Lord God took man and placed him in the garden **to work it** and watch over it (HCSB)*". Therefore, it couldn't possibly be the outcome of it. Furthermore, before He ever created man or placed Him in the garden, God revealed His intent for the characteristics that should dominate man along with his work: *Blessing, fruitfulness, multiplication (see Genesis 1:28)*. After man fell, we see a shift in the originally intended dominion: *Cursing* replaced *blessing, Thorns and Thistles* replaced *fruitfulness and multiplication, the sweat of the brow* replaced *the cool of the day,* and *painful toil* replaced *pleasurable work (Genesis 3:17-19)*. Adam messed up and the ground — His work — was left to pay the debt of his disobedience. Thankfully, the "curse" wouldn't last forever. As soon as that first nail pierced the hand of the "second Adam" (Jesus), drawing blood from His body for the fifth time, the payment for the debt was made. In that very moment, He was "reversing the curse" on "our work" as prophesied by Isaiah who declared,

> *For as the rain and the snow come down from heaven, And do not return there without watering the earth and making it bear and sprout, and furnishing seed to the sower and bread to the eater*
>
> *So will My word (**JESUS**) be which goes forth from My mouth; It will not return to Me empty, without accomplishing what I desire (**REDEMPTION OF THAT WHICH WAS LOST**), And without succeeding in the matter for which I sent it.*
>
> *For you will go out with joy and be led forth with peace; The mountains and the hills will break forth into shouts of joy before you, And all the trees of the field will clap their hands.*

Instead of the thorn bush the cypress will come up, and instead of the briar the myrtle will come up, and it will be a memorial to the Lord, For an everlasting sign which will not be cut off (Isaiah 55:9-13).

What was once fruitful, meaningful, and pleasurable and had become frustrated, meaningless, and painful would now be returning to its original state. . . . FOREVER.

OUR WALK — *The 6ᵗʰ shedding of His blood — Psalm 22:16; Luke 24:39; John 20:20*

Most home owners would agree that there's a massive difference between attaining a home and maintaining a home. Both are phases of ownership that require a different focus. The first focuses on *becoming the owner* while the second focuses on the *being the owner*. The sixth shedding of Jesus' blood is unique from the others because it is here that He is shifting the focus of acquisition from redemption (becoming the owner) to responsibility (being the owner) — where the emphasis becomes more about the care of the property than the contract on it.

When my wife and I finally purchase our next home, once we have fulfilled all the demands of the contract, that will make it totally and completely ours. However, it would be foolish to think that our new property will be void of any on-going responsibilities beyond those initial purchase agreements. The reality is, meeting those obligations ensures there will be a new set of demands, such as those that come with taking care of the home. The better we are at keeping these commitments, the greater the impact it will have on our new home's value.

Jesus was fully aware of the "ownership shifts" that come with the acquisition of new properties and the direct impact it will have on their value. Even more so, He anticipated it and made provision for it. As the hour drew near for Him *"to leave this world and go to the Father"*, Jesus *"got up from the meal, took off His outer clothing, and wrapped a towel around His waist'* and *'began to wash His disciples' feet"*. When He came to Simon Peter, who said, *"No, you shall never wash my feet"*. Jesus answered, *"Unless I wash you, you have no part with me."* Peter responded, *"not just my feet but my hands and my head as well!"* To which Jesus answered, *"Those who have had a bath need only to wash their feet; their whole body is clean, and, you are clean, but not all of you"*. (John 13:1-11). The washing that Jesus was referring to was the washing of His blood on behalf of their "walk" which was provided for when His feet were nailed to the cross. Unlike the other times that His blood was shed, it would not be for their salvation (contract), rather, it would be for their sanctification (care) — the on-going commitment of *being an owner*.

OUR GENERATIONS — *The 7ᵗʰ shedding of His blood — John 19:33,34*

The seventh and final time that Jesus' blood was shed came after His death. John records it in his gospel from an eye-witness account writing,

> *But when they came to Jesus and found that **he was already dead**, they did not break his legs. Instead, **one of the soldiers pierced Jesus' side with a spear, bringing a sudden flow of blood and water**. The man who saw it has given testimony, and his testimony is true* (John 19:33-35).

There are two unique distinctions that I've highlighted about this shedding because they each point to a third hidden element covered by "the new covenant": **our generations**.

The first distinction to notice is that it came after His death. Death marks the end of a life, or, the end of a generation. The end of His life meant the beginning of another. Just as John the Baptist passed the baton to Jesus (see John 3:30), Jesus was now passing the baton to the next generation — a baton dipped in His blood and handed off with the command, "*I gave you a pattern, that as I did to you, you also should do. Truly, truly, I say to you, a servant is not greater than his master, nor a messenger greater than the one* having sent him. If you know these things, you are blessed if you do them (John 13:15-17 BLB)".

If there's one thing Jesus was keen on, it was *"patterns"* and the momentum of blessings or curses they can bring. More specifically, He understood the impact they can and will have on many succeeding generations (including the innocent bystanders) if not set properly. In fact, He came to re-calibrate the settings of the first Adam, and, in turn, change the generational pattern of "sin and death" to a pattern of "righteousness and life". How would He do it? It's so simple, yet, so wise. He'd go straight to the source of all generations — the family — starting with the very first (Adam and Eve).

This brings us to the second distinction, which came when "one of the soldiers pierced Jesus' side with a spear". We've already made a reference to Him being called "the second", or the "last Adam". Still, it's worth repeating. Why? It forces us to look to the first and see that He, too, had his side opened:

> So the LORD God caused a deep sleep to come over the man, and he slept. God took one of his ribs and closed the flesh at that place. The LORD God fashioned into a woman the rib which He had taken from the man, and brought her to the man (Genesis 2:21,22).

Eve was taken from Adam's side. The result? Earth had its first family and, naturally, the commencement of its first generation. When the blood poured out of Jesus' body for the last time, it was for each one of our families and the generations that would follow them — a promise that the benefits of this new covenant would be made available to them just as it has been made available to us.

WHAT MORE

What more could He have done to prove how much we are worth? What my friend said is true: *value is always determined by the price someone is **willing** to pay for it.* Seven times He showed His willingness. Through it all — the agony, the beatings, the piercings, even unto death He kept going. And, He did it because He believed YOU ARE WORTH IT!

REFLECTION QUESTIONS

#1. Jesus willingly laid down His life to purchase yours. Does this change the value you have for yourself?

#2. As proven by the chapter, His blood covered more than we may realize. What personal revelation is coming to you as you work through each one?

#3. Are there any specific areas "blood bought" areas that stand out to you? Why?

#4. Will this change how you "eat His flesh" and "drink His blood" in the next communion you take (see John 6:25-59)?

MEDITATION/APPLICATION

To revisit our past, apart from the blood of Jesus, is to welcome deception in that we are visiting something that no longer exists. —Bill Johnson. Selah.

13

NATURAL BORN CONFORMERS

"Value is determined by who/what surrounds you"

Just a few short years ago we, as a nation, experienced an economic collapse — a crisis considered by many economists to have been the worst financial crisis since the *Great Depression* of the 1930's. The more recent *Greater Recession* lasted from December 2007 to June 2009. As some of you may call, the igniting catalyst responsible for setting it in motion was the bursting of the near $8 trillion dollar housing bubble (caused by financial institutions approving "favorable" loans that borrowers should have never been approved for and, as it turned out, couldn't pay for). During this time, the country went into survival mode when it came to spending which heavily and negatively impacted the bottom line of businesses — large and small. As a result, many of them were forced into extreme budget cuts, which led to job losses, which led to foreclosures which soared to all-time highs (*by 2009 almost 3 million homeowners received at least one foreclosure filing, setting a new record for the number of people falling behind on their mortgage payments* [CNN Money]).

THE STRUGGLE IS REAL

Needless to say, the crisis was scary, detrimental, and even became fatal for some. Even so, as it is with most things, there's always a "silver lining". My wife and I didn't lose our home, however, we definitely felt the effects of losing its original value due to the number of foreclosures surrounding us. We originally purchased the home in August of 2006 (our timing is impeccable isn't it?) for $110k. By 2009, when the collapse was in full effect, the appraisal value of our home had dropped to $92k, meaning, we were officially "upside-down" and couldn't sell it unless we were willing to take a significant loss. I was stunned to discover all of this when attempting to sell our home shortly after it had ended.

In my late 20's, fresh out of college, newly married, first-time business owner and home owner, I didn't know nothing about nothing (as the old folks were always sure to let me know in my younger years). Honestly, I was sort of oblivious to the seriousness of it all and never really grasped the gravity of what we were facing until I was slapped in the face with a $20k reduction in our home's value. Thankfully, that *slap* woke me up to a lesson I'll forever cherish. A lesson that reaches into every single area of our lives and that is this: **value is always determined by who and what surrounds you.**

It only took three foreclosures in my neighborhood of 40-50 homes for me and my neighbors to see an average decrease of $15k in the individual assessment of each of our homes. What's true with value of homes is also true with the value of humans. Yeah, I know what you're thinking. *Oh no! Here we go! Another lecture on how I need to change my friends, or change the places I'm choosing to hangout if I want to change my life.* And, you'd be right!

Here's the deal. I'm not just going to tell what you need to do, I'm going to give you context. I'm going to show you the *why* behind the *what* because I know what it is to have a person, most times someone you look up to — a leader, a teacher, a pastor, a coach, or some other type of mentor or role model — say to you something to the effect of, "if you really want to change then you need to get rid of your old friends". Just one problem. While you know in your heart of hearts that the "things" the group is doing is not good for the life you're trying to live, you also know in your heart of hearts that the individuals in that group, at their core, are not really bad people. You've done a lot of life together. They've been a shoulder to cry on during tough times and a hand to high five during high times. They've had your back when nobody else, including some of your own family, did. They've seen you at your worst and didn't *get rid of you*, so, how in the world could you possibly consider getting rid of them?

Trust me, I know all-to-well the pain of change, the loneliness of the road less traveled, and the confusion of comparing the life you used to live with the life you are now trying to live and concluding "that one" (the old one) seemed to be the more attractive of the two — more fun, more satisfying, and more friends. As the young people say these days, "the struggle is real". I have some unfortunate news for you — it doesn't get any easier. Why? If you're not growing, you're dying. And, your ability to grow — to "level up" in life — is forever linked to your ability to embrace and make changes. If you thought going from a *bad* life, filled with *bad* people, and *bad* environments to a *good* life, filled with *good* people and *good* environments was challenging, wait until you're faced with the *change demands* of going from a *good* life to a *great* life. Mark my words! It will happen. Just as there was an inspiring impetus — a person, a testimony, a book, a movie, or a message — that caused you to want to stop using drugs and start living clean, there will be another inspiring impetus that will spark a discontentment in you that will make you want to "move" once again. This time, however, it will be to reach beyond living clean into, perhaps, helping others learn how to live clean. No matter the level, you can rest assured something will have to change in order for you to move from where you are to where you want to go.

CHANGE THE TANK

Before we go any further, I want to tell you what I wish my early teachers would've told me: **the ridding requirements often associated with change are usually not as much about getting rid of or removing yourself from the people, places, or things as much as it's about getting rid of the limitations that come with them.** Two years ago, I wrote a post on Facebook that I'll share with you to help you understand what I mean by the previous statement:

MORNING MOTIVATION: What's up FB fam? Let me give you a warning before reading further-this will be vulnerable, raw, real, and a little lengthy, but I promise it will be worth reading until the end. Let me thank you ahead of time for taking a few minutes to continue. Someone shared a thought with me a few years ago that made a lot of sense when it comes to being a positive influence in the lives of others. *He said, 'what motivates you will motivate others . . . always be willing to give what you've been given and when you do BE VULNERABLE'.* With that said, I want to share a story with you that I heard about five years ago that changed my life.

First, I need to give it a short setup for it to make sense. For those of you that knew me from my high school days and previous, know that I was insecure, prideful, selfish, and had a huge case of ITC (I'm Too Cool). It's ridiculous to think about now but I let the desire to be accepted run my whole life and I hurt a lot of people along the way, ruined more friendships than I can count, and just wasn't a good person . . . AT ALL. To make a real long story short, I never wanted to do some of things I was doing and definitely reached a point earlier than most realize where I knew I needed to change and eventually desperately wanted to change but had no idea how to even begin the process. So, I started searching anywhere and everywhere — church, books, seminars, etc — and nothing seemed to help but I refused to give up bc I knew the answer was out there somewhere.

Thankfully, I came across a story of the Japanese Oranda Fish. This fish is unique as it has the 'potential' to grow up to 12" in length but its growth is completely dependent on the size of the tank you put it in. In other words, its 'surrounding' or 'environment' determines how much of its potential it will reach. This helped me realize two things. First, I had a greater potential. Second, I needed to change my 'tank' if I wanted to see it. The key difference in the fish and myself is the Oranda fish doesn't have a choice — its owner determines where it lives. I, on the other hand, do have a choice. My 'growth' is my responsibility. I intentionally began putting myself in bigger tanks. Was it intimidating? YES. Was it uncomfortable? YES. Did I want to go back at times? YES. You see, these tanks were filled with people better than me-had more money, was in better physical condition, possessed a stronger mentality, had better relationships on all sides, was more stable emotionally, and most of all, seemed extremely confident in life. It was tough to change but it was worth it. In life, we are either growing or dying. I'm not yet where I want to be but here's what I know and have found to be true 100% of the time. Enlarge your environment and you will enlarge your life. #environmentsmatter #neverstopgrowing #staytuned

Take a look around you right now! What does your "tank" look like? What do the people look like who are in it with you? What kind of attitudes do they have? What are their beliefs? What are their values? What are their thoughts? What do their conversations sound like? Do they talk about problems or do they talk about dreams? Circumstances or opportunities? If they are discussing dreams and opportunities, are they taking action toward them or do they just keep talking? How about their income? How much money are they making weekly, monthly, or annually? Are they in debt? Do they live above their means? Are they constantly saying to each other and their children things like, "we can't afford this" or "we'll never be able to do that"? *Whoa. Wait just a minute Chevis! You had me until you started this money talk. Money's not everything and I won't make decisions on who I will or will not be friends with based on money.* I get what you're saying and I agree. It's very shallow to choose friends based **only** on money or possessions. Still, we can't deny the brutal reality it can provide us with when it comes to the influence that our "tanks" have on our lives. One of the founding fathers of the personal growth and self-help industry, Jim Rohn, once said, "You are the average of the five people you spend the most time with."

> JIM ROHN, ONCE SAID, "YOU ARE THE AVERAGE OF THE FIVE PEOPLE YOU SPEND THE MOST TIME WITH."

Is he right? Let's do a personal case study and see for ourselves. First, I want to ask you to lower your money guard and understand this is not a money talk; this is a "tank" talk. We are simply using money as the mirror. Now, make a list of the top five people (if you're married, couples count as one) that you **consciously choose** to hang out with. Then, write down a guesstimate of anything that's measurable — their household incomes, their debt, the square-footage of their home, the number of bedrooms/bathrooms in it, their jobs, etc. Is it or is it not true that you and your "things" are an *average of* or are somewhat *similar to* those of your inner circle? Crazy how that happens right? Exactly how does it happen? Although it seems coincidental or accidental, it's not. It's actually an expression of our divine design as **NATURAL BORN CONFORMERS.**

IN THE BEGINNING GOD CREATED . . .
CONFORMERS

Conformity has been a grossly misunderstood subject. So much so, that some respected thought leaders and renowned authorities have passionately opposed it and have convinced many of their followers to do the same. The tragic consequence has been the mass production of generations who view victorious living more through a lens of retreat than pursuit. The intended offensive posture that we were created to carry gives way to a defensive one and we become known more by what we are against than what we are for, essentially, joining us to the ranks of those who seek security in place of opportunity, comfort in place of change, and the preference to enter the safe zone of burying talents above the risk of multiplying them (see Matthew 25:14-30). The anthem of those with such a view can be summed up in a quote I heard recently that said, *"the opposite of courage in our society is not cowardice, its conformity"*. That rolls off the tongue real good and if spoken to a crowd of people would no doubt elicit a few *ooh's* and *ah's* but it speaks against how we've been designed and causes us to place demands on ourselves and others that's absolutely impossible to fulfill.

Just as dogs bark, ducks quack, fish swim, and birds fly . . . humans conform. It is a part of our very essence put in place by the Creator Himself. Instructing us to avoid conformity is like teaching a dog he was made to swim. Can a dog swim? Yes. However, it's very unnatural for it do so. If left in the water too long the dog will eventually drown because he is attempting to be and do something he is not. Like the dog, many individuals have found themselves drowning in a pool of ineffectiveness by operating against their divine design and their self-esteem has been left to "foot-the-bill". The truth is conformity is one of the greatest powers available to us for transformation, whether personal or societal, if it is used correctly. Much like a loaded gun, it must be handled with the respectful realization that it can help us or hurt us depending on where it's aimed and the intention for its use. For us to begin to tap into this long neglected reserve of power, we have to go to the source of its origin — *In the beginning.*

As far as we know, the closest the world has ever been to perfect was during the creation of its first delegated authorities: Adam and Eve. These two were created with the intended purpose of serving as the prototypes for all humanity in both form and function. In God's divine order of creation, man ended up being sixth in line. This is an important place to pause and reflect because it is on the sixth day that He interrupted his usual pattern of creation. Up to this point, every created thing was established by Him speaking it into existence. In other words, He created something from nothing. Man, however, wasn't created this way as is recorded in Genesis 2:7: *God **formed** man of the dust of the ground.* Pay attention to the word highlighted in this verse — *formed.* God made something (i.e.: man) from something. Man is the form of another form further confirming that conformity truly is a part of our most prevailing instincts.

To conform means *to give the same shape, outline, or contour to.* God could've selected any existing substance for the construction of humanity. In His perfect wisdom, He chose dust. Why? Dust is pliable. It contains the unique ability to change shape and form. I can't think of anything in all of Creation that holds this type of capacity. What if He would've used the sun? Or a tree? Or grass? Or rocks? Or stars? Or light? Each of these were also a part of His creation, yet, none of them made the cut for the development of the first man and woman because they lacked the capacity to move in and out of form easily.

While we, the present generation of humanity, can't claim to be literal descendants of the dust, we can lay claim on being the ancestors of those who were. Meaning, we carry the same hereditary characteristics as them in that their existence pointed to something that existed before them. Think with me for a moment! How did you and I get here? There was a sperm and an egg. The two met and you and I were formed. Just as the mother and father of the entire human race couldn't exist without dirt, so it is that we couldn't exist without the sperm and egg. This fact alone is enough to bring infallible proof to the idea that we're working with, but it didn't stop at our conception. As we progressed and made our eventual debut on planet earth, we arrived as entirely dependent beings. We couldn't do anything for ourselves. It's easy to forget that our current competencies are the result of someone else's tireless efforts in assisting us toward becoming independent, functional beings. Simple tasks such as walking, talking, feeding ourselves, dressing ourselves, going to the restroom, or giving ourselves a bath were once impossible feats to accomplish on our own. Therefore, someone had to show us. They had to set a consistent example and we had to follow it, or mold ourselves to it, until it became a habitual part of our lives.

The inherent ability to conform has always been a crucial cornerstone of our growth and development. We were made to be the expression of another's impression. Acknowledging this as a reality of our nature exposes the flaws that we've long held high as immutable laws for triumphant living allowing us to re-position ourselves to work with the flow of our natural design instead of against it.

RISE AND FALL

The traditional concern of "the fall" has been on what was lost as a result. A closer look, however, reveals that what could be lost by partaking of the forbidden tree was not nearly as concerning to God as to what would be gained. It is in the dialogue between the serpent and Eve which led to the fall that we find what God was attempting to keep man from and what the enemy was after.

> *"Indeed, has God said that you shall not eat from any tree in the garden?" The woman said to the serpent, "From the fruit of the trees of the garden we may eat; but from the fruit of the tree which is in the middle of garden, God has said, 'You shall not eat from it or touch it, or you will die.' The serpent said to the woman, 'You surely will not die!* **For God knows that in the day you eat from it your eyes will be opened, and you will be like God, <u>knowing good and evil</u>"** (Genesis 3:1-5)

Man, along with his realm of influence (earth) gained the "knowledge of evil". Knowledge, in its Hebraic description, holds a bi-fold meaning: "to ascertain by seeing" and "to know by experience". Because "seeing" and "experience" can be multi-faceted, it's important to note in this particular passage that seeing is mental, not physical and experience is actual, not theoretical. By eating the fruit, evil was injected into the mind and motive of man, thereby, creating the needed pathway for it to enter into their magistracy as well.

Before this catastrophic event, the entire world harmonized in a perfect order called "good". This is proven at the end of God's seven day creative binge when it was recorded, *"God saw all that He had made, and behold, **it was very good"***. All of Creation was the flawless reflection of its Creator's "image" (see Psalm 136:1 and I Timothy 4:4). In fact, the place Adam and Eve called "home" was the Garden of Eden, which is translated as the Garden of Pleasure.

Pleasure is a unique word as it can find definitive roots as a noun, adjective, or verb. In other words, it has an all-inclusive meaning that sets itself apart by exhibiting an unusual ability to touch every aspect of life. This is no accident. God, the master orchestrator of life, knew exactly what He was doing when he made everything subject this idea. As a noun, pleasure is revealed as a person. As an adjective, it describes the person. As a verb, it becomes an expression of intimacy and influence with the person. The obvious common denominator is "The Person", who is God, who is called "good" (Psalm 107:1). To miss the Person is to miss the point. Apprehending the fullness of the garden requires us to have the Person present. Without it, we'll be unable to capture the true value of the world Adam and Eve were favored to "dress and keep" (Genesis 2:15). All things flowed together in harmonious agreement with the image it was born from. Looking through the lens of natural sight, it would've been impossible to see any sign of divided lines. There was no segregation, no separation, and most of all, no degradation. Our best imaginative attempts pale in comparison to what it must have been like. What we've come to refer to as "unusual visitations of God's Presence" was the "usual habitation of their daily being". They were surrounded by "good" and only "good". They were surrounded by God.

DON'T FIGHT IT, DIRECT IT

The question is not IF we will conform; the question is who, or what, will we conform to. Mark Twain said it best:

The person you will be in five years is based on the books you read and the people you surround yourself with today.

And, guess what? You hold the power — the power of decision to become whoever and whatever you want to be. All you have to do is be aware of what's inevitable and what's available. It doesn't matter how strong you think you are or how much will-power you think you have. If you expose yourself to a group of five people who are alcoholics, or drug addicts, or poverty stricken long enough, it's just a matter of time before you are number six.

Once again, we are natural born conformers — that's the inevitable recognition we must force ourselves to live with. The sooner you can accept it and stop fighting it, the sooner you can move into recognizing what's been made available to you through His name, His word, His blood, and, finally, His presence. And, once this happens, you will see yourself as He sees you and, most of all, you will begin to value yourself the way He values you. With the realization of what will cause your personal "stock" to rise and what has caused it to fall, you will be ready to be an immunizing force to the plagues, the problems, and the crisis of the world. You will be ready to make your mark on the world by not only knowing who you are, or what you're worth, but also by knowing why you're here.

REFLECTION QUESTIONS

#1. *Value is determined by who/what surrounds you.* Past or present, good or bad, can you attest to the truth of that statement and give a few examples (naturally and spiritually)?

#2. Are there any "tanks" that you need to get out of so that you can grow to the size of person God intended? How about any "tanks" that you need to get in?

#3. *Dogs bark, duck quack, and humans conform.* Have you been working against your natural design? What are some shifts you can make to start working with it?

MEDITATION/APPLICATION

The concept of environments being extreme influencers on our lives is nothing new. What is, however, is why. We've spent an inordinate amount of time trying to "abstain" from and the fight the "urges" within without realizing that it's an impossible battle to win because we are fighting against our God-given design as "conformers". Genesis 1:26 proves it, saying, "Let Us make man in Our image". Within that statement is not only "who" we've made to be, but also the "how" driving it: *images.* More simply stated, we conform to images, whether they be mental (internal) or environmental (external). Now you can see reason environments are so powerful: they provide "images" for us to see and what we see enough of we become. Change what you see and you'll change what you see.

For more in-depth information on practical, yet, powerful truths concerning this, study Malcolm Gladwell's, *The Power of Context,* theory from his book, *The Tipping Point.*

PART III
PURPOSE
WHY AM I HERE?

*"The greatest tragedy in life is not death,
But a life without purpose."*

—MYLES MUNROE

14

THE UNHOLY GRAIL

"Me, I want what's coming to me . . . The world, Chico, and everything in it."

—SCARFACE

*Go, make disciples of all nations, **baptizing them in the name of . . . the Holy Spirit**.* There has not been a more heavily debated or divisive topic than the baptism of the Holy Spirit. Those who choose to participate in such debates generally find themselves in one of two categories: relevance or evidence. Group A, which we'll call "the minority", argue over relevance with half contending the Holy Spirit is still for the present time and the other half contending that He is not. Group B, which we'll call "the majority", debate and divide over "evidence" with the contending differences being as numerous as the approximate 38,000 Christian denominations in existence today.

FREEDOM THROUGH CAUSE

Yes, you saw it correctly. 38,000 Christian denominations, or, more accurately stated, Christian *dissensions*. It's no wonder why we keep reproducing more confusion than conclusion, why we're not more appealing or attractive to those on "the outside", and why our impact still seems minimal at best, although, there are more churches (options) in existence today than we've ever had in history. We've yet to realize our contentions between one another are worthless — dead-end arguments — because, as is the case with one of the leading causes of denominational separations (the baptism of the Holy Spirit), we are attempting to reach common ground through *complements* instead of *causes*. A lesson I learned the hard way.

I came up in a group who holds to the doctrinal position that, "a person baptized in the Holy Spirit must speak in tongues as the initial evidence of his or her baptism". I was convinced of this myself for many years as it was difficult to question the passion behind their promotion or the supporting scripture they had backing it. I've stood in countless lines with many other hungry, desperate, Spirit-deprived believers begging God to baptize me in His Spirit. I know what it is to *fake* it in order to satisfy (and get away from the embarrassment of) the mature Spirit-filled believer who is laying hands on you shouting, "there He is, there He is, there He is, I can feel Him", all the while, feeling absolutely nothing myself (except maybe like I was going to hell for being a phony). I also know what it's like to try and *"force"* it — to strive and strain in fasting and prayer for days and hours on-end only to arrive at a belly on empty and needing to be fed instead of one that's full and over-flowing *with rivers of living water (see John 7:38,39)*. Trust me, I know all-too-well the constraints of a limited doctrine. One that simply doesn't fit when "trying it on". One that's too small and too limiting — almost like trying to squeeze into a pair of the ever-increasing-and-I-have-n o-idea-why skinny jeans that I see people wearing these days (kidding . . . not really). But, you know what else I know? The freedom of being released by an evidence based on *cause* as opposed to an evidence based on *complement*.

Quite frankly, I got sick and tired of being sick and tired — of coming up empty and feeling like I was in an endless cycle of disappointed outcomes. So, I set out on a journey that led me to a tri-fold discovery and revealed a world (and a newfound aim) much bigger than the one I had been in.

First, I uncovered eight other *gifts*, besides tongues, that seemed to be able to serve as decent candidates of baptismal proof (see I Corinthians 12:1-11). Second, I discovered there also nine *fruits of the Spirit* (Galatians 5:22,23) in addition to the "gifts" that I assumed grew like any other fruit — with water (aka: baptism) — and, considered, maybe, just maybe, if I could see any of these in myself then I could already be baptized. Finally (the most freeing of all), I discovered during Jesus' baptism when the *"Holy Spirit descended on Him, in bodily form, like a dove"*, that He didn't speak in tongues. You know what He did do however? The very next verse says He, *"began His ministry"* (Luke 3:21-23). I believe it was from this perspective that He released the concluding marching orders of the Great Commission: *Go, make disciples of all nations, baptizing them in the cause (name) of the Father, the Son, and the Holy Spirit.*

GONE WITH THE WIND

Tongues, along with the other spiritual gifts are important, and should be "earnestly desired" (see I Corinthians 14:1). Still, we must pursue them as complements to the cause and not the cause itself. Our disillusionment has not been that we've sought demonstrative evidence of a baptism; it's been that we've sought it through an effect that has promised and proven to be a *moving target*. I Corinthians 12:11 states,

> *"All of these (spiritual gifts) are the work of One and the same Spirit, **and He distributes them to each one, just as He determines**."*

Jesus also made reference to life 'in the Spirit' in a similar manner, describing it this way:

> *The wind blows wherever it wants. Just as you can hear the wind but can't tell where it comes from or where it is going, so you can't explain how people are born of the Spirit* (John 3:8 NLT).

Naturally speaking, we know how foolish it is to think we can "control" the wind and we would never attempt to do so in our everyday lives. Spiritually speaking, however, this is exactly what we've done. We've gotten *caught up in* and *confused* by the wind of a single event known as the "Day of Pentecost" (see Acts 2:1-4). We've attempted to trap (control) what it blew in (tongues of fire) in a box of denominational doctrine so that we can offer it as a predictable gift to our congregations of hungry and thirsty followers only to realize upon opening it that it has disappeared. Instead of anticipating the next "gust" from a different direction (with different evidence) we keep looking in the empty box trying to convince ourselves and those we're leading that although we can't see it, it's right there.

As the wise writer of Ecclesiastes says, *"chasing the wind is vanity"* (see Ecclesiastes 1:2,6) — a meaningless pursuit akin to a worthless and purposeless existence. This is what you can expect when you choose to chase and exalt complement: A life without cause. A life gone with the wind.

IMMERSION OF INFLUENCE

The cause (name) of the Father is to immerse (baptizes) us in our identity answering the question of *"Who Am I"*. The cause of the Son is to immerse in our inheritance answering the question of *"What Am I Worth"*. And, finally, the cause of the Holy Spirit is to immerse us in our influence answering the question of *"Why Am I Here"*.

While it's impossible to predict *how* the Holy Spirit is going to come, we can predict *why*. Any place you find Him (more specifically, His baptism) you will find a purpose and a partner. His cause is your cause. That doesn't necessarily mean He comes to strong-arm you into His agenda forcing you to be a partner of His purpose; it means He comes to expose you to yours (the one He helped God fashion for you before the world began) and make Himself a partner of it.

The events on the day of Pentecost, when those in the upper room received the baptism of the Holy Spirit were wild, to say the least. Included within it was *"a rushing mighty wind"*, *"tongues of fire"*, and an extremely bold, corrective, and inspired sermon from Peter *(see Acts chapter 2)*. But, do you know the *cause* for the events? In the previous chapter (Acts 1), Luke, the writer of the book, unveils it through quoting Jesus:

> *You will receive power when the Holy Spirit comes upon you. And you will be my witnesses, telling people about me every-where—in Jerusalem, throughout Judea, in Samaria, and to the ends of the earth* (Acts 1:8).

Did you see it? He came to give them *"power to be wit-nesses"*. Stated otherwise, He empowered them for a purpose. If you ever get a chance to attend an event or conference that I'm speaking at, you will often hear me say, "A Spirit-filled life is a purpose-filled life". Any supposed HS encounter that leaves you void of a higher pursuit, a greater ambition for living, an elevated vision, or a bigger dream than you had before it, you have right to question.

Just as Peter echoed,

> *"This is what was spoken by the prophet Joel: In the last days, God says, I will pour My Spirit on all people; your sons and daughters will prophesy, your young men will see visions, and your old men will dream dreams* (Joel 2:28, 29).

The Holy Spirit baptism, is, above all else, an immersion in visions and dreams. My question to anyone who is questioning their "could-be" baptismal experience is "when you got up off of the floor, did you walk away with more lint on your clothes or more purpose in your heart? When the goosebumps disappeared, did a new dream appear? When there were no more tears in your eyes, was there a new vision for your life"? That is the *cause* of His coming — to reveal to us the reason for the breath in our bodies, to instill in us a confidence to declare, "*for this reason I have been born and for this purpose I have come into the world*" (see John 18:37), so that, we, like Jesus during His baptism, can "*begin our ministry*".

> ANY SUPPOSED HS ENCOUNTER THAT LEAVES YOU VOID OF A HIGHER PURSUIT, A GREATER AMBITION FOR LIVING, AN ELEVATED VISION, OR A BIGGER DREAM THAN YOU HAD BEFORE IT, YOU HAVE RIGHT TO QUESTION.

A LANGUAGE BARRIER

The county I currently live in is Whitfield County — located in the foothills of the Blue Ridge Mountains in Northwest Georgia. We are referred by most as "*the Carpet Capital of the World*" due to being the headquartered home of several of the flooring industry's leading manufacturers. Being a predominantly manufacturing community has also made us home to a surprisingly large Hispanic community (*the state of Georgia's highest percentage for the past two consensus in a row*). Some areas show a percentage as high as 47%. Many of them have become my friends and many others have not, mainly because, there's a language barrier preventing us from having a conversation much less building a friendship or partnership. They don't know how to speak English and I don't know how to speak Spanish. With that said, I have the benefit of living in a daily reminder of just how important language is. Not only to our ability to connect and comprehend, but also to our ability to influence and transform.

The reason I tell this story is because I don't want a word like "ministry" to scare you, to shut you down, or to drive you away. It has been adopted, accepted, and promoted as a dialect of the church. And, worse yet, the accompanying interpretation has been that it references the "select, chosen, or favored few" who have been blessed with the more superior *sacred* call of God to full-time church work with the remaining being left as inferior financial supporters through their *secular* work. As I'm going to show you in the pages ahead, nothing could be further from the truth.

The languages we've created have not only placed a barrier between *us* and *them*; they have also placed a barrier between *them* — the brave few who have found a way to accept us in spite of us — and their *real* purpose. Even in their acceptance, they still end-up on another end of our self-made linguistic spectrum: pressured into the unfortunate pursuit of a more sanctified *"position"*. One that forsakes the *secular* for the *sacred*, trades the unholy grail of worldly influence for the holy grail of religious influence, and abandons the "high places" of society for the supposed "higher call" of souls. The resulting consequence thus far has been individual salvation without national transformation, positional enhancement without kingdom advancement, and revival monuments without revolutionary or reformational movements.

Does the concluded chaos of the religious dialect sound like an extreme theory to you? It shouldn't. Especially, when you consider what all language begets: interpretation. Not only have we interpreted our religious jargon in a way that's made *secular* work seem sinful and their workers inferior. We have also deceivingly called it "the language of God", which doesn't fit into where they are, so, they think they need to change where they are to fit in. They end up selling their multi-million dollar businesses, stepping down from their governmental ranks, hanging up their professional jerseys, or getting away from the bright lights of acting in order to go on the missions field or into full-time ministry because, let's be honest, they don't hear tongues in the boardroom of a business, or see people falling out in the Spirit on Wall Street, or hear scripture being quoted by potential govern-mental leaders during an election. As fate would have it, when they find themselves in one of "those" places, the only natural conclusion (interpretation) is "I must be in the wrong place — in the middle of a wrong purpose — because it doesn't "sound" like church (God) here and they leave. Then, after a short time, another dilemma emerges. They begin feeling claustrophobic from the overly crowded religious sector and guilt-ridden for being "tempted" by the desire to go back to their former "worldly" careers — a place where they actually mattered and where they were actually making a difference.

BEEN THERE, DONE THAT

Shame on us! Shame on the *by us, for us* language we've created! And, shame on how we've made the church *God's superior vehi-cle* of meaningful and impactful work. Vehicle to what exactly? Save the world? Who knows? It's usually left as an open-ended statement glorifying, once again, those with the "higher calling of Christ". Since its left open, let me be the first to fill in the blank. **The church is God's vehicle to . . . <u>equip the saints for every good work</u>** (see II Timothy 3:17; Ephesians 4:12-14). *"Every good work"* means there's more than one — such as the work of a business man, like Abraham; or the work of a king, like David or Solomon; or the work of a bodyguard, like Benaiah; or the work of craftsman and artistic designer, like Bezalel; or the work of an advisor and consultant, like Joseph or Daniel; or the work of a mother, like Mary. Changing the world is going to be hard to do if there's none left "in the world" to do it — if we are all in the church preaching and prophesying to each other because that's what we've translated (or have had translated for us) as being the more significant, superior, or sacred call.

At this point, the tone of my writing may seem more aggressive or intense. And, it is because I've been there and done that. 15 out of the 16 years of being a Christian I sat behind the wheel of a vehicle I really wasn't made for — a vehicle given to me by someone else, through prophetic words, so, it had to be God, right? It sounded nice, looked nice, smelled nice, felt nice, and drove nice, but, truthfully, it never was my car. It was theirs. In all fairness, I don't believe for a second that their intent was malicious or that their "words" were entirely false or made-up. I believe they did what most of us do when trying to help someone move onto a better, more productive, and more significant path: they prophesied, advised, and counseled from the perspective, with the language, and according to a purpose they knew — one they had the most experience with and felt they could equip me the best in.

You would think I'd be upset about this period of my life. I'm not at all. In fact, I'm so thankful for that time and for those people. God knows I needed it and them. Looking back, I'm fully convinced that it was never really about the accuracy of the words being spoken; it was about the revelation of purpose in them. While those giving me direction may not have been highly accurate, they were highly inspired (by the Holy Spirit, who comes, as you may recall, to give us purpose). I may not have walked away knowing exactly what my reason for living was; I did, however, away knowing I had a reason for living. And, it was all by divine design.

Ironically, it was that season — the season of *wrong words* that turned out to be the *right path*. Proverbs 19:21 says, *"Many are the plans in a person's heart, but it is the Lord's purpose that prevails"*. Translation: God has made it impossible to miss His purpose because He has made every "plan" (regardless if it's yours, someone else's for you, or the devil's) a path to it. Some paths may be the long-way-around, full of regret, pain, misguidance, sabotage, or confusion. Nevertheless, He promises that you will still get there (see Romans 8:28).

Some of their *plans* for me were to be "a shepherd in God's house", a "soul-saving, fire breathing evangelist", "a soldier in the Lord's army", and a "prophetic intercessor to the nations". God's *purpose* was to take me on a 14 to 15 year journey so that I could write this book to help you discover yours.

Before we get into that discovery, I need to be up-front with you. I'm not as interested in giving you a direct or specific prophetic word of what you should be doing with your life as I am in giving you some keys for identifying it yourself and sending you on your way to discover it (just like I've had to do and am still doing). Even if you and I were to sit down together and I was able to somehow see your life's purpose with pin-point accuracy and crystal-clear definition, I'm not real sure I would tell you what it is for fear that I may be robbing you of the greater good that only a personal process can give you and teach you: the ability to lean into and trust the greatest prophetic voice you will ever have — your own. With that, we come to the first of five keys to identifying purpose:

1. <u>PASSION</u>: *The Language of the Heart*

The language of the heart is passion. And, like any language, it comes with an innumerable amount of accents, which can range from love to hate, compassion to frustration, motivation to irritation, joy to anger, interest to indifference, excitement to boredom, admiration to rejection, and everything in between. Without a doubt, these accents can make it somewhat tricky to navigate. Even so, we must discipline ourselves to learn because regardless of how it sounds when it speaks, when it comes to our purpose, there is not and never will be a more reliable voice than the one in our hearts.

What do you love? I'm not talking the things you say you love because someone told you should, or the things you force yourself to love because someone you love (a spouse, a friend, a parent, a child) loves it. I mean what do you really love? What gets you going, excites you, or causes you to lose sleep when you know you're getting to do it the next day? What have you done that you can't stop thinking about since you've done it? Where have you experienced a timeless-awareness — where eight, ten, or twelve hours didn't seem long enough; where you wished it could go on forever?

What do you hate? Again, let me clarify! I'm not talking about the political party or the president you *act* disgusted with when you're trying to fit into a political discussion with a group of friends who are also acting to sound intelligent. I'm asking, what do you hate deeply? What pisses you off on a level that you have to be you, in your physical body, to truly comprehend it? What injustices do you see that you can't tolerate — that you think about wanting to confront and destroy?

Don't be shocked if answers emerge from each set of questions presented. As vastly different as they are, every one of our hearts carry the ability to love deeply and to hate deeply, to show compassion and to show aggression, to soften and to harden. The beginning of knowing why you are here starts with accepting the dominating accents that your heart speaks with.

Some, like Martin Luther King, Jr. will enunciate themselves with more anger, hate or aggression while others, like Mother Teresa, may express themselves more through the opposites. I think we can agree both were world-changing, society shifting, planet shaking reformers, although each did it "in their own way". You see, we can't (and shouldn't try to) control how our hearts speak, but we can control how we hear (see Luke 8:17,18).

Disney released a children's movie this past November (2016) called *Moana*. Since then, it has taken the world by storm with both children and adults alike. The Brooks household is no exception. We absolutely love it. What started out as a trip to the movie with my daughter to get a little quality time in quickly became an all-time favorite of my own. Obviously, our attractions are for very different reasons. Avery is drawn to it for its entertainment factors — music, songs, cute little animals, action — while I'm drawn to it for its inspirational and spiritual factors — quotes, finding your calling, facing your fears, taking risks, and going after your dreams. Since I don't want to ruin it for you if you haven't seen it, I'm not going to go into great detail on the plot or summary. I will, however, let you in on a small part that fits perfectly into our *"passion"* discussion. At point during the movie, Moana finds herself wrestling with her "calling"- in a tug-o-war between the safe and familiar (the island of Motunui) or the dangerous and unfamiliar (sailing beyond the reef). She, like many of us, has been told by those around her (many of which love her) who she should be and what she should want for her life. Inside, however, she feels a pull to something else — something much bigger. As she struggles with the growing tension within, she eventually has a conversation with the "island crazy lady": her super-spiritual, super-weird grandmother, *Gramma Tala*:

> Moana (frustration @ it's peak from her Gramma's vagueness): *"If there's something you wanna tell me, just tell me! (Slight Pause) Is there something you want to tell me?"*

> Gramma Tala *(looks back @ Moana, smirking):* *"Is there something you want to hear?"*

Let me present the same question to you: **Is there something you want to hear?** Whatever you want to hear, God is already saying. It's in what you desire the most. Desire is a two-part Latin word: *"De-",* meaning *"of"* and *'-Sire'* meaning *'father'.* Translation: that (the voice, the emotion, the longing) which is in your heart is of the Father. You miss it, I miss it, the majority misses it more times than not because it sounds a lot like us — like our voice — and we're waiting on permission to pursue it never realizing the desire is the permission. And, the voice is yours. It's the voice of the Father speaking through the accent of your heart. All that's left is the courage to trust it and the confidence to pursue it.

2. **PROBLEM(S)**: *Calling in Chaos*

One of the most familiar and inspirational lives in all of history is Martin Luther King, Jr. He will forever be marked as one of the greatest reformers to have ever walked the earth. The willingness he had to step out as a hated minority, looking demons of prejudice in the eyes while intentionally placing himself in front of hostile crowds in order to become the voice of equality makes him, without a doubt, the epitome of courage. His unwavering fight for freedom is no less than impressive as it paved the way for a culture we now consider normal. The only real way to bring honor to his life is to make sure his story is never forgotten. Regardless of color or ancestral background, we all have been greatly impacted by his fight. He wasn't a literal soldier. Figuratively, however, we would be hard pressed to find another individual — past, present, or future — who more closely resembled one. He waged violent wars on the battlegrounds of injustice against the enemy of racism with the weapon of his dream. Although he died without personally experiencing the fulfillment of his heart's cry, his fight doesn't fall on empty ground of wishful thinking, nor is it still a prisoner of "one day". We are the "one day" of his dream — a living testament of heirs who get to hold in our hands the tangible reality of what He held in his heart and so artistically painted a word picture of during his monumental "I have a dream" speech on August 28, 1963.

Mobilizing a movement to put an end to racism, demanding justice and liberty for all, and giving one of the most moving speeches ever from the steps of the Lincoln memorial to a crowd of 250,000 people sounds like the make-up of a man who had found his life's purpose doesn't it? MLK was that man. He had found the purpose for why he was born and was living in the middle of his greatest passion, yet, there's more on display than we realize. His life and legacy teaches us that a purpose-filled life will be a life that's not only full of passion, but is also full of problems.

Problems are the part of purpose nobody really wants to talk about or consider. It's much more exciting and much less stressful to live in the anticipation of being a world-changer than it is to actually live in the middle of the issues that need to be changed. Even so, it doesn't remove the fact that just as MLK's calling emerged from the chaos of his day, so will ours. And, it will vary greatly from one to another — in size, in location, and in category.

Some will identify their purpose through societal issues, like racism, leading them to become equality reformers. Others will identify theirs through personal issues, like a fatherless upbringing, leading them to become identity reformers. Others, still, will identify theirs through first-time parenting issues, like potty-training, leading them to become potty-training reformers. Whether it be on a home-scale or a world-scale, the issue is not the size of *this* problem compared to *that* problem. The issue is realizing that the problems you feel a passion for are those you've been "anointed" to solve (see Isaiah 61:1-4). At the end of the day, solutions are solutions. As long as you are bringing them in an area you love, then you are living in your purpose.

3. <u>PERSONALITY</u>: *God don't make no mistakes!*

The voice we hear within sounds like us because IT IS us. The expressions (passions) of the heart come through the accents of our individual personalities. While personalities can be similar, they'll never be exact. It is this undebatable truth that allows us to declare and to believe with full certainty that there is no such thing as "Plan B" in God's kingdom or in His calling.

A common scare tactic that's been used to get people to protect and value their purpose is "God will raise up another to accomplish His work if the one currently carrying it doesn't steward it right". My first issue with this approach is that it induces fear, which doesn't come from God (see II Timothy 1:7). The second and main issue I have with it is that it makes it seem as if God actually has a *plan B* — as if He were capable of making a mistake in *plan A*. Those who use this method can argue from the reference of David replacing Saul all day long, but, it's an argument that hasn't taken into consideration the "other side" of the story: Saul's.

The story of David and Goliath is an extremely familiar story (to believers and unbelievers alike). An innumerable amount of messages have been preached on it. And I've even preached it myself, yet, we all speak from the same side of the story: David's. Walk with me for a moment and see, in light of making our point, the story from Saul's perspective.

Before the battle with the giant, David comes to Saul and Saul gives him his own armor to go into battle with. There's just one problem: the armor didn't fit.

> "*David* **tried to walk but he couldn't** *because he wasn't use to wearing them. I can't fight with all this," he said to Saul, "I'm not used to it". So he took it all off* (I Samuel 17:39 GNT).

The way we usually interpret the story is don't try to be like anyone else. Stick to what you know and what God has given you. Even if it doesn't look mighty in the eyes of the world, it is mighty in God. This interpretation is accurate and needs to be preached many more times, but, we must recognize David's revelation was also accurate for Saul. While Saul's armor may not have fit David, it did fit Saul. What's the revelation? **<u>NO ONE CAN WEAR YOUR ASSIGNMENT LIKE YOU!!!</u>**

Think about this! Which one is more effective for battle — the armor or the slingshot? Obviously, the armor. A willingness to make an argument for the slingshot because it was in the "anointed hands" of David is foolish. Don't forget Saul was also "anointed" by the same person as David (Read I Samuel 10). For those unwilling to see there's more to the story than what meets the religious eye, I will ask the question a different way. Considering that both David and Saul were God's "anointed", which weapon is more effective for battle? An anointed man with armor is always better equipped than an anointed man with a slingshot. It is equally as foolish and blind to contend that it wasn't about anointing at all, rather, it was about David's extreme faith and trust in God. After all, His battle cry became *the battle is the Lord's*. Could it be that David made this his war cry, not because he was so full of faith, but because he knew he wasn't *equipped*? The hidden insinuation of David's cry was the battle was not his own. The battle had to become the Lord's because the one (Saul) best equipped for it was afraid to fight. With all my heart I believe in, celebrate, and acknowledge David's courage and trust in God. It proved to be monumental for the entire nation of Israel. Nevertheless, it still doesn't remove the fact that he stepped into a situation he wasn't equipped for and he knew it.

God's gift and call upon Saul's life was irrevocable (Romans 11:29). Irrevocable means "not able to be changed, reversed, or recovered; final". There are two points illustrated in this irreversible truth regarding God's call. First, a clear point should be made that Saul was God's choice just as David was God's choice and the idea that David was raised up to "replace" him makes God a liar and David a second class copy. And, we know, *"God is not a man who lies, or a son of man who changes his mind. Does He speak and not act, or promise and not fulfill? I have indeed received a command to bless; since He has blessed, I cannot change it (Numbers 23:19,20 HCSB)"*.

The discipleship training that I received about "taking from Saul and giving to David" tormented me for years. It's both frustrating and freeing

> THERE ARE NO SUCH THINGS AS "REPLACEMENT" PROMISES.

to know that it was incorrect. This fear-driven agenda must stop. When obedience is the product of fear, law and religion are conceived; when it is the product of faith, grace is born. Law and religion require, while grace enables (Bill Johnson). The former dilutes my relationship with God as it places me in a striving posture to gain acceptance through works. The latter enhances my relationship with God as it places me in a posture of acceptance empowering me to live *from* the acceptance instead of *for* it. With that being said, let us graciously live with this truth: There are no such things as "replacement" promises.

To believe in such is filth. It reduces God down to our size and gives His promises an opportunity to be counted as mistakes. In the words of my southern ancestors, "God don't make no mistakes". He is perfect. . . . PERIOD! Anything he does is perfect, His call is perfect, and His promises are perfect. We are not replacements or copies. "*We are God's masterpiece. He has created us anew in Christ Jesus, so we can do the good things he planned for us long ago (Ephesians 2:10 NLT)*". Accept it! Live from it! Pour into it! Stir it up! Empower it! **You are an original and nobody can do "you" like you can do "you". There is no plan B when He calls you. It's a reckless abandon on his part. His chips are all in . . . ON YOU.**

4. <u>PATH</u>: *Start Here, Go Anywhere!*

As we made reference to earlier in this chapter, God makes it impossible to miss His purpose for our lives because He has created many plans, or paths, to it. Often times, purpose and plans get placed into the same category and are referred to as the same thing when really they are not. Purpose is the destination. Plans are the routes (paths) to it. Although, we've touched on it, I still want to go deeper with you so that you can free yourself from being anxious over whether or not you're going to "miss" His destiny (purpose) for your life. For my own peace of mind, you need to know the following information is meant to give you permission to stop worrying, not permission to start living without restraint. *For the LORD watches over the path of the godly, but the path of the wicked leads to destruction (Psalm 1:6 NLT).*

I want you look down right now! The place you're standing– the present — is the path to your purpose. And, it doesn't matter what the ground underneath your feet looks like — whether it's a prison floor that Nelson Mandela would've been looking at during a certain period (27 years) of his life. Or, whether it's the floor of a failed business that Henry Ford would've been staring at with his first two car companies. Or, whether it's the floor of a locker room that Michael Jordan would've saw after being cut from the basketball team his sophomore year of high school. Or, whether it's the floor of section-8 government housing for an extremely low-income, struggling Pastor like Bishop T.D. Jakes. Where you are is the path, as bleak and hopeless as it may seem, that God is using and will use to get you to your purpose.

Nelson Mandela went on to become South Africa's first black elected head of state and first democratically elected President. Henry Ford rose from the ashes of his failures, founded the Ford Motor Company, through which he revolutionized the automobile industry by creating a simple, reliable, and, most of all, affordable car, that the average American worker could afford — making him one of the richest men to have ever lived. Bishop TD Jakes' view has changed a little as he now finds himself preaching on and in many of the world's largest, most iconic stages and venues (including his own estimated 20,000 member church, *The Potter's House*, in Dallas, TX), "fathering" some of the biggest names in Hollywood and professional sports, writing best-selling book after best-selling book, and, now, quickly making his mark as a movie producer. Michael Jordan? Enough said.

My friend Richie Hughes wrote a book in 2011 titled, *"Start Here, Go Anywhere"*. The premise of the book is no matter where you are today, with God's help and through leveraging the power of choice, you can go anywhere. The aforementioned men proved it. And, they are not alone. What do these men and those like them — with similar stories — have in common? What is it that we should be drawing from their testimony? Some would say, "Nothing. They're lucky and I'm not". That "some" would be dead wrong. These men were not lucky; they were decisive. They all decided, in the motivational words of Bishop Jakes, to make '"their setbacks a setup for a spring back". They decided not to stay down after getting knocked down. They decided to see their present realities as *perfect starting places* instead of *final resting places*.

Please don't die in the "defeat" that you've come to assume is your destiny. I know you want it to be different. I know you wished it could be easier. I know you regret the decision(s) you've made (or that someone else made for you) that brought you "here". "Here" is where you are. It's not where you have to stay, but it is where you have to start. The important thing is not that you know exactly where to go. The important thing is that you GO (see Hebrews 11:8). When you "go", you may have to "go" from (start from) a divorced path, an abandoned path, a painful path, a delayed path, a regretful path, a scary path, an unclear path or an unfair path. You "go" knowing regardless of the path there is a way to your purpose from it because the guide of purpose — the Holy Spirit — lives in you. You "go" believing the same command and promise which rested on the father of "goers", Abraham, rests on you as well:

Now lift up your eyes and look from the place where you are, northward and southward and eastward and westward; for all the land which you see, I will give it to you and to your descendants forever (Genesis 3:14,15).

What does that mean? All directions are covered. No matter which one you take —north, south, east, west — it is *the* direction to your purpose.

5. <u>PLATFORM</u>: *Where's Your Mountain?*

Up to this point, the emphasis has been on our purpose as individuals. We've learned how to use our own unique passion, our own unique personality, our own unique problem, and our own unique path to identify what our own unique reason for breathing may be. In this final section, we're going to stay in the flow of the "individual" picture by talking about the individual platform or platforms that we could go into. And, we're going to use it to connect us to the "bigger picture": *that the kingdoms of this world become the kingdoms of our Lord and Savior Jesus Christ.*

Nobody is a purpose in, of, or unto themselves. Every individual's mission is a part of and subject to the greater mission. Kris Vallotton puts it this way: *"When you're in submission to His primary mission, you will be commissioned".* Finding and living in your purpose with a co-mission mindset will guard you from a life of *"selfish-ambition or vain conceit"* (see Philippians 2:3). It will also keep you from advancing or building the wrong kind of kingdom: the kingdom of the flesh.

One of my good friends, Stan Lester (who also happens to be my Pastor), often says, "We are all characters in God's story, He is not a character in ours". Yet again, another great reminder that although we can speak and search in terms of what makes us unique as individual characters, the reality is we are still only a part of a much bigger narrative than our own personal lives.

Oddly, the very things that set us apart are the same things that connect us. That's the nature of purpose. It operates much like a battery in that a positive and negative must co-exist for the "charge" (the over-arching purpose) to be accomplished and seen. The same is true for us. For the overarching mission of *"Heaven on Earth"* to be completed, the various platforms of purpose, what Lance Wallnau has termed 'The Seven Mind-Molders of Society' (Religion, Government, Family, Education, Media, Entertainment, and Business), must be individually identified and co-missionally invaded.

This is why I'm such a fan of Dr. Wallnau and the *"Seven Mountain Strategy"* that he has promoted for the better half of a decade now. It is a strategy that demands a transition in where our focus has been so that our impact can go where it was meant to go and be what it was meant to be. A transition where a church focus shifts to a kingdom focus, where *ministry* shifts from being a clerical word designated by-the-few-for-the-few to being a missional work assigned to all for all, where 'worldly' positions shift from being an unholy call to a call to the unholy, and where the measurement of success shifts from conversions (of souls) to occupation (of territory). These shifts, should we be brave enough to embrace them, will allow us to play the game at the level it was meant to played — *for entire nations* — because the wealthy business man will no longer be ashamed of climbing to the top of his mountain in the name of Jesus. The young man who wishes to be President or Prime Minister of his country will no longer feel the need to abandon that call and his country to be a missionary in another country to another group of people. The teacher who thought she needed to be a good behind-the-scenes-Pastor's-wife will step to the forefront of her field as a voice of educational reform that truly leaves "no child left behind". The professional football player will retire his bishop's gown, pick his jersey again, and reach far more in this uniform on a Sunday than he ever could have in the other. The mainstream media leaders will shift from lies to truth, from bad news to good news as they begin to understand that evangelists are not the only ones whose calling is to promote a gospel (aka: good news) agenda. The stay-at-home-mom whose ministry has become raising the youth of her own home will shift from believing that motherhood is the sacrifice of a former career to the stewardship of future generations. She will see that her duties extend far beyond being the manager of "good manners" into being a manager of "great missions".

GOING PRO IN GOING INTO THE ALL THE WORLD

In 2010, the NCAA (National College Athletic Association) released a commercial celebrating 100 years of the student-athlete. If you're an avid Saturday consumer of college football during the fall you'll remember it. The commercial opened with a statistic: *There are over 360,000 NCAA student-athletes.* Then, it followed with the promotional tag-line for every "100 years of student-athlete" commercial thereafter: *And, just about all of us will be going pro in something other than sports.*

There is zero-doubt in my mind that some of you will be called into the religious sector — maybe as a Pastor, a Christian Author, a Missionary, or an Evangelist. And, we need you there. However, we need you there *celebrating* (and equipping) "the day of the saints" instead of *celebritizing* (and exalting) "the work of those in ministry" because "just about all of us (7.5 billion people on the earth at the present time) will be going pro is something other than full-time ministry".

REFLECTION QUESTIONS

#1. Do you believe that a person absolutely **must** speak in tongues as **the** initial evidence of the Holy Spirit's baptism?

#2. Have you ever been baptized in the Holy Spirit? What were the after-effects? Did you *see* — dream of, envision — a better life?

#3. What are some of your celebrations and/or concerns embracing purpose as the Holy Spirit's *cause*?

#4. Have you ever felt that the "Holy Grail" of *calling* was full-time church ministry? Now, that you know there are other options of *callings*, what adjustments do you feel need to make in your personal approach or in your teaching (if you're a pastor)?

#5. Do you feel the church (or *your church* if you're a pastor) has done a good job at equipping the saints for "every good work" and not just "church work"? Why or why not? If not, what can we do to change that?

MEDITATION/APPLICATION

Read Revelation 11:15, Habakkuk 2:14, Isaiah 2:1-3:

Especially considering the passage in Isaiah, we can see that one potential strategy for this prophecy being fulfilled is to help others identify their "mountain" and take possession of it. What are some other practical strategies we should consider implementing in order to mobilize such a movement? How can we work together to do it?

15

INTENTION DEFICIT DISORDER

"Never ignore a gut feeling, but never believe it's enough."

–ROBERT HELLER

An inspirational life is a legacy worth pursuing. Making that dream a reality starts with knowing what inspires us as inspiration always reproduces inspiration. In the words of entrepreneur and best-selling author, Janet Grace Shier, *"What moves you will move others"*. That's what the last chapter was all about: discovering what moves you through identifying the **instinctive** passions of your heart so that you can determine where your platforms lie and begin carving out the path to get yourself there in order to solve the problems therein. With that, there's something you must know. Instinct alone will not be enough to complete *your* mission. **There's a big difference in finding your purpose and fulfilling your purpose**. To finish, you will have to tap into the *other part* of yourself — the often overlooked and under-celebrated practical part of yourself: your intention.

GAINING EQUILIBRIUM

We can all agree and attest to the fact that instinct is a very powerful trait. What makes it dangerous, though, is that it's reactive in nature possessing no real boundaries. Those who operate through instinct alone (animals) have proven to be highly unpredictable.

Lions are my most favorite animals on the planet. I am drawn to their many symbolisms such as royalty, leadership, courage, and strength. As captivated as I am by these powerful creatures, I wouldn't dare bring one home as a pet to introduce to my three and half year old daughter. The reason is obvious. Even if I were to get it as a cub, train it to be "nice", and show it all the love and attention in the world there would still come the inevitable day where its instincts will get the best of it and someone will be seriously hurt or, worse, killed. The lion would be punished to the maximum penalty of death by me or someone else, but the truth is he didn't know what he was doing and had no way of controlling it because lions are entirely instinctive creatures. He would simply be doing what is natural for him to do with no realistic way of governing it.

While God wanted us to embody all of the incredible benefits of instinct, He was also keen to its unpredictability if left to act alone. Therefore, He added within our coding an accompanying buffer to serve as a taming, yet, predictable partner and guide. This buffer came in the same *breath* as its counterpart when it was breathed into man making him a living soul (Genesis 2:7). The word for it is "Neshammah" and it's defined as "divine inspiration and intellect". So, humanity is part-instinct and part-intention. Although nowhere near as discussed or desired, it is the intentional part of us that sets the human being apart from the other "life beings", thereby, making us God's highest form of creation.

Stewarding these two as co-existing realities can be challenging, especially when paired with a belief system deeply cemented in a cultural conditioning that's made eventual enemies out of predetermined allies. The result of such belief systems is that we remain plagued by a spiritual vertigo that continuously causes the world around us to seem as if it's spinning out of control and we find ourselves left in a state of disempowerment, discouragement, and disillusionment. All the while, we carry on accepting these things as our chosen lots in life without questioning the source behind our '*dis*' style of life. Like it or not, we are in a very real war with a very real enemy who is skilled at what he does. He is not a natural source and will not be defeated through natural means (II Corinthians 10:3-5). With that said, a confrontation is in order.

THE ART OF WAR: LEVERAGING "BEFORE"

The serpent is introduced to us as being "craftier than any beast of the field". Now, I'm convinced this is not to be taken as a statement of praise regarding his "talent". It is given, instead, to warn us of his "tactics". In his book, The Art of War, Sun Tzu writes, *"If you know the enemy and know yourself, you need not fear the result of a hundred battles. If you know yourself but not the enemy, for every victory gained you will also suffer a defeat. If you know neither the enemy nor yourself, you will succumb in every battle".* Positioning one's self for victory in battle, whether it be natural or spiritual, does not begin on the battlefield. It begins off of it. Again, echoing the writings of Sun Tzu, *"Every battle is won or lost before it is ever fought".*

As a football coach, everything starts in the film room. Without fail, with each new game, we would come together as a coaching staff and start, by first, studying our opponent. We wanted to "know" them — their strengths, their weaknesses, and their tendencies. This process was critical to every new game week as it set the course for our entire agenda leading up to and through the game from practice schedules, to player preparation, to play calling. What were we doing? We were doing our best to position ourselves for victory BEFORE the battle began.

In the natural, this is a common practice among proven winners in nearly every sphere of society. Surgeons spend many years in preparation ***before*** operating on a patient. Lawyers spend many hours preparing their arguments to present their cases ***before*** walking into a courtroom. Coaches, as used in my example, watch countless hours of the same film over and over and over ***before*** walking onto the practice field, much less the game field. Business owners had a business plan ***before*** they had a business. No matter the sphere, planning and preparation is required if success is desired. In the words of Benjamin Franklin, *"if you fail to plan, you are planning to fail"*.

When it comes to the spiritual side of life, however, it seems the exact opposite is true for many of us. We live plagued by an intention deficit-disorder approaching the days of our lives without a plan in the name of "trusting our gut", never realizing that this "gut trusting approach" is going to leave us with a "gut-wrenching reality" : we are presenting ourselves unprotected, unequipped, and unprepared for the inescapable battle awaiting us. Paul gave a strong command in his letter to the Ephesians, writing:

> *Finally, be strong in the Lord and in the strength of His might. Put on the full armor of God, so that you will be able to stand firm against the **schemes of the devil**. For our struggle is not against flesh and blood, but against the rulers, against the powers, against the world forces of this darkness, against the spiritual forces of wickedness in the heavenly places* (Ephesians 6:10-12).

While many points can be taken from this passage, there is one main idea that serves as the over-arching purpose of his command: **that we would be able to stand firm against**

the wiles of the devil. Paul and Sun Tzu had something in common — they both knew that victory began by being prepared and more importantly, by being prepared, first, with *"knowing"* your enemy.

The enemy has a weapon of mass destruction that has wreaked havoc on generation after generation from the days of Adam and Eve until now. He has used it so effectively and so consistently that we've fallen prey to accepting it as the norm and worse yet we have taught our children to do the same. It gives confidence the appearance of pride and makes humility look weak. It defines dreams and desires as selfish ambitions and turns the expression of gifts into vain conceit. It exalts theory above experience, the opinion of man above the plan of God, poverty above prosperity and feelings above faith. It convinces us that the top is the bottom and the bottom is the top. It tells us that we can love without liking, forgive without forgetting, and reap without sowing. It is everywhere and every one of us have been impacted by it. What is "it"? LIES.

In one of His conflicts with the Jews, Jesus says about devil, *"There is no truth in him. Whenever he speaks a lie, he speaks from his own nature, **for he is a liar and the father of lies**"* (John 8:44). Often times, his lies are difficult to detect because they are offered with an element of truth attached. A simpler way of saying this is he "distorts the truth". Recall the dialogue with Adam and Eve where told them, *"You will surely not die. God knows that when you eat the fruit you will be like him."* The distortion was they were already made in image of God and this "truth" blinded them to the lie they were presented with.

Later, while tempting Jesus in the wilderness, the devil used the phrase *"It is written"* in an effort to distract him with an ever-so thin layer of truth from the hidden agenda of destruction that he was after. As we all know the word is called "truth" (John 17:17). Today, we are faced with the same dilemma of a higher quality. The present scheme of his temptation has evolved from an outside-in strategy to an inside-out. His ultimate goal is to make us a "divided house" (Matthew 12:22-28) by taking what is "true" about our inherent make-up and turning it against itself.

"Divided" literally means "to separate (distinguish) one part from another'". By getting us to distinguish between the strengths and weaknesses (truths) of our dual nature, he is able to make our lives very unstable. Stabilizing ourselves for victory begins the moment we become clear on, embrace, and learn how to use the entirety of our heavenly disposition: instinct as well as intention. And, we begin doing that by understanding that . . .

1. Instinct is not above intention and intention is not above instinct

Due to the vast benefits that come with instinct or intention as components of our God-given nature, it's easy to separate them while trying to highlight the power residing within each. This is a point well proven by the number of books that have been written by many great authors on one or the other as the main topic. While we can assume it was never the pursuit of these authors to create a conflict, the resulting problem in separating these "twin powers" is that it has led to a grudge match of internal and external comparisons that result in making them and their "carriers" (us) enemies of one another.

Those with a more instinctive bent are generally seen as the "risk takers" and "dreamers" while those who are more inclined toward intention are seen as being more "realistic, calculated, and logical". The first says, "ready, fire, aim" and the other says "ready, aim, fire". As you can see, depending on which message resonates with us, we choose the tribe we feel we are most like or the tribe we feel we most want to become like and begin the subtle process of turning either from or against the "other".

The truth is instinct is not above intention and intention is not above instinct. They each have an immense value in our make-up and was purposed by God to work together with one's strength complementing the other's weakness and vice versa. The leap-without-looking mantra of the instinctive need the logical perspective of the intentional in order not to *leap* to a premature death. On the hand, the "calculated" approach of the intentional need the faith and courage of the instinctive in order to move from planning to action. Both are powerful weapons that no enemy can withstand if we can train ourselves to bring them and their functionality into unity.

2. Instinct resides in the "Right Brain". Intention resides in the "Left Brain".

The devil's credited "craftiness" in our introduction to him is revealed in his ability to implement well-designed "schemes" in the pursuit of his objectives. Another word for "scheme" in Paul's writing is "deceit". Deception performs best in the presence of confusion and we know the enemy is *"the author of confusion"* (I Corinthians 14:33). But, what is confusion? While there are many ways to define it, confusion is nothing more than a conflict of perspectives and perspective is simply *"a point of view"*. Depending on the *"view point"*, it's easy for two people to *see* the same thing and come to totally different conclusions. Take the following sentence for example:

They fed her dog meat

The sentence can be read as *normal* or *nasty* depending on the dominate perspective. Either "they fed HER dog meat" or "they fed her DOG meat". Who was fed? Her or the dog? Obviously we're having a little fun here, yet, this is no laughing matter when the confusion tends to be more internal than external.

I'm sure most of us have heard the term "getting our wires crossed". This is the simplest way to explain how the enemy works. He is very competent at "crossing the wires" of our internal perspectives. Perhaps this is why James warned us "a double-minded man is unstable in all of his ways" (James 1:8).

Again, instinct and intention were both given with the purpose of helping us, not hurting us. The challenge is they operate in completely separate hemispheres, therefore, offering us completely different "ways of seeing" the world around us. **Instinct resides in the "Right Brain" hemisphere while intention resides in the "Left Brain" hemisphere.** Keep in mind this is one brain with two separate functions. Take a look at the drawing:

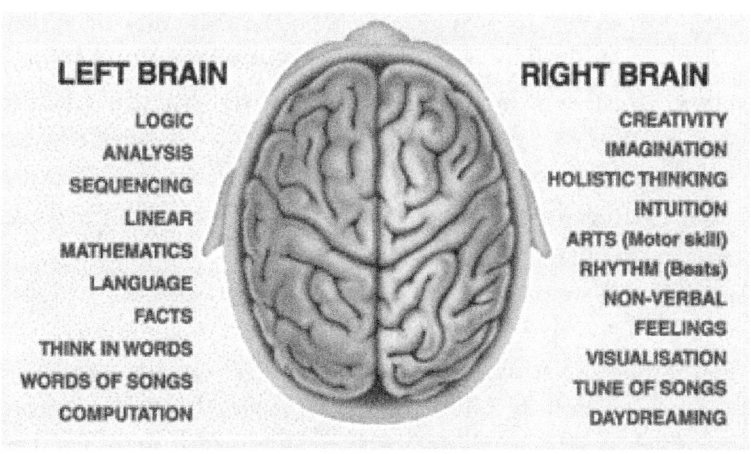

As you can see, the perspectives of the "instinctive, right brain" hemisphere and the perspectives of the "intentional, left brain" hemisphere couldn't be more different from one another. God's plan was that these differences would be complementary instead of conflicting — that we would be an "undivided (aka: unconfused) house". I believe each of us have experienced moments in our lives where these differences have been *the best of friends* and *the worst of enemies*. By understanding the origin of it all, we'll find that we are in more control over how they will operate with each other than we like to take credit for as it's always easier to blame outside influences than take personal responsibility.

We've been taught to see the devil as our enemy and we spend, or more accurately stated, waste our days "binding, loosening, and casting out" things that are nothing more than smoke-and-mirror deceptions keeping us from identifying who and where the real enemy is. Let me break it down for you: ENEMY. EN-E-MY. IN-NER-ME. INNER ME. WE. ARE. OUR. OWN. WORST. ENEMY. We've tricked ourselves into thinking that "enemy" is the role the devil seeks in our lives. Although he is rightfully referred to as our adversary, that is not the primary title that he desires to carry. In fact, his plans hold a greater chance of success if he can shift that title from him to us making us an enemy of, against, and within ourselves. This is why he operates through ever so subtle schemes of confusion to move us into a state of "double-mindedness" which leads us to a stance of "unstableness" (James 1:6-8).

A divide in our inner world is created when logic views creativity as messy, analysis makes a worthless fairy-tale out of imagination, big picture, holistic thinking becomes frustrated with the slow paced planning of sequencing, intuitive gut feelings are questioned by linear fact findings, mathematical number crunching takes precedence over forward motion, and daydreams, or visions, aren't given permission to be taken seriously because there's no computed, detailed path toward the destination. Little by little, we begin to take on the same self-deprecating posture as Adam and Eve who turned their eyes on themselves and felt "shameful" over what they saw (Genesis 3:7 NLT). As this happens, we slowly begin to forfeit the rights of our influences through inaccurate self-judgments of worth and capabilities. We eventually stop defining ourselves by the "image of God" and lower the standard of our identities to the world around us instead of the world above us.

From the days of the fall until now, this has been the norm. Starting now. Starting here. IT ALL CHANGES. Our true worth, capability, and identity was never really lost. It was buried beneath a pile of lies by "the Father of lies" himself in conjunction with our own choice to participate in those lies. All that's needed is a revelation of truth and a revolution of thought in conformity with that truth to be free. That's what this book is about — exposing lies, revealing truth, and setting you free to become the REAL you. You are instinctive and you are intentional.

3. Instinct gives us our calling. Intention gives us control.

Over the last ten years, I've had the privilege of being married to an incredible woman with an incredible voice. As we say in the south, "that woman can SANG". I've watched her sing solos and I've watched her sing with groups. In either situation, I am amazed at her talent but for totally different reasons.

In her solo performances, she's leading a song and that takes real courage. All eyes and all ears are on her. Being live, on stage, in front of crowd is a place that offers very little forgiveness for mistakes. Forget the words and everybody in the room knows it (especially when it's blasted on the big screen for everyone to see and sing along with). Sing too high or too low and the crowd cringes. A pace faster or slower than the band and everyone becomes distracted. It's a high pressure place to be in and I have to say my wife embraces it well and I'm always extremely proud to say "that's my lady". Her voice is breath-taking and her courage is inspiring, nevertheless, I have a confession to make. Whether she knows it or not, the solo performances that I have grown to love the most are those without a stage and without a crowd. These performances are done while washing the dishes, or cleaning the clothes, or putting on make-up. Sometimes I wonder if she knows she's singing at all. There's an extremely soft tone that would be impossible to hear if you weren't in close range and many times the song is given in pieces — scattered and incomplete (those who live with singers know what exactly what I'm talking about). At times, she opens in the middle of a song that's running through her mind. Other times, she'll simply hum the chorus. And the best one of all is when she flows in and out of conversations with myself or our daughter and immediately picks back up where she left off before "tending" to us. I watch in awe as the innate part of her design emerges. Through this observation over the years, I've come to realize something. Her singing is not as much about *want* as it is *need*. She absolutely MUST sing. It's irresistible to her. It has nothing to do with the crowds and everything to do with her calling. Without a doubt she is passionate about it. Her desire, however, points to the greater revelation of her calling which surfaces from the depths of her instinct. She was made to sing.

When she sings in a group, she's assisting a song and that takes control. That control is displayed through the role of harmony. Harmony could be defined as the agreement of similarities and the allowance of differences. It celebrates who a person is, or what they have to offer, without stumbling over who they're not, or what they lack. Every person in the group brings a strength of tonality, which also means they bring a weakness of tonality. One may be a soprano, another may be an alto, and others may be a tenor, bass, or baritone. The soprano can't do what the baritone can do and the alto can't do what the bass can do, nor do they ask each other to. The goal of the group and the success of harmony depends on each person utilizing his or her strengths as complements to the other's weaknesses. I'm not sure if there's another moment in life where I feel I'm able to capture a more accurate picture of what God had in mind when designing us for life with others. As they move in and out of harmony, neither of them are in a mode of comparison. They are not looking to compete, they are looking to complete. A group that sings with flawless harmony is able to maintain the uniqueness, or strength, of each individual's sound without destroying the uniqueness of their partners sound in the process. They allow differences without destruction and similarities without struggle. The only way this can happen is for each member to be intentional about maintaining control over their voice so as to highlight the group and not themselves.

Learning to live instinctively, with calling, requires that we also learn to live with intention, or control, as an equally important attribute. Our calling is God's gift to us and, in turn, becomes our gift to the world around us but it was never meant to operate single-handedly. Because we receive it as an individual, it's easy to become trapped by the assumption that our calling was meant to be a solo performer displaying itself as the *"main event"* in every event. As powerful as our calling can be by itself, the vastness of its true potential can only be tapped into in the presence of its pre-determined harmonizing partner. **While instinct gives us our calling, intention gives us control**. Too much calling and we become reckless. Too much control and we become cautious. The beauty of my wife's gift is not always in the sound of melody produced from her vocal chords. Sometimes it's in the silence. She has learned the art of harmony, not just in her music, but also within herself. In fact, I believe what I hear in her music is a reflection of what's in her person. And that is why I am amazed.

LIVING IN THE LEFT

As a man dominated by the "right-side" of his brain, I stand guilty of doing whatever I can — finding more right-brain friends, reading more right-brain books, listening to more right-brain speakers, quoting more right-brain scriptures — to live there. Admittedly, I do it because it's more comfortable.

It doesn't take near as much effort, doesn't feel near as boring or constricting, and gives me way more excuses that I can make for those times that I "come up short" as I've found that blaming a deficit is always easier than admitting defeat.

Lately, however, I've had a rude awakening that's brought me face-to-face with an extremely hard reality: a large majority of my life and a large majority of your life will spent and lived in the "left" — in the pragmatic and/or normal side of life. I don't know about you, but the greater portion of my days aren't filled with burning bushes, or seas parting, or heaven breaking open in the sky, or angels manifesting themselves to hand-deliver God's messages to me. No, they look more like washing the dishes, or folding the laundry, or meeting deadlines at work, or having lunch with a friend, or writing this book, or going to the gym, or playing with my daughter. So, what about these passions that I've identified in my heart to be "a world-renowned speaker, trainer, teacher, and author", "to have influence with influencers", "to build great wealth in every area of my life", "to travel the globe", or "to be the 'go to' transformational leader that nations call when in a crisis"? What do I with them? What do you do with yours? What do we do when there is no burning bush or when an angel has never tangibly appeared to hand-deliver a message to us? What do we do when we *see* ourselves traveling and changing the world and the farthest we've traveled this year is the gym and the greatest change we've brought is that of a diaper or pull-up? You take what life is giving you and GET INTENTIONAL about where you are and where you're going because, like it or not, living IN purpose will require that we learn to live ON purpose.

> LIVING IN PURPOSE WILL REQUIRE THAT WE LEARN TO LIVE ON PURPOSE.

And, there are five simple ways to starting doing just that: By . . .

1. PARTICIPATING
2. PRETENDING
3. MODELING
4. VISUALIZING
5. AFFIRMING

PARTICIPATING: *PARTICIPATION IS REQUIRED!*

Do you want to know how to *really* manifest your destiny, how to *really* make your dreams come true, how to *really* turn your vision into reality? PARTICIPATE. Waiting is not participating. Complaining is not participating. Praying for what He has already promised is not participating. Participating is participating.

Jesus' life (and death) was one big prophetic word. Time after time, He would say things like, "This is to fulfill what spoken by the prophet" or "that is so the scripture may be fulfilled". The secret behind the fulfillment was not just Him knowing what was said about Him. The secret was Him participating in it when the opportunity presented itself. What would've happened had he not have participated? The assignment most certainly would've been delayed, or, worse. And, it would've been completely His fault, not the prophets and not God's. God did His part by inspiring the prophet to speak and by making sure Jesus knew what was said about Him. Jesus had to do his part by deciding (intending) to engage.

Your assignment is awaiting *your* engagement. It's waiting on you to realize that where you are *is* where you are going, that your current path is *the* path to your destiny, and that you are already *on* route now it's time to get *in* route. The reality is no matter how many continents you leave your footprint on, how many nations call you, how many magazine covers you end up on with global leaders, how many stages you speak on, or how much wealth you acquire, the dishes will still get dirty and need to be cleaned, the laundry will still need to be washed, dried, and folded, the wife will still need to be taken on dates and given quality time, and the children will still need your guidance throughout the various stages of their lives. So, instead of becoming depressed by the verity of our normalcy, let us be encouraged by what it tells us: that we are "halfway" there. And, let us never lose sight of where we come from so that we'll always know how to get back because in addition to being our launching pad, it will also be our haven of rest and peace, as well as the much needed reminder of the other part ourselves that is often overlooked, but is ever-so important.

PRETENDING: *ACT AS IF!*

Dictionary.com has an interesting way of defining the word "Practical":

1. *Of or relating to **practice** or action*
2. *Consisting of, involving, or resulting from **practice** or action*
3. *Engaged or experienced in actual **practice** or work*

British dictionary definitions add:

1. *of, involving, or concerning with experience or actual use; not theoretical.*

Your present, as gut-wrenchingly average, normal, mundane, or uninteresting as it may seem, is not a *waiting room*. it's a *training room*. It is God's chosen location of preparation for your passion — __the__ place where you will "practice", or "act as if", you're already where you ultimately desire to go.

By nature, I am a coach. At the time of this writing, I have more than a decade invested coaching athletes in the area of speed and strength as well as a few years coaching high school football. I would venture to say that coaching is one of the more rewarding professions you can be in. And, it is also one of the most strenuous and frustrating. The reason for that is practice.

In football, we practice way more than we play. Case in point. In the state of Georgia, if the stars line up just right we will play a 14 or 15 game season depending on the year and schedule (that's the amount of games to get to and win the state championship). Games do not begin until the end of August each year. We begin our practices in the spring during what is known as spring practice. This is usually about a two week stretch of time getting acquainted again with the playbook, seeing what you have as a team, getting adjusted to the loss of the previous year's senior class, and getting familiar with the incoming freshmen. This is a very exciting time of year full of anticipation, expectation, and practice. With all that said, "practice" is a word I understand on many different levels.

First, practice doesn't make perfect, it makes prepared. It is all about using the present as a time to prepare for, not wait on, the future. We as, coaches, will intentionally try to set it up in way to mimic, or mirror, the upcoming game and opponent as much as possible. We will choose players for our "scout teams" to work against who most resemble the players from the other team — from the way they look, to the way they move, to the way they breathe. Once we have those impersonating players in place, we will then set them up in the exact offensive or defensive alignments (depending on what we're preparing for that day) and will have them run the exact plays out of those alignments according to what we've seen on film. Can you imagine what would happen if we took the same approach with our teams and their futures that we take with ourselves and our own futures? It wouldn't go as desired would it? We would arrive at "the anticipated day"; we just wouldn't arrive prepared for it because we didn't take the time to get the reps in.

This bring us to the second huge benefit of getting practical in our purpose through practicing: It is all about repetition, although not for repetition sake; it is for habit (skill) sake. Coaches understand that *repetition is the mother of all skill (Tony Robbins)*. This is why, in our world, reps must have an intentional, definite focus of quality within the quantity in order to create the outcome we want. We are aware that the habitual skills we're looking for is in the quantity of quality within each rep instead of the quantity of the reps themselves. Get around any pure-bread coach long enough and you'll quickly realize how "OCD" we are about this. Bad reps will create bad skill. Good reps will create good skill. I have a saying that may help us better understand what I mean when it comes to instilling the correct habits in our players. It's something I used to tell the players that I had the benefit of coaching: 'If you train fast, you'll be fast. If you train slow, you'll be slow. In football, we want to be fast.' I know it sounds simple, but it takes thousands and thousands of the "right" kind of reps to create the "right" habitual skills — those you don't have to think about when game-time" comes; you just do them.

You see, it's not enough to be called to a purpose. You also need to be skilled in that purpose. And, you want to make sure that skill is habitual (doesn't require a lot of thought) when you get there. I want to end this section by bringing the idea of practice to each of our individual passions. How do you use *your* present to prepare yourself for "game day"? It's easy to do with a football team, but how can a date with your spouse prepare you for the "call of nations"? Easy! You make your spouse the "head-of-state" in that moment. How would you *act* differently on a date if you pretended your husband or wife were the leader of the nation that called you and you just sat down for dinner to discuss the issues at hand? Would you be highly engaged in the conversation or would you be looking down at your phone the whole time you were with them? Would you be "into the details" of what he or she was saying or would you have that zoned-out-looking-but-not-listening face? The truth is my spouse (and yours) IS the "head-of-state" in our home (just ask our daughter). They are dignitaries of the highest value that I must give my attention to and learn to work with first because if I can't partner with her in handling the affairs of our home, how can I expect to handle the affairs of an entire nation?

MODELING/MENTORING: *SUCCESS LEAVES CLUES!*

"Modeling" is a term and technique that I came across and began leveraging in my own life almost 11 years ago while reading Tony Robbins book, *"Awaken the Giant Within"*. In the book, Tony writes:

The way to expand our lives is to model the lives of those people who are already succeeding. It's powerful, it's fun, and these people are available all around you.

"Modeling" is just another word for "mentoring and/or discipling" and has proven to be the absolute best practical approach in turning the invisible desires of the heart into the visible reality of life. The idea behind it is that "success leaves clues". We don't have to reinvent the wheel to see success (in our case, the fulfillment of our purpose). All we have to do is learn from the best. Whatever you want in life, someone has already discovered how to get it. All you have to do is identify who that someone is (preferably the best of the best in your chosen passion or field), make sure they've produced consistent results over time, get into close proximity, and look for the "clues" because people who succeed consistently are not lucky; they're just doing something different that sets them apart. They've found a strategy that works and if you follow the same strategy, sowing the same seeds, you will reap the same harvest.

These people, the mentors and models, are truly available all around you. Here's the kicker. You're going to have to go to them as they are more than likely not going to come to you. Remember it was Jesus who said it is the "asker" who is "given what he asks for", the "seeker" who "finds", and the "knocker" who has "the door opened to them" (see Matthew 7:7). In your "asking, seeking, and knocking", don't get so caught up in the doors that give you direct access to direct mentors. Those are extremely nice to have, but, they can also be extremely busy and mostly unavailable (if you are truly searching out the "best of the best"). Indirect models can bring just as much value and, honestly, can be much easier to find with an availability that is subject to your own, whether it be through a book they've written, a conference that you can attend they're holding (or one they're speaking at), or through the click of a mouse taking you to an interview or message they've posted on YouTube, Facebook, Instagram, or Twitter — all incredible, practical, easy-to-use resources to help you find a mentor or as many mentors as you'd like.

Many of those that I would call my personal "mentors" are indirect. They've never met me and I've never officially met them, yet, they've still impacted my life tremendously. And, the best part is, all that was really required was a little bit of intentionality on my part to start searching.

VISUALIZING: *SEE IT, FEEL IT, BELIEVE IT!*

Conor McGregor is the first person in UFC (Ultimate Fighting Championship) history to hold two World Championship belts simultaneously in two different weight classes (145lb and 155lb divisions). As great as he is in the octagon, his fighting prowess is not what has made or continues to make record-breaking pay-per-view buyers tune into his fights. What draws the masses is the Muhammed Ali-like verbal abuse he hands his opponents before he ever steps into the ring with them combined with the eerily accurate way he predicts the outcomes of his fights (and his life).

For example, in November 2014, he wrote the following message on his Twitter account:

"Two belts and shares in the company"

The first of those two belts came just over a year later — December 12, 2015 — against Jose Aldo, who, at the time was considered the best pound-for-pound fighter in the world with a decade-long winning streak to back it up. By the time they fought, everyone thought McGregor was nothing more than a good trash-talker. One could only imagine how absurd and out-of-his-mind he must have sounded in the pre-fight press conferences leading up to the main event matchup predicting that he would "KO" (knockout) Aldo inside of the first round. Not only did he do it; he did it in 14 seconds exactly *how* he said it would:

He'll (Aldo) over-extend his right hand, I'll slip, and bang the left hook to the chin and he'll be KO'd unconscious.

Then, eleven months later — November 12, 2016 — as fate would have it, the original "tweet" prediction had come to full fruition in the second-round of his Lightweight (155lb) title fight against Eddie Alvarez, who he also KO'd to obtain the second belt.

He's gotten his forecasts right so many times that he's been dubbed with the nickname, *Mystic Mac,* which the ever-so confident McGregor took a liking to and wears with just as much pride as he does his two belts. In most of his interviews, the mesmerized media will ask about this mysterious ability, to which McGregor usually smiles and says:

*If you can **see it here** (pointing to his head) and you have the courage enough to speak it, it will happen. So, **I see** these shots. **I see** these sequences. And, I don't shy away from them.*

A lot of times people believe in certain things but they keep to themselves. They don't put it out there. They don't truly believe in it. If you become vocal with it, you are creating that law of attraction and it will become reality.

Recently, he set his sights on another so-called impossible feat: bringing boxing great, Floyd Mayweather, out of retirement and challenging him to a boxing match, or what McGregor calls, *a contest where the rules of Mayweather's sport will keep him alive.* Most said it would never happen, some titled it a circus act, and others said he'll get destroyed if it does. True to form, McGregor persisted in his vision and has gotten his wish. The two just inked a deal to fight in Las Vegas on August 26 of this year (2017).

Obviously, the news has spread like wildfire causing an absolute media frenzy (as if it should really come as surprise to any of us anymore) with McGregor adding fuel to the fire through an Instagram post of a massive, freshly painted mural on the wall of his gym showing him connecting with a precise, clean left to Mayweather's chin and commenting, "I predict these things"(check it out: https://www.instagram.com/p/BVs nwNjASXf/?taken-by=thenotoriousmma&hl=en).

McGregor fans are laughing and cheering. Mayweather and Boxing fans are ridiculing and doubting. Fan or not, it would serve all to step back and catch the real science behind *"Mystic Mac"*. He's a very skilled fighter who has and continues to put in a ton of physical work in order to be the two-weight world champion that he is. The real method to his madness, however, lies within the equal and intentional training that he gives to his mind.

The mystique behind *Mystic Mac* is really not mystical at all. It's a simple technique that's available to any one of us and has been used throughout the ages (especially among the successful) with athletes and non-athletes alike. It's called *"Visualization"*.

Visualization is really quite simple. You sit in a comfortable position, close your eyes and imagine — in as vivid detail as you can — what you would be looking at if the dream you have were already realized. Imagine being inside of yourself, looking out through your eyes at the ideal result. –Jack Canfield, Author of "Chicken Soup for the Soul"

It's the basketball player lying in bed at night and just before going to sleep, imagines himself shooting free throws. He "feels" the shape of the ball in his hands, the faint breeze of the air-conditioning blowing across his body, the small beads of sweat rolling down his face. He takes in the all-too-familiar scent of the quiet empty gym. He "hears" the soft buzz of the electricity running through the building providing him with the needed light to practice. The lingering "taste" of the rubber is still on his tongue from licking his finger to get a better grip before shooting. He "looks" at his target before going through his pre-shot routine of three dribbles, slight pause, and shoot. Again, He "feels" the perfect release and "sees" the ball float effortlessly through the bottom of the net. The perfect free throw shot. He rewinds it all and does it again and again and again . . . 25-50 shots. . . . all in his mind. This is visualization — accessing all the senses of your body through mental rehearsal in order to put yourself in possession of the perfect shot, or the ideal spouse, or the greatest speech, or your dream life.

Right now, what would it look like if you already had the passions you've identified in your heart? Go ahead. Have fun. Be a kid again and put your imagination to work. For those getting stretched beyond your Christian comfort zone, do what God told Habakkuk to do:

Write down this vision;
clearly inscribe it on tablets
so one may easily read it.

For the vision is yet for the appointed time;
it testifies about the end and will not lie.
Though it delays, *wait* for it,
since it will certainly come and not be late.
(Habakkuk 2:2,3 HCSB)

The most important thing when doing this exercise is don't try to sound smart. Don't worry about being grammatically correct or getting caught up in the attempt to spiritualize it, or spelling it all out in "Christianese". Focus more on the clarity, the feeling, and the repetition. If it's not *clear* don't write it. If you can't feel it, don't write it. If it's not going to pull you back to it tomorrow and the next day and the next, don't write it. Without detailed clarity, emotional intensity, and constant repetition, you won't be able to reprogram (aka: Renew: see Romans 12:1,2) your mind, or more specifically, your subconscious mind, and, therefore, will be unsuccessful in planting and watering the seeds of your passion so that it may become the fruit of your experience. SEE IT, FEEL IT, REP IT, BELIEVE IT, HAVE IT.

AFFIRMING: WORDS CREATE WORLDS!

A few years back I went through a nine-lesson money management course developed and taught by Dave Ramsey called *Financial Peace University (FPU)*. During one of the first two or three classes, Dave began teaching on the importance of budgeting, which he defines as *"as a way to spend your monthly income on paper, **on purpose**, before the month begins"*. What really branded the concept in my mind, however, is when he went on to explain that budgeting puts you in the driver's seat making you the master of your money instead of your money being the master of you because, *"you're making every dollar behave by giving every dollar a name"*. In doing so, you initially minimize and eventually eliminate the chances of *"accidental spending".*

This part of the lesson resonated with me because I had tasted the fruit of accidental spending (negative bank accounts, embarrassing "insufficient fund" declines, and overdraft fees) one too many times and I hated it. Just as Dave promised, budgeting *(intentionally giving every dollar an assignment)* was just what I needed. It put me back in control, drastically reduced the reoccurring deficits I was experiencing in my bank account, and, much to my surprise, became a transformational strategy that could easily transfer and be applied in other areas of my life as well.

Proverbs 18:21 tells us, *"Life and death are in the power of the tongue, and those who love it will eat its fruit".* We know it, we quote it, and we live it. However, we tend to live it much like I used to live financially: more accidentally than intentionally. We allow external influences to determine how we will spend our words instead of predetermining how our words will be spent. As a result, we find ourselves in a constant state of recovery — always having to "climb out of a hole" we've dug for ourselves by saying things we don't really mean or impulsively speaking things that we don't really want to happen. And, the account that takes the hit remaining insufficient, overdrawn, and undeveloped is that of our purpose.

Words create worlds. That can be a world where visions live or a world where they die. This is why we can't take any chances — why we must take responsibility for what comes out our mouths by intentionally creating a "word budget" to live from so that we can minimize and eliminate any *accidental speaking* and begin seeing more of our dreams come to life.

Having a vision is powerful, but, God Himself, proved "in the beginning" that vision alone will not be enough to turn intangible passions into tangible creation. There must be an accompanying declaration, or affirmation, of the vision for that to happen.

Like most things classified as "spiritual", affirmations have been taken to some weird extremes. Regardless, we have to be careful not to reject it altogether if we want our visions to *"certainly come and not be late" (Habakkuk 2:3)*. Affirmations are the "word budget" we need. They are a way to "spend our words" on paper, on purpose, before anything or anyone else does it for us. It's a way for us to affirm and align what we are saying with what we are seeing so that we can tap into the creative power of agreement (see Matthew 18:19). Like Jim Rohn once said, *"If you don't design your own life plan, chances are you'll fall into someone else's plan. And guess what they have planned for you? Not much"*.

When developing an allocation plan (a list of affirmations) for our words, there are five main categories they need to be assigned to:

1. AFFIRMATIONS MUST BE WRITTEN, READ, AND SPOKEN IN <u>PRESENT-TENSE</u> FROM A <u>FIRST-PERSON POINT OF VIEW</u> :

"I am a son of God"

"I am a world-renowned speaker, trainer, and teacher"

"I am an international Best-Selling Author"

"I am a child of God"

We are made in the image of God (Genesis 1:26-28). And, the first image we have of Him is that He is creative (Genesis 1). Paying attention to *how* He created provides insight into *how* He has made (and expects) each of us to create as well: **in the present-tense from a first-person point of view.**

First, *"He calls those things which are not as though they are"* (Romans 4:17). In other words, He doesn't "tell it like it is"; He tells it the way He wants it to be as if it already is. You see, in the beginning, the earth was *"formless and void; and darkness covered the face of the deep"*, yet, God never spoke about any of that. Instead, He simply said, *"Let there be"* and the earth responded accordingly. This is a massively important example to all of us as most, *in the beginning* of our transformational process, will find ourselves surrounded by the same kind of "formless, void, and dark" realities. By following God's example and leveraging the creative capacity of our words — by speaking those things that are not as though they are — we will see the same kind of results.

Second, you'll remember from one of the earlier chapters that in original Hebrew text, *"Let there be"* and *"I am"* are the same word: *Hayah*. Essentially, every time God said, *"Let there be"* this or that, He was calling it in the present-tense from a first-person point of view ("I am"). Likewise, by structuring our affirmations with "I am", we are saying "Let there be" or "Let it become". The power lies in the permission of the present. Affirming, "I want to be an international best-selling author" tells the desire, "someday". Affirming, "I am an international best-selling author" tells the desire, "today". Timing is not in God's hands, it's in yours. The fact that you've desired it says "now" is the time because "Now, faith is . . ." (Hebrews 11:1). You're not waiting on it, it's waiting on you, on your voice, and on your word. Now speak it.

2. AFFIRMATIONS MUST BE WRITTEN, READ, AND SPOKEN IN THE <u>POSITIVE</u> (AS OPPOSED TO THE NEGATIVE):

"Positive thinking won't let you do anything, but it will let you do everything better than negative thinking will" (Zig Ziglar).

The same is true when it comes to affirmations. The purpose of writing, reading, and speaking them in the positive (as opposed to the negative) is that it gives you a focus of where you want to go instead of where you don't want to go. Wherever you're aimed (wherever your focus is aimed) is exactly where you'll end up. For example, "I am not like my father" puts my focus where? On all the traits of my father I'm wanting to avoid. Ironically, I still end up at a place I didn't want to be because although I wanted to be going in the opposite direction I wasn't. What if I said, instead, something to the effect of, "I am an incredible, loving, caring, and present father to my children"? That sets my focus in a different direction doesn't it? And, best of all, I end up exactly where I want to be. Make sure you're aimed in the direction you actually want to go when it comes to your affirmations.

3. WRITTEN, READ, AND SPOKEN AFFIRMATIONS MUST <u>PROVOKE</u> EMOTIONS:

Affirmations that don't *move* you (emotionally) won't *move* you (physically). What excites you ignites you. The greater you feel about what you're reading, writing, and speaking, the more likely you'll be to actually believe it and to start taking action toward it.

Action is the bridge between seeing it in your head and holding it in your hand. Until you "feel" like you can have it or until you "feel" like it you deserve, however, you simply won't do anything about it. Those who believe they can, do; those who believe they can't, don't. It's really that simple. And, you are in full control. When it comes to your affirmations you can actually try "feeling" the emotion you would have as if you were in already in possession of it. If that doesn't work, you can voice the emotion: *I am so excited now that I am a world-renowned, in-demand, speaker, trainer, and teacher, or, I am so happy and grateful now that I am traveling the world with my family.* By voicing it, your physiology will follow. You already know what "happy", "excited", and "grateful" looks like. They have a physiology just like "depression", "anger", and "disappointment". **Be intentional about your emotional state because it will always become your *real estate*.**

4. WRITTEN, READ, AND SPOKEN AFFIRMATIONS MUST BE <u>PERSISTENTLY</u> REPEATED.

In the morning when waking up, at night just before going to bed, and/or as a "pattern-interrupting" replacement to the old ways of thinking and feeling when they arise, affirmations must become a persistently repeated daily ritual. Their ultimate goal is to re-condition our thoughts, feelings, and actions in order get a different result — an outcome where we move from internally desiring to actually living. Conditioning doesn't happen without adaptation and adaptation can't happen unless a new, unfamiliar stimulus is introduced consistently or repeatedly. Set aside two to three times a day, preferably in the morning when waking up and just before retiring for bed at night, to re-affirm your desires.

5. AFFIRMATIONS MUST BE WRITTEN, READ, AND SPOKEN <u>PRESICELY</u>:

Prioritize precision when it comes to your affirmations. Be sure they are congruent with your vision. Include as much detail and specificity as possible remembering that "*a house divided cannot stand*". If your passion is to "speak, train, and teach", once you get the opportunity to do it and it doesn't go the way you thought it would, don't walk away (like I've done) saying, "I'm a terrible speaker" or "I did an awful job communicating tonight". Those are affirmations as well. Instead, use the concept of precision as a reminder of what may be missing (specificity) and add to your original affirmation something like, "I am an internationally recognized, in-demand, speaker, trainer, and teacher. My mind is sharp, my communication is clear, my delivery is dynamic, my message is inspiring, and the masses are being greatly impacted by what I say. I am proud of myself for giving the best I had to give and grateful for every opportunity knowing with absolute certainty that I am getting better with each new experience gained."

WAITING IS MOVING

God will live WITH us, ON us, IN us, and THROUGH us (to the extent that we allow), but He will not live FOR us. Remember, this is a CO-mission: a partnership where the completion (fulfillment) of the assignment (the purpose) is dependent on Him doing his part and us doing ours. His part is the inspiration. Our part is the intention. Therefore, the prophetic word, the dream, or the vision that He inspired you with 5, 10, 15, 20 years ago that you've been "waiting on Him" to bring to pass has been waiting on you to bring to process.

From His perspective, waiting is not forgetting, or settling, or setting aside for a later day. Waiting is moving. It's flying at heights that others can barely breathe in, running at a pace that most grow weary in, and walking distances that many faint in (Isaiah 40:31). This is why "putting your dream on the shelf and waiting on God to bring it to pass" is a terrible idea. Your dream wasn't made for the shelf; it was made for you. So, find the shelf, grab your dream, knock the dust off of it, get intentional, and move.

REFLECTION QUESTIONS

#1. *Living __in__ purpose begins by living __on__ purpose.* Have you been intentional about your purpose? Are there any other action steps you can add to the list in the chapter to get more intentional?

#2. *The enemy laces lies with elements of truth.* Can you think of areas in your life where this has happened? What did you do to identify it and overcome it?

#3. What promises have you "put on the shelf" that you need to take down?

MEDITATION/APPLICATION

I'll never forget the day one of my previous mentors stole a quote from Thomas Edison and put his spin on it saying, "Most people "miss" God's purpose for their lives because it's dressed in overalls and looks like work". It was hilarious, to say the least, but I'm so grateful he had the audacity to put it out there because it taught me that God will live on me, in me, and through me, however, He will not live for me. Have you depended on God to do everything "for" you?

16

A TIME FOR WAR

"I didn't come this far to only come this far"

–ANONYMOUS

Who do you think you are? Nobody is going to read this and if they do they won't like it. You're wasting your time. What makes you any different from the thousands of others who have written on the same topic? This arena is too crowded with too many voices. Your voice will never stand out or make a difference. Everybody is going to make fun of you. They'll think you're weird. You'll fail. You'll let your family down . . . again. You'll be a disappointment and an embarrassment to those you're closest to. You're nothing more than a fantasizer who will forever be dreaming while never accomplishing. You'll start this and stop this just like you have with other endeavors you've began. Even if you get off to a good start, you'll find a way to sabotage it. What will you do if it is successful? You're not equipped to handle a huge demand of people seeking answers? You don't have enough answers, much less enough money, enough talent, or enough time.

These are just a few of the voices I've heard **every single day** for the past 11 months since I made the decision to not only start, but also finish this 14-year old dream of writing a book. You read it right, *voices*, as in many different ones coming from many different angles. Some are self-induced, others are background-induced, and the remaining I'll say is "the devil" (in my best southern Pentecostal preacher voice). No, I do not have multiple personality disorder, nor am I demon possessed. I am simply a living, breathing example of what every dream-seeker before me had to endure and what every dream-seeker after me will have to endure if they wish to inherit *their* "Promised Land": **Opposition**.

FIGHT THE *ITES*

Inspiration and intention are enough to bring you to the borders of your purpose. They'll even take you as far as allowing you to spy it out. Still, if you wish to take possession of it — to make it your "home" — you must be willing to embrace the opposition that is sure to come with the invasion as there is no such thing as occupation without confrontation. A point well-proven by the children of Israel whose 40 years of wilderness wandering was a direct result of an unwillingness to go to war for their promise. Were they inspired by the vision of Canaan? Absolutely! Who wouldn't be inspired by *"an angel as their guide" "God as their defender", "blessings on their food and water", "promises of no sickness, no barrenness, no miscarriages, and no early or premature deaths (full life spans)"* [see Exodus 23:20-26]? Were they intentional about moving toward it? You bet. They would've never made it as far they did (to the southern border of the Promised Land) or been able to "spy it out" if they hadn't been. They like so many of us, never moved beyond a "preview" because they just didn't believe they had what it took to fight the "ites" and win.

Who are the "ites"? The Hittites, Girgashites, Amorites, Canaanites, Perizzites, Hivites, and Jebusites. The seven nations that God told Israel they would have to face in order to possess the land (see Deut. 7:1). They are the inhabitants to every inheritance. Although they are "familiar" foes, you probably won't recognize them by the natural names. You will, however, by their spiritual names:

HITTITES	Sons of Terror	*Subliminal torments, phobias, terror, depression, deceit*	*FEAR*
GIRGASHITES	Clay Dwellers	*Focus on earthliness, unbelief in what cannot be seen*	*DOUBT*
AMORITES	Mountain People; Renowned	*Obsession with earthly fame and glory, domineering*	*PRIDE*
CANAANITES	Lowlands People	*Addictions, perversions, exaggerated people pleasing*	*LUST*
PERIZZITES	Belonging to a village	*Limited Vision, laziness, low self-esteem*	*INSECURITY*
HIVITES	Villagers	*Vision limited to enjoying an earthly inheritance; hedonism*	*VANITY*
JEBUSITES	Threshers	*Suppression of spiritual authority to fellow believers; legalism*	*GUILT*

Biblical scholars have estimated that over 1,000,000 people died in the wilderness. In a 14,600 day (40 years x 365 days) span of time, that's an average of just over 68 people PER DAY. Can you imagine losing 68 friends and family every single day for the next 40 years of your life? That was the brutal consequence for a generation who chose cowardice over courage: they traded a *tomorrow* "full of milk and honey" for a *tomorrow* full of death and wandering. To make matters worse, that trade resulted in 1,000,000 people who perished with their purpose still locked within them. All because of the "ites". And, here's the most bizarre part: the "ites" never had to lift a finger to do it. They never had to engage in one battle or bring out one weapon because no one (with the exception of Joshua and Caleb) was courageous enough to challenge them.

How many more lives since then do you think fear, doubt, and insecurity have been responsible for? How many more promises never came to pass because of lust or pride? How many more visions have fallen victim to vanity or guilt? More importantly, when do you think we will reach a place where enough is enough? When will we choose to fight instead of fear, to believe instead of doubt, to try instead of die? When will we stop depositing our lives and our dreams into the bank account of the cemetery making it richer than it already is?" Les Brown once said:

> *The graveyard is the richest place on earth, because it is here that you will find all the hopes and dreams that were never fulfilled, the books that were never written, the songs that were never sung, the inventions that were never shared, the cures that were never discovered, all because someone was too afraid to take that first step, keep with the problem, or determined to carry out their dream.*

I have made it my life's mission to "Bankrupt the Graveyard" — to do whatever it takes to make sure that no more cures, no more businesses, no more books, no more inventions, no more artwork, and no more songs are deposited there because our dreams are always an answer to someone else's problems. Without a doubt, starting a business (if that's in your heart) could bring great personal rewards to you and your family. And, God wants that for you. However, He also wants you to recognize that it was made to bring rewards to many other families, such as those you employ, by providing them with means to an income so that they and 'theirs' are fed, clothed, and sheltered as well.

If you're the one holds the cure for cancer, it could bring you great fame and fortune. The true wealth, however, will be in the great healing, joy, and happiness it will bring to those it was made for. That's how purpose works. It's given in order to be given. And, that's why you can't die with it still inside of you because it's not just you dying with unfinished business; it's you dying with another's cure, another's happiness, another's healing, another's provision, another's purpose.

Out of the first 68 people that perished, how many of the 1,000,000+ do you think they were responsible for taking with them? How many of them do you anticipate they contained the solution for — if not directly, then most certainly, indirectly? How many lives is your purpose connected to?' How many would you be robbing, or, more sobering, how many would you be killing if you decided to flee instead of fight?

YOU CAN RUN, BUT YOU CAN'T HIDE

King Solomon in the third chapter of Ecclesiastes opens saying:

To everything there is a season, and a time to every purpose under heaven (Ecclesiastes 3:1)

Then, he begins to go through a list of unavoidable "seasons" that all of us will have to endure on this side of eternity starting with, *"A time to be born and a time to die".* Those two make sense to be *the* leaders of a portfolio of inescapable life realities. What doesn't are the subsequent "times" Solomon goes onto record (see Ecclesiastes 3:1-8). Nevertheless, he counts them the same, including "a time for war".

Believe it or not, like it or not, war, according to the wisdom of God, is as inevitable as dying. In other words, we don't really have a choice in the matter, regardless of how hard we try to avoid it. We can build our homes on the highest hills, move to the most secluded places on earth, become the most dearly beloved human to ever grace the planet having not one admission of dislike concerning us, still, war, like death, will visit us. Our lack of success in avoidance won't be because we're unable to identify the highest hill or the remotest place. Neither will it be because we lacked some skill set in making everyone we meet love us, or, at the very least, tolerate us. It will be because "*our battle is not against flesh and blood, but against the rulers, against the authorities, against the world powers of darkness, against the spiritual forces of evil in the heavens*" (*Ephesians 6:12 HCSB*).

While there are many places we can go to avoid confrontation with each other (flesh and blood), there is nowhere we can go to avoid the confrontation of "spiritual forces". Fear of what you will think about this book has been present with me whether I've been sitting in front of my computer writing it or whether I've been sitting in a beach chair in front of an ocean thinking about writing it. Doubt about the impact it will have has been with me whether I've been swimming in a pile of papers on my desk at work or swimming in the pool with my daughter after work. Nearing the completion of this book, the tension increases daily between being pleased with my accomplishment or becoming prideful. And, once again, the tension is there regardless of where I'm at or what I'm doing. So, I've found the better pursuit is not in making our homes unreachable or in making ourselves invisible or more admirable; the better pursuit is in making our "positions unassailable".

UNASSAILABLE

In his book, *The Art of War*, Sun Tzu writes:

> *The art of war teaches us to rely not on the likelihood of the enemy's not coming, but on our own readiness to receive him; not on the chance of his not attacking, but rather on the fact that we have made our position unassailable.*

To be unassailable means to be in "such a strong position that you cannot be defeated". Naturally, the question for you and me becomes, how do we create such a position for ourselves as we embrace the inevitable fight ahead in pursuit of our purpose?

#1. First, we have to recognize that positions are dictated by commissions.

The reason that war can be considered an art is because no two battles, like no two canvases, are the same; which means that no two approaches toward a finished picture of victory will be the same either. For Sun Tzu and his warriors, their "readiness" was defined in terms of *receiving their enemy*. In other words, they carried a commission that called for a defensive position– one whose anticipation and preparation was predicated on the enemy making the first move. Sun Tzu was a brilliant strategist who understood that the art of war is the art of flexibility. He knew how to adapt to the given situations at hand allowing him to put himself and his soldiers in the best possible positions for victorious outcomes, ultimately, branding him as a legend among legends in the military world. As great of a tactician as he was, however, his genius didn't really lie in his understanding of alignments; it lied within his understanding of assignments. Because he was clear on the commission, he was able to be clear on the position.

#2. The next logical step then in becoming unbeatable is to **know *your* assignment and implement the proper, congruent alignment.**

When I coached football, we would never run a defensive alignment when it was time for an offensive assignment. Seems like an overly-logical statement to make until you look around (or look within) and realize that's exactly what we've been doing when it comes to the purpose for our lives. We've been handed a mandate to "GO", yet, we're not going. We've been given a dream to write books and we're not writing them. We've been authorized and baptized to teach nations and we're not teaching them. We've been given permission to build businesses and we're not building them. We've been ordered to "possess the land" and we're not possessing it. We've chosen security over opportunity, comfort over challenge, caution over chance, defense over offense, and have successfully hedged our lives from the possibility of failure. However, in doing so, we've also hedged it from the possibility of fulfillment. We've taken alignments that are incongruent with our assignment. And, although we've done it out of a response to the 'ites', we've considered it "savvy", even going as far as calling it "wisdom". I must warn you, *"If you live cautiously, your friends will call you wise. You just won't move many mountains (Bill Johnson0".* Nor will you possess many promises because you will be taking a stance when you've been commissioned to make a charge.

#3. Finally, **taking positions in alignment with His commission guarantees His protection and leads to our possession.**

Our assignment is one that demands a "readiness" defined by and led by aggressiveness — where our expectation and subsequent preparation is driven by us "firing the first shot". It is one that courageously engages the enemy instead of dodging him or waiting for him to engage us. It writes in the face of fear, sings in the presence of insecurity, dances in spite of doubt, preaches regardless of pride, leaps despite the lust, advances against the vanity, and goes in opposition to the guilt. And, we are willing to take such risks — to put ourselves in the line of fire — because we know that a position in alignment with His commission, though it may appear to be dangerous to those around us, guarantees His protection and leads to our possession.

> "THE SAFEST PLACE IN ALL THE WORLD IS IN THE WILL OF GOD".
> —WARREN WIERSBE

Over the past 16 years, since giving my life to the Lord, I've often had to be reminded of the famous words of Warren Wiersbe:

"The safest place in all the world is in the will of God".
—Warren Wiersbe

I've also had to accept the fact that most of the time "the will" of God will place me "among the wolves" (Luke 10:3), or "in a wilderness being tempted by the devil" (Luke 4:1), or "in a war against nations greater and stronger" (Deuteronomy 7:1) than me. All hostile places that logic would tell us to avoid, nevertheless, these are the places that He has given me and that He has promised to be with me in (to protect me) if I'll just go (Deuteronomy 31:1-8).

NOW IS THE TIME

We are not waiting on our promise. Our promise is waiting on us. One of my greatest concerns is that what we've come to call and somehow honor as some type of divine "waiting" has really just been a well-disguised cover-up and excuse for "wandering". "*I wonder when 'it' will happen. I wonder when that prophetic word will come to pass. I wonder when I'll get to preach to the nations. I wonder when I'll get to open the business. I wonder when I'll get to write the book. I wonder when God is going to open the door."* I wonder when . . . ? I. WANDER. And, God is thinking, "I wonder when they're going to realize that My commission carried My permission, that My "Go" was my "Yes", and that the "appointed time" is no longer with ME, it's with them.

When we decide that now is the time for the book to be written, it will be written. When we decide that now is the time to start the business, it will be started. When we decide that now is the time, it will be the time. So, stop standing and waiting at the borders of your promise and decide that now is the time to advance and occupy!

GO! Write the book that you were born to write. *GO!* Sing the songs you were born to sing. *GO!* Preach the word you were born to preach. *GO!* Own the businesses you born to own. *GO!* Invade the nations you were born to invade. *GO!* Step into your heavenly identity, embrace and embody the value of one worth dying for, and become all that God has purposed for you to become.

GO!!!

REFLECTION QUESTIONS

#1. Have you ever been stopped by the "ites" at the border of your purpose? Which specific "ite" has been the most difficult to overcome? Why?

#2. *God has given you permission through His commission.* Have you given yourself permission to GO get what's yours?

#3. *War is as inevitable as dying.* What thoughts or feelings emerge when you read that?

#4. *The Lord rejoices in the beginning of a work.* What step can you take today towards your purpose? Better yet, who can you take it with?

MEDITATION/APPLICATION

And Jesus sent them out two by two (Luke 10:1)

It's not wise to go into battle alone. Jesus never sent His disciples anywhere by themselves, which is the reason, I believe He needed an even number of them (twelve). Is there anyone in your life today that is willing to go into battle with you and that you're willing to go into with? What can you do together that ensures you're never without a partner in war?

NOTES

The Forgotten Commandment

1. Daniel Sweet, "The Four Types of Love: Unconditional Friends, Romantic Family," http://www.gods-word-first.org/fruitofspirit/biblelove-agape-phileo-eros-storge.html, accessed July, 2016.

Jesus Loves Me This I Know

1. Formless, Void, Darkness. *Strong's Exhaustive Concordance: New American Standard Bible.* (Updated ed.). Retrieved from http://biblehub.com/parallel/genesis/1-2.htm

2. Commandment. *Strong's Exhaustive Concordance: New American Standard Bible.* (Updated ed.). Retrieved from http://biblehub.com/greek/1785.htm

Last Words

1. Mark Rowh, "First Impressions Count," American Psychological Association, http://www.apa.org/gradpsych/2012/11/first-impressions.aspx, accessed August, 2016.

2. Lance Wallnau, "What is Your First Impression?," https://lancewallnau.com/what-is-your-first-impression-no-matter-what-the-product-you-sell-you-are-alw/, accessed August, 2016.

3. Valentine Cowley, "Leonardo Da Vinci's Last Words," http://scientific-child-prodigy.blogspot.com/2006/12/leonardo-da-vincis-last-words.html, accessed August, 2016.

4. "Patriot Nathan Hale was Hanged September 22, 1776", America's Story from America's Library, http://www.americaslibrary.gov/jb/revolut/jb_revolut_hale_1.html, accessed August, 2016.

5. Simpson, Mona. "A Sister's Eulogy for Steve Jobs", *NY Times,* 30 Oct. 2011, http://www.nytimes.com/2011/10/30/opinion/mona-simpsons-eulogy-for-steve-jobs.html?mcubz=1

6. Baptizing. *Strong's Exhaustive Concordance: New American Standard Bible.* (Updated ed.). Retrieved from http://biblehub.com/greek/907.htm

7. Name. *Strong's Exhaustive Concordance: New American Standard Bible.* (Updated ed.). Retrieved from http://biblehub.com/greek/3686.htm

Lost and Found

1. Adam. *Strong's Exhaustive Concordance: King James Bible.* (Updated ed.). Retrieved from http://biblehub.com/hebrew/120.htm

2. Let there be and I am. *Strong's Exhaustive Concordance: King James Bible.* (Updated ed.). Retrieved from http://biblehub.com/hebrew/1961.htm

I Am in the I Am

1. Christ. *Strong's Exhaustive Concordance: New American Standard Bible.* (Updated ed.). Retrieved from http://biblehub.com/greek/5547.htm

Soul Food

1. Soul. *Strong's Exhaustive Concordance: King James Bible.* (Updated ed.). Retrived from http://biblehub.com/hebrew/5315.htm

2. Breath. *Strong's Exhaustive Concordance: New American Standard Bible.* (Updated ed.). Retrieved from http://biblehub.com/hebrew/5397.htm

3. Dickens, Charles. A Christmas Carol. http://www.pagebypagebooks.com/Charles_Dickens/A_Christmas_Carol/Stave_1_Marleys_Ghost_p10.html, accessed September, 2016.

4. "Male Fertility and Sperm Count: A Numbers Game", Sperm Check Fertility, http://www.spermcheck-fertility.com/studies.html, accessed September 2016

5. Rowling, JK. (2000). Harry Potter and the Chamber of Secrets. New York, NY. Arthur A. Levine Books.

6. Allen, James. (1903). As a Man Thinketh. CreateSpace Self-Publishing Platform.

7. Schutte, Shana. "Thoughts on Real Definition of Intimacy", *https://shanaschutte.com/thoughts-on-the-real-definition-of-intimacy-2/*, accessed October 2016

Once Upon A Time

1. Inception. Dir. Christopher Nolan Perf. Cillian Murphy, Marion Cotillard, Joseph Gordon-Levitt, Ellen Page, Ken Watanabe, Michael Caine, and Leonardo DiCaprio. Warner Bros., 2010, Film.

2. Donald Miller. "How to Tell a Good Story With Your Life — or — The Four Critical Elements of a Meaningful Life," Storyline, http://storylineblog.com/2012/03/06/how-to-tell-a-good-story-with-your-life/, accessed October, 2016

3. Johnson, Bill. (2006). Dreaming with God: Secrets to Redesigning Your World through God's Creative Flow (pg. 63). Shippensburg. PA. Destiny Image Publishing.

My Father

1. Wallnau, Lance. (2007). Your Highest and Best: The New Science of Living Your Destiny by Design. Lance Learning Group.

Reclaiming Sonship

1. Transgressions. *Strong's Exhaustive Concordance: New American Standard Bible.* (Updated ed.). Retrieved from http://biblehub.com/greek/3900.htm

The God of Abraham Maslow

1. Enlightened. *Strong's Exhaustive Concordance: New American Standard Bible.* (Updated ed.). Retrieved from http://biblehub.com/greek/5461.htm

2. McLeod, Sean. "Maslow's Hierarchy of Needs," Simple

Psychology, https://www.simplypsychology.org/maslow. html, accessed November, 2016

3. Clinton, Dr. Robert J. (2012). The Making of A Leader: Recognizing the Lessons and Stages of Leadership Development. Colorado Springs, CO. NavPress.

Van Gough, Apple, and A Dead Squirrel

1. Workmanship. *Strong's Exhaustive Concordance: New American Standard Bible.* (Updated ed.). Retrieved from http://biblehub.com/greek/4161.htm

2. Elgan, Mike. "Why Apple is the most successful company in the history", ComputerWorld, https://www.computerworld. com/article/2883747/why-apple-is-the-most-successful-company-in-history.html, accessed December 2016

3. Grant, Daniel. "What's the Value of a Signature on an Art Print?", Huffington Post, 25 May 2011, http://www.huffingtonpost.com/daniel-grant/whats-the-value-of-a-sign_b_826711.html

4. To see additional references concerning specific brand value of companies: https://www.forbes.com/powerful-brands/list/#tab:rank

Natural Born Conformers

1. Christie, Les. "Record 3 million households hit with foreclosures in 2009," CNN Money, 14 Jan, 2009, http://money. cnn.com/2010/01/14/real_estate/record_foreclosure_year/

2. Knowledge. *Strong's Exhaustive Concordance: New American Standard Bible.* (Updated ed.). Retrieved from http://biblehub.com/greek/1922.htm

The Unholy Grail

1. Fairchild, Mary. "Christianity Statistics", ThoughtCo., 14 Mar. 17, https://www.thoughtco.com/christianity-statistics-700533

2. Johns, Andy. "Number of Hispanic residents in Georgia grows", Times Free Press, 18 Mar. 18, http://www.timesfreepress.com/news/news/story/2011/mar/18/georgia-hispanics-grow/45211/

3. Moana. Dir. Ron Clements and John Musker, Walt Disney Animation Studios, 2016, Film.

Intention-Deficit Disorder

1. Robbins, Tony. (1991). Awaken the Giant Within: How to take Immediate Control of Your Mental, Emotional, Physical, and Financial Destiny (pg. 92). New York, NY. Simon and Schuster.

2. Canfield, Jack. "Visualization Techniques to Affirm Your Desired Outcome: A Step-by-Step Guide", Jack Canfield Maximizing Your Potential, http://jackcanfield.com/blog/visualize-and-affirm-your-desired-outcomes-a-step-by-step-guide/, accessed February 2017

A Time for War

1. Rushmore, Lewis. "How many Israelites Died in the Wilderness?", http://www.gospelgazette.com/gazette/2001/mar/page20.htm, accessed August 2017

2. "The Girgashites", Shamah-Elim, http://shamah-elim.info/girgash.htm#The_7_types_of_evil_spirits, accessed August 2017

3. Tzu, Sun. (2010). Art of War. Nabla Ltd.

ACKNOWLEDGMENTS

Honestly, this may be the most stressful part of the entire book for me due to the fact that there are so many people who deserve to be acknowledged for the "part" they've played in my life. Another book could be dedicated to just you. However, I only have one page. Please forgive me if you didn't make this one. There will be others ☺

First, to my wife, Keri, and our beautiful daughter, Avery: My ambitions are not always easy to handle and, undoubtedly, require patience and sacrifice from you. Thank you for that. Without you, I'd be hopeless.

To my mother, Debbie: Only you and God know the "full" measure of the price you had to pay to throughout the years. Thank you for not giving up when I know it would've been easy (and justified) to do so. I hope this book makes you feel like it was worth it.

To my brother from another mother, Clint Spencer: You

believed in me when I didn't believe in myself. This book would've never been possible without it. I am forever indebted to you.

To my mentor and friend, Richie Hughes: Perhaps you have no idea, but the consistency you've shown as a "man of God", the unwavering commitment you've shown to your "family", and the certainty (faith) you've shown in your pursuits, have all been major influences on my life. Thanks for setting the standard.

To my best friend, John Paul Burdashaw: Thanks for helping with some minor proofreading/editing. Most importantly, thanks for your constant encouragement and genuine interest throughout the process.

To the Swishers (Steven, Valerie, and Tori): You provided the foundation for me to begin seeing myself as God sees me. My hope is that you forever know that your love as well as your "words" fell on good soil.

ABOUT THE AUTHOR

CHEVIS BROOKS is on a mission to help others see themselves, their work, and their world *In God's Eyes*, which in his own words, "looks much different than we've been led to believe."

Through his writing, speaking, and coaching, he boldly identifies and confronts the ideologies, theologies, and philosophies that have kept individuals, organizations, and nations from seeing themselves as God sees them and, as a result, has prevented them from stepping into the fullness of who they are, what they're worth, and why they are here.

An overcomer by determination, a coach by trade, and aggressive by nature, Chevis uses a no-holds-barred, tell-it-like-it-is, no-excuse-making approach to shake the comfort zones of mediocrity, passivity, and timidity awakening the settlers within to their higher calling and design.

Chevis lives in Georgia with his amazing wife, Keri, and their beautiful daughter, Avery. Connect with him at ChevisBrooks.com.

CONTACT CHEVIS

Email
chevisbrooks@gmail.com

Or visit his website at
www.chevisbrooks.com

**You may also find him on Facebook
@authorchevisbrooks**

Printed in Great Britain
by Amazon

43820812R00178